TREASURES of the SMOKIES

Tempting Recipes from East Tennessee

The Junior League of Johnson City, Tennessee, Inc.

The Association of Junior Leagues, Inc. is an international organization of women committed to promoting voluntarism and leadership of trained volunteers. Its purpose is exclusively educational and charitable.

The proceeds from the sale of *TREASURES OF THE SMOKIES - Tempting Recipes from East Tennessee* will support community projects sponsored by the Junior League of Johnson City, Tennessee.

To order additional copies of:

TREASURES OF THE SMOKIES,
Tempting Recipes from East Tennessee
or
SMOKY MOUNTAIN MAGIC
write to:

High South Publications
P. O. Box 1082
Johnson City, Tennessee 37605

First Printing   10,000 copies   October, 1986
Second Printing   5,000 copies   July, 1994

Wine descriptions and suggested food pairings provided by Ben Scharfstein of One Stop Wines and Liquors, Inc. of Johnson City.

Special thanks also to Dr. Martha Raidl and Jennifer Camp from the Department of Applied Human Sciences at East Tennessee State University for the nutritional analysis of the light and lean section.

THE JOHNSON CITY JUNIOR LEAGUE
Johnson City, Tennessee

Printed in the USA by
WIMMER
The Wimmer Companies, Inc.
Memphis • Dallas

INTRODUCTION:

Welcome to a glimpse of East Tennessee! Here you will find the first capital of the Southwest Territory, the oldest town in our state, mountains and lakes enough for the most avid water enthusiast and outdoorsperson, the Appalachian Trail, The Smoky Mountains National Forest, and a gracious mix of farming communities and metropolitan areas.

Diverse we are, a product of all who have gone before. Like the early settlers, we come from many backgrounds with ideas of how to accommodate ourselves to this beautiful area of the Upper South - and it to us. Many of our most loved foods are southern favorites, served with innovative, nutritionally sound methods of preparation. Many are "imports" from all parts of our country and the world, improved with a Tennessee cook's special touch.

Whether you are a native East Tennessean, a new resident, or summer visitor, we know you will find Tennessee's slogan, *"America At Its Best,"* to be appropriate for the recipes selected for you. Whether you choose to dine alone or with friends, throw a black-tie gala, or host a picnic, you will be sure to find some new favorites from this excellent variety. **ENJOY!**

ABOUT THE COVER:

Special thanks to J. Scott Graham/Scott's Shots for providing the front and back cover photographs. With an eye for the unusual, Graham travels from nearby sites around his home in East Tennessee to numerous locations throughout the Blue Ridge Mountains to record the beauty and uniqueness of this region on film. His images of wildlife, beautiful mountain scenery, and wonders of nature have gained national recognition by demonstrating an artistic viewpoint and revealing a unique ability to bring a fresh focus to familiar subjects. For more information on award winning images in the Scott's Shots collection of photographs, or for a free catalog of limited edition prints, please call (615) 854-9435.

Johnson City Junior League members and friends have submitted over 1200 recipes to be tested and edited for this book. We do not claim that all of the recipes are original, only that they are our favorites. We have selected the best variety of delicious recipes to suit your every meal!

This cookbook, **TREASURES OF THE SMOKIES,** is a revised edition of **Upper Crust, A Slice of the South**. We have added a suggested wine list and a section of light and lean recipes for you to enjoy.

⧖ When you see this "hourglass", you will know that it takes only a short time (15 minutes or less) in the kitchen to prepare this recipe; this does not include the cooking time.

The following hints will be helpful when using **TREASURES OF THE SMOKIES - Tempting Recipes from East Tennessee:**

- all oven temperatures are preheated
- flour is all-purpose
- heavy cream is whipping cream
- light cream is half and half
- oil is vegetable oil

COOKBOOK COMMITTEE

Charlotte L. Anderson
Judy H. Booze
Carolyn H. Coleman
Sissy W. Jones
Susan P. Fortune
Carol L. Link
Ann R. Littleford

Pamela D. Mathis
Emilee T. Matteau
Karen J. McGahey
Ann K. Mooneyhan
Anne E. Scholl
Sheryl D. Taylor
Tonya M. Wilkes

COMMITTEE FOR THE REVISION

Susan Bolton
Serena Crowder
Anna Lee Crysel
Kim DeGennaro
Michelle Ellis
Mildred Kidd

Vikki Link
Mary Duke McCartt
Linda Mitchell
Beverly Smith
Karen Smith
Carol Utsman

Contributors List

Frances C. Abernathy
Honey Alexander
Jean T. Alexander
Marge Allen
Margaret P. Alston
Cindy J. Anders
Joyce Anders
Charlotte L. Anderson
Hallie Anderson
Elizabeth Audley-Charles
Jesse Bacon
Vickie B. Bacon
Sherri T. Bailey
Karen Baker
Sue Baskette
Mildred Bates
Katie Battista
Elizabeth M. Beaver
Edwina Beardin
Ann Bender
Peggy B. Bender
Renee Bender
Jan C. Berg
Carolyn S. Berrong
Pam Billingsley
Jane Black
Debra W. Blair
Patty S. Bolton
Sarah Bolton
Judy H. Booze
Mrs. Adam Bowman
Zeph M. Bowman
Veronica R. Brannon
Mary G. Breeding
Anne Brewer
Betsy M. Bridgeforth
William A. Bridgeforth, M.D.
Jean Brobeck
Nellie K. Broderick
Velma Bryant
Erma W. Budd
Jane T. Burdick
Leona C. Burleson
Betsy P. Burleson
Pat E. Burleson
Karen·B. Burnett
Mrs. Jasper W. Calloway
Paula W. Calloway

Ellen W. Cambell
Ella Cannon
Margaret H. Carr
Karen M. Carriger
Anna Sue Carter
Joann C. Cheek
Julia B. Clements
Karen W. Cole
Sharon M. Cole
Carolyn H. Coleman
Elizabeth A. Colonna
Mary Lou S. Conant
Jean M. Conger
Jane L. Cornett
Debbie W. Corpening
Mrs. W.S. Corpening
Patricia V. Cosby
Trisha Cosby
Amy B. Costner
Janice M. Cotter
Ella A. Cox
Dorinda L. Creech
Polly T. Crowder
Louise M. Crowe
Margaret Crumley
Jean Darr
Deanna Davis
Shiela S. Dodson
Thelma Dodson
Elizabeth Dolfi
Emma Lou S. Doughty
Janelle M. Dunbar
Mrs. Winfield Dunn
Marjorie L. Dyer
Martha S. Eldred
Michelle A. Ellis
Marcella T. Epperson
Suzanne W. Ervin
Celeste T. Eversole
Jan H. Feazell
Jodie Ferguson
Mrs. Jimmy Fletcher
Mary B. Ford
Susan P. Fortune
Jenny C. Fowler
Janice E. Freeman
Connie B. Freemon
Hazel D. Fulton

Lura Gano
Theresa A. Gibbons
Dottie V. Gibson
Betty Glasgow
Marianna J. Gallong
Ann Goins
Betsy H. Gordon
Cathy Grant
Mary B. Graybeal
Karen C. Green
Michele J. Green
Sally B. Griffin
Vickie S. Grist
Kay H. Grogg
Mrs. Carl Groner
Novice H. Gross
Lucy K. Gump
Harriet A. Hager
Judy J. Hale
Jane Hales
Katherine H. Hall
Christine L. Hammond
Helen M. Hankins
Hannah Harris
Max T. Harrison
Lucy T. Hart
Diane W. Haynes
Audrey A. Head
Jacqueline L. Heath
Jo R. Hemphill
Ann G. Herndon
Nancy F. Herrin
Donna L. Herron
Bettye B. Hillman
Vickie M. Hinton
Clyta P. Holmes
Valda C. Holyfield
Patricia Hone
James D. Horton
Judy Myron Horton
Beth T. Imes
Margaret D. Ingram
Clarinda Jeanes
Virginia B. Jennings
Evine Jennings
Mrs. Arlie S. Johnson, Jr.
Evelyn Johnson
Betty M. Jones
Brenda Jones

Debby E. Jones
Elizabeth (Duffie) B. Jones
Lida W. Jones
Sissy W. Jones
Emily W. Jordan
Virginia M. Jordan
Rosalie J. King
Phyllis S. Kirk
Lori K. Kiser
Sandy D. Lauderback
Laura L. Lawrence
Joann Lawson
Nancy P. Lawson
Valerie B. Leath
Wanda G. Ledford
Esther A. Leonard
Amanda C. Link
Carol L. Link
Vertie Little
Ann M. Littleford
Cabell W. Lonon
Beth F. Lowe
Nancy J. Lowe
Holly Loy
Donna A. Lyon
Jill C. MacLean
Jacqueline Maddock
Mary Beth W. Malone
Beverly Matherly
Alyne Mathes
Beverly Matherly
Pamela D. Mathis
Emilee T. Matteau
Carolyn B. Mauk
Cathleen McComas
Carolyn McCracken
Sandra McGaha
Karen J. McGahey
Tim McGahey
Elizabeth A. McGowan
Vickie G. McGowan
Agnes McIlhaney
Carolee P. McKinstry
Ada H. McLeod
Aliesa Taylor Meade
Linda N. Medlin
Margaret Meechan
Martha Nan G. Meredith
Mindy Meredith

Mrs. Agnes S. Miller
Gay T. Miller
Mary Mitchell
Marjorie S. Mitchell
Judith Moody
Linda S. Mooney
Ann K. Mooneyhan
Suzanne W. Moore
Mary Will Morgan
Janice Morgan
Pat L. Moss
Eva T. Myron
Marjorie Nicholson
Joette D. Norman
Lynda D. Nystrom
Ginger P. Oaks
Susan C. O'Connor
Claire T. Oldham
A.K. Oldham
Ann O'Quinn
Mary Ostermeyer
Barbara F. Parker
Deborah L. Pakrul
Sandy Perkins
Lisa W. Pendelton
Ann B. Phillips
Peg M. Pickens
Barbara J. Pierce
Mary Lea D. Pittman
Pam M. Pittman
Frankye B. Poole
Brenda S. Porterfield
Maxine C. Preas
Billie G. Price
Frankie Y. Price
Suzanne Redmon
Ginny Reister
Carolyn W. Repass
Hazel D. Rice
Margaret G. Roberts
Vivian V. Rockwood
Virgnia N. Runge
Alison B. Runyan
Marty H. Runyan
Bonnie F. Sampson
Janie D. Sanders
Jeanette Saylor
Anne Elizabeth Scholl
Dot R. Scholl

Katherine Scholl
Mary Lou M. Scholl
Jan S. Scott
Louise D. Sells
Julie Seward
Cathy M. Shearin
Lucy Shelley
Judy G. Shelton
Rachel Shipley
Sandra W. Shumaker
Kitty Fuller Simmons
Lucy Skelton
Lisa T. Smalling
Carol P. Sloan
Kathie M. Souza
Beverly M. Smith
Karen M. Spannuth
Carolyn Speed
Sue O. Speer
Linda J. Spence
Shirley Stafford
Mrs. Mary Steffey
Amy Parker Stover
Betsy T. Street
Suzanne C. Street
Linda Streight
Mary L. Stribling
Verna B. Strickland
Ann T. Suedekum
Doris T. Summers
Nita W. Summers
Betty F. Swoyer
Barbara G. Taylor
Connie Cannon Taylor
Della Taylor
Jackilee T. Taylor
Jane H. Taylor
Sheryl D. Taylor
Cassandra S. Thomas
Mary P. Thompson
Patricia F. Thorton
Marjorie J. Thorp
Joanne S. Tillman
Katherine Toncray
Joyce W. Treadway
Jean S. Tucker
Polly Tyson
Lucy Vaughan
Jane W. Vermillion

Katie G. Walker
Sue Carr Walker
Mary Ellen Westbrook
Martha P. Wexler
Mrs. Hasford White
Kay R. Whitmore
Tonya M. Wilkes
Frances J. Williams
Jana L. Williams
Jean C. Williams
Martha C. Williams
Ann S. Wilson
Becky L. Wilson
Georgianna S. Wilson
Ray Wilson
Dianne D. Winn
Betty Witzke
Helen H. Wofford
Mary P. Wood
Mary S. Woods
Doris Wylie
Pat Yong
Cathy W. Young
Robin B. Young
Karen Cole
Michele Green
Mary Breeding
Betsy Burleson
Martha Eldred
Mary Graybeal
Novice H. Gross
Cabell W. Lonon
Suzanne Moore
Carol P. Sloan

Betsy Street
Lou Kieser
Carolyn Repass
Tonya Wilkes
Cathy Young
Jill Maclean
Janice Reid
Debra Blair
Robin Young
Allison Runyan
Suzanne Redman
Mrs. Winfield Dunn
Polly Crowder
Elizabeth Dolfi
Margaret Roberts
Hazel Rice
Ann Gilmer
Judith Moody
Marty Runyan
Lucy Shelley
Ann Suedkum
Tamara Younce
Clarinda Jeans
Hazel Fulton
Ellen Hodges
Alyne Mathes
Ann Goins
Linda Mooney
Cathleen McComas
Janice Freeman
Sandy Perkins
Sandy Lauderback
Renee Leach

Thank you to all the people who helped with recipes, testing and proofin

TABLE OF CONTENTS

BEVERAGES & APPETIZERS

"CURIOUS GEORGE'S SHAKE"

yield: 2 servings

3 large ripe bananas, peeled
1 (8-ounce) carton vanilla yogurt
  or 1 pint vanilla ice cream
2 Tablespoons peanut butter

Combine all ingredients in blender. Blend until smooth. Recipe can be doubled. Children especially enjoy this one!

FRUIT SLUSH

yield: 10-12 servings

1 (10-ounce) package frozen
  raspberries
1 (12-ounce) can pink lemonade
  concentrate
1 (12-ounce) can orange juice
  concentrate
1 (8-ounce) can crushed pineapple
  and juice
4 medium bananas, finely chopped
1 (32-ounce) lemon-lime carbonated beverage
¾ cup sugar
10-12 paper or styrofoam cups
  (3-ounce)

Thaw frozen items to slushy consistency. Mix all ingredients, pour into cups, and freeze. Thaw slightly in the microwave; it will return to a slushy consistency for serving. You may also add any other fruits in season.

A terrific snack or dessert!

HOT APPLE CIDER

yield: 8 cups

8 cups apple cider
½ cup brown sugar
1 teaspoon allspice
1 teaspoon whole cloves
¼ teaspoon salt
Dash nutmeg
3-4 cinnamon sticks

Mix together, simmer for 25 minutes, and strain.

A cheesecloth bag would save the straining.

FRESH MINT TEA

yield: 3 quarts

4 tea bags
12 mint leaves, large and fresh
3 cups water, boiling
1 cup orange juice
¼ cup lemon juice, fresh
1 cup sugar
6 cups water
Mint sprigs
Orange slices

Put tea bags and mint in a 3-quart pitcher. Add 3 cups boiling water; steep until cool. Discard tea bags and mint leaves. Add orange juice, lemon juice, sugar, and 6 cups water to tea mixture. Stir until sugar is dissolved. Serve over ice garnished with mint sprigs and orange slices.

Refreshing any time! — and with anything!

FRUIT TEA PUNCH

yield: 50 servings

2½ cups sugar
1 cup water
2 cups strong tea
1 cup lemon juice
2½ cups orange juice
2 cups pineapple juice
2 cups frozen strawberries
1 quart gingerale

Make a syrup of the sugar and water. Add the tea, lemon juice, orange juice, pineapple juice and additional water to make 1½ gallons. Stir in frozen strawberries and gingerale before serving.

HOT CRANBERRY PUNCH

yield: 25 servings

8 cups cranberry juice
1 (46-ounce) can unsweetened
   pineapple juice
2-4 cups water, to taste
⅔ cup brown sugar
3 cinnamon sticks
1 Tablespoon whole cloves
1 Tablespoon whole allspice
2 whole lemons, halved or
   quartered

Pour cranberry juice, pineapple juice, and water in the bottom of a large coffee maker. Place remaining ingredients in coffee basket and perk. Serve warm. Leftovers can be refrigerated and reheated.

BANANA SLUSH PUNCH

yield: 54 6-ounce servings

4 cups sugar
8 cups warm water
12 medium bananas
1 cup lemon juice
8 cups pineapple juice
5 cups orange juice
3 (2-liter) lemon-lime sodas

Dissolve sugar in warm water. Combine bananas and lemon juice in blender or food processor and pureé. Add to juices and water. Freeze. Thaw to a slush and add soda. This will not freeze after adding soda. To keep bananas from turning brown, when they float to the top pour a small amount of additional lemon juice on the top after freezing.

You may add rum to Punch! A cabana and a bottle of suntan lotion — PARADISE!!

O. J. DELIGHT

yield: 10 4-ounce servings

1 cup sugar
2 cups boiling water
1 (6-ounce) can frozen orange juice
1 (15¼-ounce) can crushed
    pineapple, undrained
3 medium bananas, sliced
2½ Tablespoons lemon juice
Fresh mint for garnish (optional)

Combine all ingredients. Refrigerate for 24 hours, stirring occasionally. After 24 hours refrigeration, freeze overnight until firm. Set out of freezer 15 minutes before serving to soften slightly. Serve in individual small bowls or champagne glasses.

May be frozen in paper cups for a children's party.

ORANGE JUICE DRINK

yield: 8 6-ounce servings

1 (6-ounce) can frozen orange juice concentrate
½ cup milk
1½ cups cold water
¼ cup sugar
½ teaspoon vanilla
10-12 ice cubes

Combine all ingredients in a blender and blend well.

TANGY FRUIT PUNCH

yield: 40 6-ounce servings

1 (3-ounce) package lemon gelatin
2 (6-ounce) cans frozen lemonade concentrate
1 (46-ounce) can pineapple juice
1 (46-ounce) can orange juice or 2 (6-ounce) cans frozen orange juice
2 quarts water
2 teaspoons vanilla extract or 1 teaspoon almond extract
2 cups sugar
1-2 (28-ounce) bottles gingerale, chilled

Combine gelatin, lemonade, pineapple juice, orange juice, water, vanilla extract and sugar. Chill. It is even better when it is frozen solid and allowed to thaw 2 hours before serving. It will have ice crystals and be very cold. Add gingerale and serve.

This is a very flexible recipe that can be adapted to personal taste.

HOT CHOCOLATE SUPREME

yield: 10-12 servings

3 (1-ounce) squares unsweetened
  chocolate
½ cup cold water
½ cup sugar
⅛ teaspoon salt
½ cup cream, whipped fairly stiff,
  no substitutes
1 teaspoon vanilla extract
Hot milk

Over low heat, combine chocolate and water. Stir until melted and smooth. Add sugar and salt; bring to a boil for 5 minutes. Cool. Fold in cream and vanilla; refrigerate. To serve put 2-3 teaspoons in a cup and fill with hot milk.

Variation: To make chocolate sauce just omit cream.

FROZEN WHISKEY SOUR

yield: 4-6 servings

1 (6-ounce) can frozen lemonade,
  thawed
1 (6-ounce) can frozen orange
  juice, thawed
3 cans water
1½ cans (9-ounce) bourbon
2 Tablespoons sugar
2 Tablespoons maraschino cherry
  juice
Maraschino cherries to garnish

Mix all ingredients and freeze in individual high ball glasses or a pitcher. (Does not freeze solid). Thaw 10 minutes before serving. May use a blender by omitting water and adding one tray ice cubes. Serve immediately. Garnish with cherries.

SECRET WHITE HOUSE EGGNOG

yield: 30 4-ounce servings

1 gallon commercial eggnog mix
2½ cups bourbon
1⅔ cups rum
1⅔ cups brandy
1 quart eggnog (saved) or ice
   cream
Vanilla, to taste
Nutmeg, to taste

Mix eggnog, bourbon, rum and brandy. Add saved eggnog or ice cream. Add vanilla and sprinkle nutmeg on top. After making eggnog, reserve 1 quart. Store sealed in refrigerator to use in next batch. Tastes best if made 2 months before serving.

This recipe was given to me by my brother. He was head of the English Dept. at St. Stephen's School, Alexandria, Va. The wife of the White House Pastry Chef gave him this recipe. John Ficlin, the White House maitre d' says, "We keep it in the refrigerator, all sealed up. Nothing's going to go bad — after all, liquor stores keep milk and liquor mixtures on the shelf for a long time. I like to make a new batch at least a week before I serve it. It would be better if we made it in October for December. I like to make it for the whole season."

TOASTED ALMOND

yield: 2 servings

1½ ounces coffee liqueur
6 ounces vanilla ice cream
1½ ounces Amaretto
1 ounce sweet cream

Blend all ingredients on low speed of blender for 15 seconds.

MOUNTAIN WINE

yield: 1 gallon

½ cup water, warm
1 cake yeast, no substitutions
2 (12-ounce) cans frozen grape
   juice thawed
4 cups sugar
1 gallon glass jug (small neck)
1 10-inch balloon

Dissolve yeast in water. Add thawed grape juice and sugar, mix well. Pour mixture into gallon jug and fill almost to the top with water. Cover top of jug with the balloon. Place jug in a cool 'Happy Spot', and do not disturb for 30 days.

You may have to replace the balloon if it over inflates. You may also substitute any fruit juice appropriate for wine.

QUICK SANGRIA

yield: 5 quarts

2 (12-ounce) cans frozen pink
   lemonade concentrate, thawed
1 (33.8-ounce) bottle rosé, chilled
1 (33.8-ounce) bottle Burgundy,
   chilled
Juice of 2 limes
2 (33.8-ounce) bottles club soda,
   chilled
1 lemon, thinly sliced
1 lime, thinly sliced
1 orange, thinly sliced

Combine lemonade, wines and lime juice, mixing well. Slowly stir in club soda. Garnish with lemon, lime and orange slices. Serve over ice.

BRANDY SLUSH

yield: 1 gallon

7 cups water
1 cup sugar
3 tea bags
1 (12-ounce) can lemonade, concentrate
1 (12-ounce) can orange juice, concentrate
2 cups brandy or rum
Lemon-lime soda or ginger ale

Combine water and sugar. Boil, stirring until sugar is dissolved. Steep the tea bags in the hot water and sugar solution until water is cool. Remove tea bags. Add orange juice and lemonade concentrate, then brandy or rum. Put into plastic container and freeze.

To serve: Fill glasses ⅔ full with frozen mixture. Fill glass with soda. For punch, put all of frozen mixture into punch bowl. Add 2 quarts soda.

TUMBLEWEED

yield: 2 servings

2½ ounces light cream
1½ ounces brandy
1½ ounces Tia Maria (no substitutes)
1½ ounces dark crème de cacao
3 teaspoons crushed ice
Vanilla ice cream, to desired thickness
Chocolate curls

In standard size 4 cup blender combine cream, liqueurs and ice. Fill blender with ice cream. Blend well, adding more ice cream to desired thickness. Garnish with chocolate curls.

HOT BUTTERED RUM

yield: 1 gallon

Base:
1 pound powdered sugar
1 pound brown sugar
2 cups butter, softened (no substitutes)
2 Tablespoons cinnamon
1½ Tablespoons nutmeg
½ gallon vanilla ice cream, softened
Rum
Boiling water

Base: Mix together sugars, butter, cinnamon, nutmeg and ice cream. Store in refrigerator up to 3 weeks.

To serve: Spoon 3 tablespoons of base into large mug. Add 2 ounces of rum and fill with boiling water. Stir well.

Divide into decorative jars — makes a lovely Christmas or hostess gift. Your friends will eagerly await their Christmas gift each year. Suggested accompaniments: A SWISS CHALET!

PLANTATION COFFEE

yield: 1 serving

Sugar
1 ounce dark rum
1 ounce dark crème de cacao
1 ounce Tia Maria
Brewed coffee, hot
Whipping cream

Wet rim or very edge of coffee glass (or mug) and dip in plate of sugar. Measure rum, crème de cacao and Tia Maria into glass and mix. Fill cup ¾ full with coffee and top with freshly whipped cream. Serve immediately.

GREEK ANTIPASTO

yield: 10-12 servings

¼ cup water
2 cups carrots, cut in 2-inch slices
½ head cauliflower, cut in flowerets
2 or more stalks celery, cut in
   1-inch slices
1 green pepper, cut in 2-inch strips
1 (4-ounce) jar pimientos, drained
1 (3-ounce) jar green olives, pitted
¾ cup wine vinegar
½ cup olive oil
2 Tablespoons sugar
1 teaspoon salt
½ teaspoon oregano or Italian
   (spices) seasoning
¼ teaspoon pepper
1 (3¼-ounce) can black olives,
   pitted
Cherry tomatoes, optional
Salami, optional

Excellent with pasta!

In large skillet combine all ingredients except black olives. Bring to a boil, reduce heat, simmer 5 minutes. Add black olives and cool. Refrigerate at least 8 hours. Cherry tomatoes or salami may be added when served.

To increase recipe: Double the vegetables and triple the spices, oil and vinegar.

ARTICHOKE DIP

yield: 8-10 servings
oven temperature: 350°

1 (14-ounce) can artichoke hearts,
   drained and chopped
1 (6-ounce) jar marinated artichoke
   hearts, drained and chopped
1 (4-ounce) can green chilies,
   drained and chopped
6 Tablespoons mayonnaise
2 cups Cheddar cheese, grated

Mix all ingredients together. Place in 1½-quart casserole. Bake at 350° for 20 minutes. Serve with corn chips or other party crackers.

Variation: 1 cup mayonnaise
         1 cup Parmesan cheese
         1 (14-ounce) can artichoke hearts, drained, chopped.
         Mix and bake as above.

MARINATED ARTICHOKES AND MUSHROOMS

yield: 10-12 servings

1 envelope Italian dressing mix,
   made with twice the amount of
   cider vinegar
1 bay leaf
1 clove garlic, cut in half
1 teaspoon peppercorns
¼ cup fresh parsley
¼ teaspoon oregano
2 pounds mushrooms, halved if
   large
2 (14-ounce) cans artichoke hearts

Combine dressing and herbs; shake well. In a large bowl, combine mushrooms and artichokes. Pour dressing mixture over vegetables and toss to coat them. Chill 24 hours, tossing occasionally. Serve with toothpicks.

ARTICHOKE FRITTATA

yield: 60 appetizers or 8 luncheon servings
oven temperature: 325°F.

3 (6-ounce) jars marinated
  artichoke hearts, chopped
3 bunches green onions, chopped
1 clove garlic, chopped
8 eggs, beaten
10 soda crackers, crushed
½ bunch parsley, chopped
1 pound Cheddar cheese, grated
Dash hot sauce
Dash Worcestershire sauce
Salt, to taste
Pepper, to taste

Drain the oil from artichokes and use it to sauté the onions and garlic until they are limp. Add the crackers to the eggs and beat. Add artichoke hearts, parsley, cheese, hot sauce, Worcestershire, salt and pepper, beating after each addition. Bake in a greased 8 x 12 inch pan at 325° for 35 minutes or until firm.

This may be served hot or cold.

TANGY ASPARAGUS ROLL-UPS

yield: 40 roll-ups
oven temperature: 350°F

4 ounces blue cheese
4 ounces Roquefort cheese
8 ounces cream cheese
1 egg
1 Tablespoon mayonnaise
40 slices white bread, crust
  trimmed and flattened to paper
  thin with a rolling pin
2 (14½-ounce) cans asparagus
  spears
½ cup butter, melted
Paprika

Blend blue cheese, Roquefort cheese, cream cheese, egg and mayonnaise with mixer. Spread on both sides of the bread. Place 1 or 2 spears diagonally on the bread and roll up. Dip into butter seasoned with paprika. Bake at 350° for 15 minutes.

MARINATED MUSHROOMS

yield: 8 servings

1 (8-ounce) can whole mushrooms
½ cup tarragon vinegar
½ cup dark brown sugar
½ teaspoon black peppercorns
1 bay leaf
1 clove garlic, sliced

Drain mushrooms, reserving juice. Add enough water to juice to make 1 cup. Put in pan and add all other ingredients. (You may put spices in cheesecloth if desired.) Bring to a boil. Pour over mushrooms. Cover and refrigerate at least 24 hours.

BACON STUFFED MUSHROOMS

yield: 2 dozen mushrooms
oven temperature: 450°F

1 pound mushrooms, fresh
  medium size
2 Tablespoons butter
4 slices bacon, crisp, crumbled
3 Tablespoons mayonnaise
1 Tablespoon lemon juice, fresh
½ teaspoon garlic salt
1 Tablespoon Parmesan cheese

Remove mushroom stems. Sauté mushroom caps in butter 10 minutes or longer until brown and soft. Drain thoroughly between paper towels. Combine remaining ingredients. Fill mushroom caps and arrange on a cookie sheet. Sprinkle with additional Parmesan cheese. Bake at 450° for 10 minutes or until cheese browns.

MUSHROOM CANAPES

yield: 24 canapes
oven temperature: 350 °F

1 (8-ounce) can mushrooms, chopped and drained
2 Tablespoons margarine
½ teaspoon garlic salt
½ teaspoon instant minced onion
1 teaspoon lemon juice
1 teaspoon Worcestershire sauce
1 (8-ounce) can crescent rolls
1 (3-ounce) package cream cheese, softened
¼ cup Parmesan cheese, grated

Brown mushrooms in a skillet with margarine. Stir in salt, onion, lemon juice and Worcestershire sauce. Cook until liquid evaporates. Separate crescent dough into 2 rectangles. Press into the bottom of a 9 x 13-inch pan and ¼-inch up the sides to form a crust. Spread the cream cheese over the dough then top with mushrooms and Parmesan cheese. Bake 20-25 minutes until golden brown. Cool 5 minutes and cut into bars or triangles. Refrigerate any leftovers. To reheat, wrap in foil; heat at 350° for 8-10 minutes.

ONION TOAST APPETIZER

yield: 96 appetizers

1 loaf bread
1 (4-ounce) can Parmesan cheese
3 ounces cream cheese
1 small onion, grated
1-2 Tablespoons mayonnaise to cream ingredients together
Cayenne pepper, to taste

Cut bottom out of Parmesan cheese can. Cut 4 rounds of bread from each slice using bottom of can. Mix all ingredients together except bread. Spread on bread rounds. Place on cookie sheet and broil 2-3 minutes.

May be frozen before cooking.

SAUSAGE CANAPES

yield: 70 canapes
oven temperature: 350° F

1 pound ground chuck
1 pound ground sausage
1 pound processed Mexican style
  cheese spread
1 teaspoon garlic salt
1 teaspoon soy sauce
1 Tablespoon oregano, ground
3 Tablespoons Mexican salsa, if
  desired
2 loaves party rye bread

Cook ground chuck and sausage; drain well. Cut cheese into cubes and add to meat. Return skillet to low heat. Cover skillet until cheese melts. Add remaining seasonings. Spread on bread and freeze on cookie sheet, transferring to freezer bag or container when completely frozen.

When ready to serve, remove number of canapes desired and place on baking sheet. Bake at 350° for 11-12 minutes or until bubbly and hot.

⧗ MARINATED OYSTERETTES

yield: 1 pound

1 cup oil
1 package ranch style dressing mix
1 Tablespoon dill weed
1 (1-pound) box oyster crackers

Spread crackers on jelly roll pan. Mix oil, ranch dressing and dill weed. Pour over crackers and mix well. Put in an airtight container. Shake often to mix and let set overnight.

You may substitute blue cheese or another flavor dressing mix for variety.

CUCUMBER CANAPES

yield: 32-36 sandwiches

1 loaf party rye bread slices
2 medium cucumbers
1 (8-ounce) package cream cheese
2 Tablespoons mayonnaise
3 Tablespoons dried chives
1 teaspoon parsley
1 teaspoon basil
1 Tablespoon lemon juice, freshly
  squeezed (approximately ½
  lemon)
Mayonnaise (for spreading)
Green olives, halved
Paprika

Trim crusts from rye slices. Slice unpeeled cucumbers and drain on paper towels. With electric mixer cream the cheese, mayonnaise, chives, parsley, basil and lemon juice. Spread each slice of rye bread with mayonnaise; top with cucumber slice and a dollop of the cream cheese mixture. Drain green olives on paper toweling. Top each canape with olive half and sprinkle with paprika. The olive may be secured with a toothpick, if desired.

The cream cheese mixture may be prepared ahead. Canapes have an especially attractive appearance if cream cheese mixture is piped from a pastry bag.

MAMA'S HOLIDAY PECANS

yield: 3 cups
oven temperature: 250 °F

3 cups pecan halves
½ cup salted butter, melted
Chili powder, optional

Place pecans on cookie sheet. Drizzle butter over pecans. Bake at 250° for 1 hour. Sprinkle chili powder over nuts after baking. Cool and store in covered container.

CREAM CHEESE PASTRY

oven temperature: 350°F

1 cup butter, softened
1 (8-ounce) package cream cheese
½ teaspoon salt
2 cups flour, unsifted
1 egg yolk
2 teaspoons cream or milk

Beat butter, cream cheese and salt together in mixer until completely smooth. Work in flour to form a smooth dough. Flatten dough in foil to form an 8 x 6-inch rectangle. Chill overnight. Remove from refrigerator 8 to 10 minutes before rolling.

Divide dough in half. Roll ½ of dough on a floured pastry cloth with a floured rolling pin or between 2 sheets of waxed paper. Shape as directed for variations. Beat egg yolk with cream and brush tops of pastries. Chill before baking.

Dough may be made and chilled for several days before baking. Dough freezes well — add 5 to 10 minutes to baking time and bake without defrosting.

This recipe may be used as the pastry for the following three recipes: Parmesan Twists, Poppy Seed Rolls and Dill Sticks.

PARMESAN TWISTS

yield: 2 dozen
oven temperature: 350°F

½ recipe cream cheese pastry
½ cup Parmesan cheese
1 egg yolk
2 teaspoons cream or milk

Divide dough in half and roll each half into a large ¼-inch thick rectangle. Sprinkle heavily with cheese. Press cheese lightly into dough with rolling pin. Fold dough over itself into thirds; roll again. Sprinkle with more cheese, press again with rolling pin and fold into thirds. Roll into a 4 x 8-inch rectangle ¼-inch thick. Beat egg yolk with milk or cream. Brush dough with egg mixture. Cut into strips 4 x ¾-inches. Twist strips into spirals and place on ungreased cookie sheet. Brush ends with remaining egg yolk mixture. Chill 1 hour. Bake at 350° for 15 to 20 minutes or until crispy and golden. Carefully remove from pan at once.

POPPY SEED ROLLS

yield: 2 dozen
oven temperature: 350°F

½ recipe cream cheese pastry
Butter, softened
Poppy seeds
1 egg yolk
2 teaspoons cream or milk

Divide dough in half. Roll each half ⅛-inch thick. Fold dough over itself in thirds. Roll again and fold again. Roll once more ⅛-inch thick. Cut into 2½-inch squares with a scalloped pastry wheel.

Brush lightly with soft butter, sprinkle heavily with poppy seeds. Press poppy seeds into dough with rolling pin. Beginning at one corner roll to opposite corner. Moisten ungreased cookie sheet. Beat egg yolk with cream. Brush tops of rolls with egg mixture and sprinkle with more poppy seeds if desired. Chill 1 hour.

Bake rolls at 350° for 15 minutes or until puffed and golden.

DILL STICKS

yield: 6½ dozen
oven temperature: 350°F

½ recipe cream cheese pastry
1 teaspoon dried dillweed
Dill seed
Coarse salt

Add dillweed to pastry dough, chill overnight. Divide dough in half. Roll each half ⅛-inch thick and fold dough over itself in thirds. Roll and fold again. Roll into rectangle ⅛-inch thick. Cut into 2 inch strips and roll into ropes. Cut into 4-inch sticks. Beat egg yolk mixture. Sprinkle with dill seed and coarse salt if desired. Place on ungreased cookie sheet and chill 1 hour. Bake for 15 to 18 minutes.

SESAME CHEESE STICKS

yield: 6-7 dozen sticks
oven temperature: 350°F

⅓ cup butter or margarine
1 cup flour
½ teaspoon sugar
14 ounces Cheddar cheese, grated
¼ teaspoon salt
½ teaspoon ginger or cayenne
    pepper
2 teaspoons water
1 egg yolk
¼ cup sesame seeds

Cut butter into dry ingredients until mixture resembles coarse meal. Add water, egg yolk and sesame seeds and mix well with hands. Roll to ⅛-inch thickness. Cut into ½ x 2-inch sticks. Bake on ungreased cookie sheets at 350°F for 12-15 minutes; or until lightly browned.

HONEY ALEXANDER'S CHEESE STRAWS

yield: 6 dozen
oven temperature: 350°F

½ pound extra sharp Cheddar
   cheese, grated
½ cup butter, softened
½ teaspoon salt
⅛ - ¼ teaspoon cayenne pepper
1½ cups flour
Paprika
Salt

Mix all ingredients into a dough that is soft and pliable. Squeeze through a cookie press with a number 1 disc; make long strips and place on an ungreased shiny cookie sheet. Bake at 350°F for 20 minutes. Cut into 2-inch pieces while still warm, but let cool on pan. Sprinkle lightly with paprika and salt. Store in airtight container.

If you don't have a cookie press just roll the dough out and cut into strips.

ALMOND CHEESE ROUNDS

oven temperature: 350°F

1 cup butter, softened
8 ounces sharp Cheddar cheese,
   grated
2 cups flour
Dash of salt
Dash of cayenne pepper
Almonds, crushed
Powdered sugar

Cream butter and cheese; add flour and seasonings. Chill for several hours. Roll thinly and cut with small biscuit cutter. Sprinkle with crushed almonds. Bake at 350° for about 30 minutes or until golden brown. When cool, sprinkle with powdered sugar.

SWISS CHEESE PUFFS

yield: 20-24 puffs
oven temperature: 450°F

½ cup water, hot
¼ cup butter
⅛ teaspoon salt
⅛ teaspoon sugar
½ cup flour
¾ teaspoon dry mustard
Dash cayenne pepper
2 eggs
½ cup (2-ounce) natural Swiss
  cheese, shredded

In saucepan combine water, butter, salt and sugar. Beat until butter melts and mixture boils. Stir in flour, mustard and add cayenne pepper all at once. Continue stirring until mixture leaves sides of pan forming a ball. Remove from heat and add eggs one at a time. Stir in cheese. Drop by teaspoonfuls onto a cookie sheet.

Bake at 450° for 10 minutes. Reduce heat to 375° and continue baking for 15 minutes. Turn off oven and let puffs sit in warm oven for 3 minutes. Serve immediately.

For smoother puffs use a pastry tube to drop onto cookie sheet. Gruyere cheese may be substituted.

ZESTY CHEESE SPREAD

yield: 2½ cups
oven temperature: 350°

1 cup sharp Cheddar cheese,
  grated
1 cup mayonnaise
1 cup onion, finely chopped
  (preferably Walla-Walla or
  Vidalia)

Mix all ingredients. Bake uncovered 15 to 20 minutes at 350°. Serve with crackers.

FETA CHEESE TARTS

yield: 40 miniature tarts
oven temperature: 350°F

2 (3-ounce) packages cream cheese
1 cup butter, no substitutes
2 cups flour
1 cup light cream
1 pound feta cheese
3 eggs
1 teaspoon cornstarch
½ teaspoon dried thyme
1 garlic clove, crushed
Pepper, to taste
12 black olives, sliced

PASTRY: Blend 3 ounces cream cheese with ½ cup butter and cut in 1 cup flour. Repeat the process in a separate bowl. DO NOT DOUBLE! Chill the dough 1 hour. Evenly press a 1-inch ball of dough into each tin of a 1½-inch tart pan. Prick the sides and bottoms of each tart with a fork and bake at 350° for 7 to 8 minutes.

FILLING: Combine the cream, cheese and eggs in an electric blender and blend at medium speed until thoroughly blended. Add cornstarch, garlic, thyme and pepper and blend 45 seconds more.

TO BAKE: Fill each tart shell almost to the top. Bake in tins at 350° for 30 to 35 minutes. Top each tart with an olive slice and serve or freeze.

These are worth the effort and everyone enjoys them, even feta cheese skeptics.

BRIE en CROUTE

yield: 6-8 servings
oven temperature: 450°F

½ cup flour
Dash of salt
¼ cup butter, chilled and beaten
2 ounces cream cheese
1 small round of Brie
1 egg yolk
2 teaspoons water

Sift flour with the salt and cut in the butter and the cream cheese to resemble coarse crumbs. Refrigerate overnight. Roll pastry out on a floured board to ⅛-inch thickness. Place the cheese in the middle and enclose with the pastry. Make a small hole in the middle to allow steam to escape. Refrigerate 1 hour.

Mix egg yolk and water and brush the top of the pastry immediately before baking. Bake 450° for 20 minutes.

Double pastry recipe for a medium round of Brie.

CORNED BEEF DIP IN RYE BREAD

yield: 3 cups

1½ cups sour cream
1½ cups mayonnaise
1 teaspoon dill seed or dill weed
1 teaspoon salt
1 Tablespoon prepared horseradish
2 Tablespoons parsley
3 (2½-ounce) pressed corned beef, chopped fine
1 (2-pound) light rye bread, round or oval loaf, unsliced

Mix all ingredients together, except bread, and refrigerate 4 hours (minimum) or overnight.

Cut a circle from the top of the bread and tear out the bread inside leaving a hole, fill with dip. Serve the torn out pieces for dipping.

HERB CHEESE SPREAD

yield: 3 cups

8 ounces whipped butter, softened
2 (8-ounce) packages cream cheese, softened
¼ teaspoon garlic powder
½ teaspoon oregano
¼ teaspoon each: basil, dillweed, marjoram, thyme, black pepper

Mix all ingredients with mixer. Refrigerate at least overnight to blend spices. Serve with crackers or on baked potatoes. Can be molded if desired.

CREAMY HERB DIP

yield: 1½ cups

1 cup mayonnaise
½ Tablespoon lemon juice
½ teaspoon salt
¼ teaspoon paprika
¼ cup parsley, chopped or dried
1 Tablespoon onion, grated
1 Tablespoon chives, chopped
⅛ teaspoon curry powder
½ teaspoon Worcestershire sauce
Garlic salt, to taste
1 Tablespoon capers
½ cup sour cream

Mix all ingredients, folding in sour cream last. Serve as a dip for raw vegetables. May be prepared 1-2 days ahead.

ORIENTAL DIP

yield: 1 cup

½ cup mayonnaise
½ cup sour cream
2 Tablespoons scallions, chopped
2 Tablespoons milk
1 teaspoon ground ginger
1 teaspoon white vinegar
4 teaspoons soy sauce

Combine all ingredients. Chill. Serve with fresh vegetables.

May substitute 1 cup mayonnaise instead of mayonnaise and sour cream.

BROCCOLI CHEESE DIP

yield: 3 cups

3 stalks celery, finely chopped
1 medium onion, finely chopped
2 Tablespoons butter
1 (10-ounce) package frozen
   chopped broccoli, cooked and
   drained
1 (10¾-ounce) can cream of
   mushroom soup
1 roll garlic cheese
Worcestershire sauce to taste
Hot sauce to taste
Crab meat (optional)

Sauté onion and celery in the butter. Add cooked broccoli, mushroom soup, garlic cheese, Worcestershire sauce and hot sauce. Simmer until all ingredients are blended well. Serve immediately in chafing dish.

Variation: You may add ½ can tomatoes and green chilies if desired, or just the juice. One pound of fresh lump crab meat is a delicious addition also.

MEXICAN CHEESE BITES

yield: 117 1-inch squares
oven temperature: 350°F

12 ounces Cheddar cheese, grated
12 ounces Monterey Jack cheese, grated
5 eggs
¾ cup hot picante sauce

Mix the Cheddar and Monterey Jack cheeses together. Sprinkle half the cheese in a 9 x 13-inch pan. Beat eggs; add picante sauce, and pour over cheese. Sprinkle remainder of cheese on top. Bake at 350° for 30 minutes. Cool slightly and cut into 1-inch squares. Serve warm with tortilla chips.

MEXICAN CHEESE DIP

yield: 12-16 servings

½ pound ground beef
1 pound American cheese
1 (5.3 ounce) can evaporated milk
¼ teaspoon garlic powder
1 teaspoon cumin
1 Tablespoon chili powder
1 (10-ounce) can tomatoes with green chilies

Cook crumbled ground beef until brown; drain and set aside. Melt cheese in top of double boiler. Mix together milk, seasonings and tomatoes in blender; blend thoroughly. Add drained beef and blended ingredients to cheese mixture and heat.

Serve with corn chips or tortilla chips.

Note: If recipe is doubled, mix blended ingredients one recipe at a time.

CHILI MUNCHIES

yield: 8-10 servings
oven temperature: 350°F

1 pound hot sausage, cooked and
  drained
1 pound sharp Cheddar cheese,
  shredded (4 cups)
1 (4-ounce) can green chili peppers,
  chopped
6 eggs, slightly beaten
½ teaspoon chili powder

Sprinkle sausage in a greased 13 x 9-inch pan. Cover the sausage with the cheese. Mix together eggs, peppers and chili powder. Bake at 350° for 30 minutes. Cool slightly and cut into bite size pieces.

Your guests will not be very polite so you'll have to make sure you get one in the kitchen before serving.

PICO de GALLO

yield: 2 cups

1 (4-ounce) can green chilies,
  chopped
1 (4-ounce) can ripe olives,
  chopped
2-3 small tomatoes, chopped
4-6 scallions with tops, chopped
1 Tablespoon oil
1 Tablespoon vinegar
1½ teaspoons garlic salt
Nachos, tortilla chips (corn
  flavor), or corn chips

Mix all ingredients and serve with chips. May be prepared several hours in advance, but it may be necessary to drain some liquid before serving.

HOT SPINACH ROLY-POLYS

yield: 75-100
oven temperature: 300°F

4 (10-ounce) packages frozen
   chopped spinach
4 cups herb stuffing mix
2 onions, large, chopped
8 eggs, beaten
1 cup Parmesan cheese, grated
1½ cups butter, melted
1 Tablespoon thyme
2 cloves garlic, minced
Salt and pepper, to taste

Cook spinach and drain well, squeezing out all liquid. Mix with remaining ingredients and blend well. Chill at least 2 hours. Roll into balls 1-inch in diameter. Bake at 300° until golden brown. If desired, freeze unbaked spinach balls on cookie sheet and remove to freezer bags when frozen. Thaw before baking or bake an additional 10-15 minutes.

HAM WHEELS

yield: 100 wheels

2 (8-ounce) packages cream cheese
10 slices boiled ham
10 green onions
Fresh parsley sprigs, garnish

Spread softened cream cheese out to edges of ham slice. Place a cleaned and trimmed green onion across short end and roll up. Trim ends of onions and pack ham roll with extra cheese if necessary. Repeat with each ham slice. Refrigerate about one hour. Cut each roll into slices about one inch long. Arrange on platter with parsley sprigs.

SPINACH TARTS

yield: 2½ dozen
oven temperature: 350°F

1 (10-ounce) package frozen
    chopped spinach, thawed,
    drained
1 egg, beaten
¼ teaspoon salt
⅛ teaspoon pepper
2 Tablespoons onion, chopped
1 cup feta, crumbled or 1 cup
    Romano, grated
¼ cup butter, melted
Cream cheese patty shells, recipe
    below
2 Tablespoons Romano, grated
Pimiento, diced (optional)

PASTRY SHELLS:
1 (3-ounce) package cream cheese,
    softened
½ cup butter or margarine,
    softened
1½ cups flour

Place spinach on paper towels
and squeeze until barely moist.
Combine spinach, eggs, salt, pepper, onion, cheese, butter and
mix well. Fill each patty shell
with 1 heaping teaspoon of
spinach mixture; sprinkle with
Romano cheese. Bake at 350° for
30 to 35 minutes. Garnish with
pimiento.

PASTRY SHELLS: Combine
cream cheese and butter; cream
until smooth. Add flour and mix
well. Shape dough into 30
(1-inch) balls. Place in ungreased
1¾-inch muffin pans and shape
into shells.

SMOKED FISH SPREAD

yield: 2-2½ cups

1 (16-ounce) can salmon, drained and flaked
1 (8-ounce) package cream cheese
1 Tablespoon lemon juice
2 teaspoons onion, grated
¼ teaspoon salt
1 teaspoon liquid smoke
1 teaspoon Worcestershire sauce
1 teaspoon horseradish
½ cup pecans, chopped
2 teaspoons fresh parsley, chopped fine

Combine cream cheese, lemon, onion, salt and salmon; mix thoroughly. Add liquid smoke, Worcestershire, horseradish and blend well. Place mixture on wax paper and shape into a log. Chill for several hours. Combine pecans and parsley. Roll log in nut-parsley mixture. Serve with crackers.

HOT CLAM DIP

yield: 1 cup
oven temperature: 300°

1 (7½-ounce) can clams, minced, drained
1 (8-ounce) package cream cheese, softened
1 Tablespoon lemon juice
1 teaspoon Worcestershire sauce
⅛ teaspoon pepper
1 Tablespoon mayonnaise
½ Tablespoon parsley, chopped
¼ teaspoon mustard
½ Tablespoon chives or onion, chopped

Mix all ingredients together. Heat in oven proof serving bowl at 300°F. for 15 minutes or microwave 2 to 3 minutes on high.

Serve with crackers or potato chips.

SHRIMP SPREAD

yield: 2 cups

1 (8-ounce) package cream cheese, softened
⅓ cup salad dressing or mayonnaise
3 Tablespoons chili sauce
2 teaspoons lemon juice
½ teaspoon onion juice
¼ teaspoon Worcestershire sauce
¾ pound small shrimp, cooked and drained
Salt, to taste
Crackers

Blend cream cheese, salad dressing, chili sauce, lemon juice, onion juice and Worcestershire sauce until smooth.

Stir in shrimp and salt.
Refrigerate until serving time.
Spread on crackers.

Variations: This would be excellent stuffed in an avocado or tomato for a luncheon. Serve on a generous bed of lettuce and chopped cucumber.

TULIP CANAPES

White bread
Butter or margarine
Cream cheese, softened
1 (6-ounce) bag frozen small shrimp
1 green pepper
Garlic, to taste
Worcestershire sauce

Cut white bread into 1 x 2-inch rectangles. Spread with butter or margarine. Spread with softened cream cheese. Put small shrimp at the top. (Note: may be frozen at this point). Place a long piece of green pepper below shrimp for the stem. Add 1 or 2 small green pepper strips at side of stem for leaves.

It is extremely pretty and really dresses up your table at a party!

SHRIMP AND CRAB SPREAD

yield: 10-12 servings

1 (10¾-ounce) can tomato soup,
  undiluted
1 (3-ounce) package cream cheese
1 cup mayonnaise
2 packages unflavored gelatin
¼ cup water
1 medium onion
1 medium green pepper
1 stalk celery
Dash hot sauce
2 (4½-ounce) cans crab meat,
  drained
1 cup shrimp, cooked

Heat soup and cream cheese until dissolved. Mix gelatin and water, add to soup mixture, let cool. Put vegetables and soup mixture into blender on high until vegetables are very finely chopped. In a large bowl, stir flaked crab and shrimp into mayonnaise and vegetable mixture. Add hot sauce. Place in a mold and let set for at least 6 hours.

CRAB STUFFED MUSHROOMS

yield: 12-14 appetizers

20 medium fresh mushrooms
1 (6½-ounce) can crab meat, flaked
2 ounces cream cheese, softened
2 Tablespoons mustard with
  horseradish
2 Tablespoons onion, finely
  chopped
1 teaspoon pepper
1 teaspoon seasoned salt
Seasoned bread crumbs, toasted

Clean mushrooms, remove stems. Combine all ingredients except bread crumbs. Stuff mixture into mushrooms. Sprinkle with bread crumbs, chill.

CRAB STUFFED SNOW PEAS

yield: 30 appetizers

1 (6½-ounce) can crab meat,
  drained
⅓ cup mayonnaise
2 Tablespoons Parmesan cheese
3 Tablespoons fresh parsley,
  chopped
1 Tablespoon lemon juice
¼ teaspoon garlic powder
30 large snow peas

Combine all ingredients except snow peas. Mix well and chill. Trim ends from snow peas. Using a sharp knife carefully slit one side of pea pod. Spoon crab mixture into decorating bag with a large tip. Pipe crab mixture into each snow pea. Cover and chill.

MICROWAVE BACON-WRAPPED WATER CHESTNUTS

yield: 6-8 servings

8 slices bacon, cut into thirds
1 can water chestnuts, drained
1 cup soy sauce
¾ teaspoon ginger
¾ teaspoon garlic

Wrap bacon around water chestnuts, securing with toothpicks. Combine remaining ingredients in bowl; mix well. Marinate water chestnuts in soy sauce mixture in refrigerator for several hours; drain. Place in glass baking dish. Microwave on high for 3 to 4 minutes or until bacon is crisp.

CARAMELIZED BACON

yield: 6-8 servings
oven temperature: 375 °F

1½ cups turbinado (raw sugar)
1 pound bacon

Spread the sugar on a cookie sheet and press the bacon into it, coating heavily. Place on two cake racks over baking sheets covered with aluminum foil (easy cleaning). It is not necessary to turn the bacon as it self drains. When bacon appears cooked, remove from oven and cool very slightly. Let it finish cooling on waxed paper.

Bacon can be made in advance and served at room temperature.

I made this thinking it would make an awful mess, but surprise! I'll do it again and again.

PÂTÉ

yield: 20-50 servings

2 or 3 chicken livers, chopped
2 Tablespoons onion, chopped
3 eggs, hard cooked
1 (8-ounce) package cream cheese
1 Tablespoon butter
1 Tablespoon mayonnaise
3 dashes hot sauce
1 teaspoon lemon juice
1 teaspoon mustard

Grind chicken livers and onion together. Separate egg yolk from white after cooking. Chop yolk and white separately. Thoroughly blend all ingredients except egg yolks. Form into ball and roll in egg yolks. Chill.

SOUPS
& SANDWICHES

HARVEST SOUP IN A PUMPKIN

yield: 6 servings

1 well shaped, medium sized ripe pumpkin (approximately 4-6 pounds)
Black pepper
¾ cup brown sugar
½ pound Gruyère cheese, grated
½ pound baby Swiss cheese, grated
¼ pound sharp Cheddar cheese, grated
3 cups heavy cream
1 teaspoon allspice
1 teaspoon nutmeg
2 teaspoons each basil and parsley
6 green onions, chopped
2½ cups seasoned croutons
1 cup cooked ham, chopped

Cut lid from pumpkin and reserve. Scrape inside of pumpkin clean leaving a good strong bottom; sprinkle with black pepper. By hand, rub brown sugar to coat inside of pumpkin. In large saucepan over medium/low heat combine cheeses, cream, seasonings, and onions. Heat until melted and blended together. Put 2 layers of croutons and ham inside pumpkin. Pour cheese mixture over croutons and ham. Cover pumpkin with foil and bake in preheated oven 50 minutes. Stir occasionally. Remove pumpkin from oven and place on serving platter. Top with the pumpkin lid.

TOMATO SOUP

yield: 25-30 servings

2 (46-ounce) cans chicken broth
3 (46-ounce) cans tomato juice
½ lemon, sliced
1 teaspoon basil
1 teaspoon salt
1 Tablespoon sugar
6 cloves
Dry white wine, to taste
Parsley, chopped

Simmer broth, tomato juice, lemon, basil, salt, sugar, cloves and wine for 30 minutes. Remove the lemons and cloves. Serve, topped with parsley.

CHICKEN CHOWDER

yield: 6-8 cups

2 cups chicken broth
1 large onion, finely chopped
2 stalks celery, finely chopped
2 potatoes, diced
1 large carrot, diced
⅓ cup butter
⅓ cup flour
2 cups milk
Seasoned salt, to taste
Cayenne, to taste
Black pepper, to taste
2 teaspoons lemon juice
1½-2 cups chicken, cooked, diced

Simmer vegetables in chicken broth until tender but firm. In a small saucepan melt butter; add flour, stirring constantly, until slightly brown. Gradually add milk, stirring until thickened. Stir into vegetables and broth. Season with cayenne pepper, seasoned salt, pepper and lemon juice. Add chicken and simmer until chicken is thoroughly heated, about 3-5 minutes.

Variations of Chicken Chowder:

Fish or Seafood Chowder

Omit from original recipe:
  chicken, seasoned salt
Substitute: 1½-2 cups poached
  trout, grouper, flounder or other
  white fish; clams, scallops, crab
  meat, or any combination of
  above
Seafood seasoning, to taste (Old
  Bay)

Follow directions for basic chicken chowder, making substitutions and changes as necessary. When possible, use fish broth or combination of fish and chicken broth.

Continued...

Broccoli Chowder

Omit from original recipe:
  potatoes, chicken
Add: 1 pound broccoli, chopped
1-1½ cups Cheddar cheese, grated

Follow directions for basic recipe; simmer broccoli with other vegetables. Add cheese just before serving and stir until melted.

Cauliflower Chowder

Omit from original recipe:
  potatoes, carrots, chicken
Add: 1 medium head cauliflower,
  chopped
Dash nutmeg
1-1½ cups Cheddar cheese, grated

Follow directions for basic recipe; simmer cauliflower with other vegetables. Add nutmeg with other seasonings. Add cheese just before serving and stir until melted.

Ham-Asparagus Chowder

Omit from original recipe: chicken
Substitute: 1-1½ cups ham, cooked
  diced
Add: ½ pound fresh asparagus, ¼
  inch slices, steamed

Follow directions for basic recipe, adding ham and steamed asparagus last.

Tomato Chowder

Omit from original recipe:
  potatoes, carrots, lemon juice,
  chicken
Substitute: 5-7 large tomatoes or 2
  large cans tomatoes, coarsely
  chopped
Oregano, optional

Follow directions for basic recipe; simmer tomatoes with other vegetables. If using canned tomatoes, DO NOT drain, but increase flour by 2 additional tablespoons.
If desired, sprinkle with oregano before serving.

CORN CHOWDER

yield: 4-6 servings

4 slices bacon, crumbled
1 cup onion, chopped
2 cups potatoes, pared and diced
2½ cups water, divided
1 teaspoon salt
¼ teaspoon pepper
2 (16-ounce) cans whole kernel
corn or 2 cups cooked fresh corn
1½ cups milk
¼ cup flour
Paprika

Cook bacon until crisp. Remove bacon, set aside, and sauté onion in bacon fat until soft. Add potatoes, 2 cups water, salt and pepper. Cover, simmer 15 minutes or until tender. Stir in corn with liquid and milk. Blend flour with remaining ½ cup water until smooth, then stir into chowder. Cook, stirring constantly, over medium heat until it thickens and heats thoroughly. Serve sprinkled with bacon and paprika.

This freezes well.

SNOWY DAY CHOWDER

2 Tablespoons butter, melted
1 pound Kielbasa, cut in ¼ inch
slices
2 cups carrots, sliced
¼ teaspoon caraway seeds
2 (10¾-ounce) cans cream of celery
soup
2 (10¾-ounce) cans cream of
mushroom soup
1 soup can milk
1 soup can water
3 cups cabbage, shredded

Sauté Kielbasa, carrots and caraway seeds in butter; cook until carrots are tender. Drain off fat. Add remaining ingredients and bring to a boil. Simmer 30 minutes.

CLAM CHOWDER

yield: 4 servings

¼ cup butter or margarine
4 Tablespoons celery, finely
chopped
2 medium potatoes, small cubes
1 medium green pepper, finely
chopped
2 Tablespoons onion, finely
chopped
2 (8-ounce) cans minced clams,
undrained
1 (10¾-ounce) can cream of potato
soup
1 cup milk or light cream
½ teaspoon hot sauce
Salt and pepper, to taste

Sauté potatoes, green pepper,
onion and celery in butter until
partially done, DO NOT
BROWN. Add clams and potato
soup; mix well. Simmer for one
hour, stirring occasionally. Add
hot sauce, salt, pepper and milk.
(If you want thick and creamy
chowder add 2-6 Tablespoons
cornstarch to the milk before
adding to the chowder). Bring
back almost to boiling point.
Serve hot.

CREAM OF CARROT SOUP

yield: 4 servings

3 carrots, peeled and chopped
1 medium onion, chopped
1 celery stalk, with leaves,
chopped
1½ cups chicken stock, divided
1 teaspoon salt
½ teaspoon sugar
Dash of cayenne pepper
½ cup cooked rice
¾ cup cream
Pimiento strips

Put carrots, onion, celery and
half of chicken stock in saucepan.
Bring to a boil, cover, reduce heat
and simmer for 15 minutes. Add
salt, sugar, cayenne and rice.
Blend on high speed in blender,
not food processor, until smooth.
Add remaining stock and cream.
Garnish soup with pimiento. May
be served hot or cold.

CREAM OF SQUASH SOUP

yield: 8-10 servings

¼ cup margarine, melted
2½ Tablespoons oil
1 large onion, minced
2 cloves garlic, minced
3 pounds yellow squash, thinly
   sliced
4 cups chicken broth
1 cup light cream
¾ teaspoon salt
½ teaspoon white pepper

Combine margarine and oil in a large Dutch oven, add onion and garlic, sauté until tender. Stir in squash and chicken broth. Cover and simmer 15-20 minutes until squash is tender. Spoon ⅓ of mixture into blender and purée until smooth. Repeat with remaining squash mixture. Return all of puréed mixture to Dutch oven and stir in light cream, salt and pepper. Cook over low heat, stirring constantly until well heated. May be served hot or cold.

POTATO SOUP

yield: 6 servings

4 large potatoes, peeled and
   quartered
6 slices bacon
¼ cup onion, chopped
2 Tablespoons butter or margarine
1 Tablespoon parsley flakes
2 teaspoons salt
½ teaspoon nutmeg
⅛ teaspoon cayenne pepper
¼ teaspoon dry mustard
1 teaspoon Worcestershire sauce
3 cups milk
½ cup Swiss cheese, grated

Cook potatoes in boiling water in Dutch oven, until tender. (About 20 minutes.) Meanwhile, microwave bacon retaining fat. Set bacon aside. Drain fat into a 2-cup glass measure cup, add onion, and microwave until onion is transparent (about 2 minutes). Add butter and seasonings to the onion and set aside. Drain and mash potatoes; then add the onion/spice mixture. Heat over low heat, stirring frequently. DO NOT BOIL. Just before serving, stir in the Swiss cheese. Top each serving with crumbled bacon.

LETTUCE SOUP

yield: 6 servings

1 large head lettuce (Romaine or Boston)
¼ cup butter
1 onion, finely chopped
2 cups chicken stock
2 cups milk or cream
Pinch of nutmeg
½ teaspoon sugar
2 egg yolks
2 Tablespoons cream
Dash salt
Dash pepper

Wash, drain, and shred lettuce. In a large skillet, sauté onions in butter until tender. Stir in lettuce and cook 5 minutes. Pour in stock, milk, nutmeg, and sugar; bring soup to simmer. Blend until smooth in blender. Pour into a double boiler and gently heat. Beat egg yolks and cream together in a small bowl. Add a ladle of hot soup and stir quickly. Return mixture to the rest of soup, stirring constantly. Reheat soup over low heat. DO NOT let soup boil. Taste and season with salt and pepper. Serve hot.

WHITE GAZPACHO

yield: 6-8 servings

3 medium cucumbers, peeled and cubed
3 cups chicken broth, cooled
3 cups sour cream
3 Tablespoons white vinegar
2 teaspoons salt
1 clove garlic, pressed
2 tomatoes, chopped
¾ cup toasted almonds, chopped
½ cup green onions, sliced
½ cup parsley, chopped

Whirl cucumbers in blender with 1 cup of chicken broth. Combine with remaining broth, sour cream, vinegar, salt and garlic in bowl. Stir just enough to mix, chill. Serve in chilled soup bowls. Sprinkle tomatoes, almonds, onion, and parsley on top just before serving.

GAZPACHO

yield: 14 servings

8 slices pumpernickel bread
½ cup olive oil
¾ cup wine vinegar
½ cup celery, chopped
½ cup radishes, sliced
½ cup green pepper, chopped
½ cup cucumber, chopped
½ cup green onion, chopped
½ cup parsley, chopped
1 avocado, peeled and cubed
1 teaspoon salt
½ teaspoon pepper
½ teaspoon garlic salt
¼ teaspoon seasoned salt
½ teaspoon basil
½ teaspoon dill weed
1 (46-ounce) can mixed-vegetable
  juice
1 (46-ounce) can tomato juice

Remove crusts from bread and cut into small cubes. Put into large bowl, add oil and vinegar and set aside for a few minutes. Add all vegetables and seasonings, stir well. Stir in juices. Chill for 24 hours before serving. Serve cold in chilled bowls.

COMMENTS: *To serve the soup as a "drink", coarsely blend bread and vegetables before mixing soup ingredients.*

MAGNIFICENT MINESTRONE

yield: 10-12 servings

1 cup navy beans, dried
2 (14½ ounce) cans chicken broth
2 teaspoons salt
1 small head cabbage, cored and shredded
4 carrots, peeled and sliced
2 medium potatoes, peeled and diced
1 (28-ounce) can Italian plum tomatoes, chopped
2 medium onions, chopped
1 stalk celery, chopped
1 large fresh tomato, peeled and chopped
1 clove garlic, minced
¼ cup olive oil
¼ cup parsley, chopped
¼ teaspoon pepper
1 cup vermicelli, broken into pieces

PESTO SAUCE:
¼ cup butter, softened (no substitutions)
¼ cup Parmesan cheese, grated
½ cup parsley, chopped
1 clove garlic, minced
1 teaspoon basil
½ teaspoon marjoram
¼ cup olive oil
¼ cup walnuts, chopped (or pine nuts)

Cover beans with water and soak overnight. Drain. Measure chicken broth and add water to measure 3 quarts. Add salt. Cook beans in broth mixture until almost tender. Add cabbage, carrots, potatoes and canned tomatoes. Sauté onions, celery, fresh tomato and garlic in olive oil; add to soup. Stir in parsley and pepper. Add vermicelli to soup 15 minutes before serving. Serve hot in bowls with a spoonful of pesto sauce in each bowl.

DO NOT OMIT pesto sauce as it contains ALL the seasonings!!!!!!

MEXICAN BEAN SOUP

yield: 8 servings

8 slices bacon, chopped
1 cup onion, chopped
1 cup celery, chopped
1 clove garlic, minced
1 (4-ounce) can chopped green
  chilies
2 (16-ounce) cans refried beans
½ teaspoon pepper
2 Tablespoons taco seasoning
2 (10½-ounce) cans chicken broth
2 cups water
1 cup Cheddar cheese, grated
Tortilla chips

In a 4 quart saucepan, cook bacon until crisp. DO NOT DRAIN FAT. Add onion, celery and garlic; cook covered over low heat for 10 minutes. Add green chilies, beans, pepper and taco seasoning. Stir in chicken broth and water. Bring to a boil; then lower heat. Simmer 10 minutes, stirring occasionally.
Serve in bowls and garnish with Cheddar cheese and broken tortilla chips.

ASPARAGUS SANDWICHES

yield: 8 servings

4 ounces cream cheese, softened
2 eggs, hard boiled, sieved
½ teaspoon seasoned salt
Juice of half a lemon
1 small can asparagus tips, drained
  and cut in pieces
16 slices of bread, crusts trimmed
Butter or margarine
Parmesan cheese

Blend together cream cheese, hard boiled eggs, seasoned salt, and lemon juice. Fold in asparagus tips. Spread on 8 slices of bread and top with remaining slices. Spread butter lightly on sandwiches then sprinkle with Parmesan cheese. Toast under boiler until lightly toasted. (Watch carefully to prevent burning.) Serve immediately.

PANE ITALIANO

yield: 4-6 servings
oven temperature: 400°F

1 loaf Italian bread
Olive oil
½ cup tomato sauce
2 cups Italian plum tomatoes,
   drained
½ teaspoon sweet basil
½ teaspoon oregano
¾ teaspoon salt
¼ teaspoon pepper
1 clove garlic, minced
¼ pound pepperoni, sliced
¼ pound Italian salami, sliced
¼ pound mozzarella cheese, diced
¼ cup Romano cheese (or
   Parmesan), grated

Cut a ½-inch slice off top of bread. Hollow out inside of loaf, leaving a ½-inch shell. Brush inside and outside of loaf with olive oil. Place loaf on baking sheet and heat at 400° for 5-10 minutes. (Inside should be dry, not brown.) In saucepan, combine tomato sauce, plum tomatoes, the seasonings and meats. Heat until bubbly; lower heat and simmer for 10 minutes. Remove from heat; stir in mozzarella cheese. Spoon into loaf and top with grated Romano cheese. Bake at 400° for 15 minutes. Cut into thick slices and serve hot.

OLIVE SPREAD

yield: 1 pint

½-1 cup stuffed green olives,
   chopped
2 (3-ounce) packages cream cheese,
   softened
½ cup mayonnaise
½ cup pecans, chopped
2 Tablespoons olive juice
Dash pepper

Mix all ingredients and refrigerate at least 24 hours. (Spread will thicken.)

SUGGESTED ACCOMPANIMENTS: Can be served on celery, crackers, finger sandwiches.

ITALIAN FILLED BREAD

yield: 12 servings
oven temperature: 425 °F

2⅔ cups lukewarm water (105° - 115°)
2 envelopes yeast
2 teaspoons sugar
6½ cups bread flour
2 teaspoons salt

FILLING:
1½ cups mayonnaise
1 cup onion, chopped
1 teaspoon oregano or Italian seasoning
1 teaspoon basil
4-5 cups summer sausage
1½ cups mozzarella cheese, grated
1½ cups Monterey Jack cheese, grated
1½ cups Cheddar cheese, grated
2 Tablespoons olive oil
2 eggs, beaten

Combine water, yeast and sugar. Stir and let stand until yeast dissolves and begins to foam, (5-10 minutes.) Stir 3 cups of flour and salt into yeast mixture and beat until smooth and bubbly. Gradually add enough of remaining flour to form a soft dough. DO NOT ADD TOO MUCH. Turn onto a lightly floured board and knead until dough is barely sticky, about 2 minutes. Place in a greased bowl and turn to coat dough. Cover and let rise in warm place until double in bulk, about 30-45 minutes. Punch down dough and turn onto lightly floured surface. Let dough rest for 10 minutes. Roll dough into 12 x 16-inch rectangle, ¼-inch thick. Combine mayonnaise, onion, oregano and basil. Spread mixture on rectangle, leaving a 1½-inch border on the two short sides. Spread with chopped beef stick and cover with cheeses. Drizzle olive oil on top of the cheese. Fold the two short ends of dough up and over filling. Dampen long ends of

Continued...

dough with cold water and pull them up to completely enclose filling, overlapping by 1-inch. Press gently to seal. Put on greased baking sheet, seam-side down and slash dough diagonally several times. Brush with eggs. Bake immediately at 425° until lightly browned, about 35 minutes. Cover with foil after 20 minutes and reduce heat to 400° if loaf is browning too quickly. Let loaf cool on rack for about 20 minutes. Cut into thick slices to serve.

Freezes well after baking!

SUNDAY NIGHT SANDWICHES

Turkey, roasted
Guacamole
Black bread

Combine roast turkey with guacamole on black bread.

Ham, thinly sliced
Brie cheese
Mustard
Raisin bread
Butter

Layer thinly sliced ham, Brie cheese and favorite mustard on raisin bread. Butter outside and grill.

Rye bread
Mayonnaise
Onion
Avocado
Tomato
Green chilies
2 strips bacon, cooked
Cheddar cheese

Spread rye bread with mayonnaise. Layer sliced onion, avocado and tomato. Sprinkle with mild green chilies and lay 2 strips of cooked bacon. Top with Cheddar cheese and broil until bubbly.

Fresh broccoli
Scallions
Cashews, toasted
Sesame mayonnaise
English muffins
Parmesan cheese

Mix barely cooked broccoli flowerettes with scallions and toasted cashews in enough sesame mayonnaise to coat. Spread on English muffins and sprinkle with Parmesan cheese. Broil until bubbly.

CANADIAN MUSHROOM SANDWICHES

yield: 6 servings

6 Kaiser rolls
Butter
1 Tablespoon bacon, chopped
2 Tablespoons onion, chopped
⅓ cup mushrooms, sliced
1 teaspoon parsley
18 slices Canadian-style bacon
    (⅛-inch thick)
6 slices Swiss cheese (1-ounce each)
6 thin green pepper rings
Paprika

Split and butter rolls. Sauté chopped bacon, onion, mushrooms and parsley for about 5 minutes. Arrange 3 slices Canadian bacon on each bottom half of roll. Top with mushroom mixture and one slice cheese. Place 1 green pepper ring on each cheese slice; sprinkle paprika inside green pepper ring. Place sandwiches on baking sheet and broil 6 inches from heat until cheese melts, about 3-5 minutes. Replace tops of rolls or serve open-faced.

HAM ROLLS

yield: 8 servings
oven temperature: 375 °F

¾ cup margarine
3 Tablespoons prepared mustard
3 Tablespoons poppy seeds
1 package baked tea rolls,
    packaged in a foil pan
1 pound ham, thinly sliced

Melt margarine; add mustard and poppy seeds. Slice entire package rolls in half horizontally. (DO NOT SEPARATE ROLLS). Spread butter mixture on both cut sides of rolls. Place sliced ham on bottom of rolls. Top with other half. Replace rolls in foil pan. Bake at 375° for 10 minutes. Cut rolls apart and serve.

CRAB MEAT MELT

yield: 2 servings

1 (6-ounce) can crab meat
1 teaspoon Worcestershire sauce
½ cup salad dressing
2 green onions, chopped
2 English muffins, split
1 Tablespoon butter
4 slices Longhorn cheese

Mix crab meat, Worcestershire sauce, salad dressing and green onions. Lightly toast English muffin halves. Spread butter on each half. Top with at least ¼ cup of crab meat mixture. Place halves on baking sheet and broil, not too close to heat, for 2 or 3 minutes. Top with cheese and broil until cheese melts.

BARBECUED BEEF

yield: 20 sandwiches
oven temperature: 250°F

1 4-pound chuck roast
1 (10¾-ounce) can tomato soup
2 cups ketchup
1 cup water
2 Tablespoons lemon juice
2 Tablespoons Worcestershire
  sauce
2 Tablespoons brown sugar
¾ teaspoon dry mustard
1 small onion, chopped
⅓ cup celery, chopped
Buns

Cook meat until very tender at 250° or about 3 hours. Cool. Remove fat. Combine remaining ingredients and simmer 30 minutes. Shred beef and add to sauce. Simmer one hour. Serve on buns.

SALADS

⌧ SLICE OF THE SOUTH SALAD

yield: 15 servings

2 (3-ounce) packages blackberry
  gelatin
2 cups blackberries
1 cup pecans, chopped (optional)

TOPPING:
1 (8-ounce) package cream cheese,
  softened
¼ cup milk, cold
½ cup sugar
1 teaspoon vanilla
2 cups whipped topping
Pecans, chopped (optional)

Mix gelatin according to package directions. If berries are frozen decrease cold water to ½ cup, add berries and nuts to gelatin and let chill until set.

TOPPING:
Mix cream cheese with milk, sugar and vanilla; fold mixture into whipped topping. Spread on gelatin and chill. Sprinkle pecans on top as a garnish.

VERY BERRY SALAD

yield: 6-8 servings

1 (6-ounce) package red raspberry
  gelatin
1 cup water, boiling
1 (16-ounce) can blueberries with
  syrup
1 (8-ounce) can crushed pineapple
  with syrup
1 cup pecans, chopped
1 cup heavy cream, whipped

Dissolve gelatin in water and let cool. Add blueberries and pineapple. Refrigerate; when almost firm add pecans and fold in cream. Refrigerate until firm.

CHERRY SALAD

yield: 12 servings

1 can sour cherries, pitted
⅔ cup sugar
1 (3-ounce) package lemon gelatin
1 (3-ounce) package cherry gelatin
1 (5¼-ounce) can crushed pineapple
½ cup lemon-lime beverage or
orange juice
Juice of 1 lemon
Rind of 1 lemon
½ cup pecans, chopped (optional)

Boil cherries and sugar. Add gelatins and return to a boil. Cool slightly; then add remaining ingredients. Pour into a 9-inch square dish and chill in refrigerator until firm.

BLUEBERRY SALAD

yield: 8-10 servings

1 (16-ounce) can blueberries
1 (15¼-ounce) can crushed
pineapple
2 (3-ounce) packages black
raspberry gelatin
1 cup boiling water
1 (8-ounce) package cream cheese,
softened
1 cup sour cream
½ cup sugar
1 teaspoon vanilla extract
1 cup pecans, chopped

Drain blueberries and pineapple and reserve liquid. Dissolve gelatin in boiling water. Add enough water to reserved liquid to make 1½ cups; add to dissolved gelatin. Pour into 13 x 9-inch pan. Chill until slightly thickened, about 5 minutes. Fold in fruit. Chill until firm.

Combine cream cheese, sour cream, sugar and vanilla; beat well. Spread over gelatin and sprinkle with pecans. Chill until set.

DORA'S CRANBERRY SALAD

yield: 8-10 servings

1 (20-ounce) can crushed pineapple in syrup
1 (3-ounce) box cherry gelatin
1 cup boiling water
1 cup pineapple syrup, reserved
1 cup sugar
1 Tablespoon lemon juice
1 cup cranberries, ground
1 orange, unpeeled and ground
1 cup celery, diced
1 cup pecans, chopped
Lettuce

Drain crushed pineapple reserving liquid. Dissolve gelatin in boiling water. Add sugar, lemon juice and reserved pineapple juice. Stir to dissolve. Pour mixture into large mold or 13 x 9-inch pan. Chill until partially set. Add cranberries, orange, celery, pecans and 1 cup pineapple. Chill until firm. Cut into squares and serve on lettuce leaves.

PRETZEL SALAD

yield: 8-10 servings

FIRST LAYER:
2 cups pretzels, crushed
3 Tablespoons sugar
¾ cup margarine or butter, melted

SECOND LAYER:
1 (8-ounce) package cream cheese
1 cup sugar

THIRD LAYER:
1 (6-ounce) package gelatin, any flavor
2½ cups water, boiling
2 cups mixed canned fruit

FIRST LAYER: Mix pretzels, sugar and margarine. Press in bottom of a 9 x 13-inch pan. Bake at 350° for 8 minutes. Cool completely.

SECOND LAYER: Whip cream cheese and sugar. Spread over cooled crust.

THIRD LAYER: Dissolve gelatin in boiling water. Chill until partially set; add fruit. Pour on top of cream cheese mixture. Chill; cut into squares to serve.

SAWDUST SALAD

yield: 20 servings

FIRST LAYER:
1 (6-ounce) package lemon gelatin
1 (6-ounce) package orange gelatin
2 cups boiling water
1 (12-ounce) can lemon lime
   carbonated beverage
2 bananas, sliced
1 (20-ounce) can crushed
   pineapple, (save juice)
1 (10½-ounce) package colored
   marshmallows
1 (4-ounce) can mandarin oranges,
   drained

SECOND LAYER:
2 cups pineapple juice
2 eggs, beaten
4 Tablespoons flour
1 cup sugar

THIRD LAYER:
1 (12-ounce) container non-dairy
   whipped topping
1 (3-ounce) package cream cheese
1 (8-ounce) package Cheddar
   cheese, shredded

FIRST LAYER: Dissolve gelatins in boiling water. Add carbonated beverage, bananas, pineapple, marshmallows and mandarin oranges. Chill until set.

SECOND LAYER: Cook until thick, cool and spread over first layer.

THIRD LAYER: Mix whipped topping with cream cheese and spread over second layer. Top with shredded cheese. This will look like sawdust.

CIDER RING MOLD

yield: 6 servings

2 envelopes unflavored gelatin
½ cup sugar
2 Tablespoons lemon juice
2 Tablespoons water
3 cups hot cider
1 cup red apples
¼ cup celery, finely diced
1 cup mincemeat

Mix gelatin with sugar in a saucepan. Add lemon juice and water. Place over low heat and stir until gelatin is dissolved; add hot apple cider. Remove from heat and chill in refrigerator until mixture is consistency of unbeaten egg whites (this can be done in the freezing compartment of the refrigerator in about 20-30 minutes).

Add diced, unpeeled apple and celery to the thickened gelatin mixture. Carefully fold in the mincemeat. Pour into a 6-cup ring mold. Chill.

Unmold on a bed of lettuce and garnish with apple wedges which have been dipped in lemon juice. Serves six.

Note: Three times this recipe, divided between two 13 x 9-inch casseroles, makes 30 square servings.

Spicy-tasting, good for holidays!

FRUIT SALAD

3 apples, diced
3 bananas, diced
1 pound green grapes, seedless
2 (8½-ounce) cans mandarin
   oranges, drained
1 (20-ounce) can pineapple chunks,
   drained (save juice)
½ cup maraschino cherries
   (optional)

SAUCE:
¾ cup pineapple juice
¼ cup water
2 Tablespoons cornstarch
1 orange, juice and rind
1 lemon, juice and rind
½ cup sugar
Pinch of salt

Prepare all fruits and combine in a bowl.

SAUCE: Cook all ingredients in a saucepan until thickened. Cool to room temperature. Pour over fruit. Let stand at least 24 hours in the refrigerator.

SPECIAL SALAD

yield: 6 servings

2 eggs, hard boiled
¼ small onion, grated
1 teaspoon ketchup
¼ teaspoon garlic salt
¼ teaspoon salt
⅛ teaspoon pepper
½ teaspoon lemon juice
1 cup mayonnaise
Avocado
Grapefruit, sectioned
Lettuce

Mash egg yolks and ¼ of one egg white with a fork. Add all other ingredients, blending well. Chill dressing several hours before serving, allowing flavors to blend.

Serve on alternating slices of ripe avocado and sectioned grapefruit on a bed of lettuce. Also good on a plain tossed salad.

⧗ FROZEN CRANBERRY SALAD

yield: 10-12 servings

1 (8-ounce) package cream cheese
2 Tablespoons mayonnaise
2 Tablespoons sugar
1 (16-ounce) can whole cranberries
½ cup pecans, chopped
1 (4-ounce) carton non-dairy
  whipped topping

Blend together cream cheese, mayonnaise and sugar. Add pecans and cranberries; blend well. Fold in whipped topping. Pour into 9 x 9-inch dish. Freeze. Cut into squares to serve. Allow to soften at room temperature a few minutes before serving.

MANDARIN ORANGE SALAD
AND DRESSING

yield: 6-8 servings

½ cup almonds, sliced
½ cup sugar
1 head romaine lettuce
4-6 green onions, chopped
1 (15-ounce) can mandarin
  oranges, drained

DRESSING:
½ cup vegetable oil
¼ cup vinegar
¼ cup sugar
2 Tablespoons parsley, chopped
1 teaspoon salt
Dash pepper

Caramelize almonds in sugar over low heat. Spread on cookie sheet to cool. Combine lettuce, onion and oranges; toss.

DRESSING: Combine all dressing ingredients and blend well. Toss salad with dressing, sprinkle with almonds and serve.

BERRY'S GREEN SALAD

yield: 8 servings

2 bunches fresh spinach, washed
   and dried
1 pint fresh strawberries, washed,
   hulled and halved

DRESSING:
½ cup sugar
2 Tablespoons sesame seeds
1 Tablespoon poppy seeds
1½ teaspoons minced onion
¼ teaspoon Worcestershire sauce
¼ teaspoon paprika
½ cup oil
¼ cup cider vinegar

Arrange spinach and berries on individual salad plates. Chill. Put the sugar, sesame seeds, poppy seeds, onion, Worcestershire and paprika in a blender. With blender running, add oil and vinegar in a slow, steady stream until mixed and thickened. Drizzle over stawberries and spinach. Serve immediately.

VARIATION: If desired, avocado may be added to the salad.

CRUNCHY LUNCHEON SALAD

yield: 6 servings

2 cucumbers, peeled and sliced
2 apples, cored and sliced
½ cup water chestnuts
½ cup fresh mint, chopped
¼ cup honey
3 cups yogurt, plain
1½ Tablespoons poppy seeds
1 teaspoon ground ginger
Salt and pepper, to taste

Mix ingredients together and chill completely.

Serve on a bed of lettuce. Garnish with sprigs of fresh mint.

CONGEALED SALAD

yield: 8-10 servings

2 (16-ounce) cans asparagus spears
2 Tablespoons vinegar
1 teaspoon salt
2 Tablespoons onion juice
Dash hot sauce
2 (3-ounce) packages lemon gelatin
Salad dressing or mayonnaise
Pimiento

Drain asparagus, reserving liquid. Place 2 rows of spears in a 9 x 13-inch pan, placing tip outward. Add the vinegar and enough water to the reserved liquid to make 4 cups. Add salt, onion juice and hot sauce and bring to boil. Remove about 1 cup liquid and add gelatin, stirring to dissolve. Return gelatin mixture to the remaining liquid. Carefully pour over the asparagus. Chill until firm. To serve, cut in squares, garnishing with a dollop of salad dressing and a strip of pimiento.

TANGY BEET SALAD

yield: 8 servings

1 cup beets, diced
1 (6-ounce) package lemon gelatin
1 cup boiling water
¾ cup beet juice
3 Tablespoons vinegar
1 Tablespoon sugar
½ teaspoon salt
1 Tablespoon onion, grated
2 Tablespoons prepared
   horesradish
¾ cup celery, diced

Drain beets, reserving juice. Dissolve gelatin in boiling water. Combine dissolved gelatin, beet juice, vinegar, sugar, salt, onion and horseradish, mixing thoroughly. Place in refrigerator and allow to thicken slightly. Stir in beets and celery; pour into prepared individual molds. Chill until set.

TOMATO ASPIC I

yield: 6-8 servings

1 (8-ounce) package cream cheese
1 (10¾-ounce) can tomato soup
1 cup water
2 Tablespoons gelatin
½ cup celery, chopped
½ cup green pepper, chopped
½ cup onions, chopped
1 cup mayonnaise
Salt, to taste
Worcestershire sauce, to taste
Pepper, to taste

Cube the cream cheese. Combine with ½ cup of the water, and tomato soup in a small saucepan. Heat until melted. Combine the remaining ½ cup water and gelatin with the cooled cream cheese mixture. Add remaining ingredients; cover and refrigerate.

TOMATO ASPIC II

4 cups tomato juice
½ cup onion, chopped
½ cup celery leaves, chopped
2 Tablespoons brown sugar
1 teaspoon salt
2 small bay leaves
4 whole cloves
2½ Tablespoons unflavored gelatin
¼ cup water, cold
3 Tablespoons lemon juice
1 cup celery, finely diced

Combine tomato juice, onion, celery leaves, brown sugar, salt, bay leaves and cloves; simmer 5 minutes. Strain. Soften gelatin in cold water; dissolve in the hot tomato mixture. Add lemon juice and chill until partially set. Add celery and pour into a 5-6 cup ring mold.

VARIATIONS: Add well drained small shrimp, crab meat or sliced olives with the celery.

MARINATED ARTICHOKE SALAD

yield: 8 servings

SALAD:
1 green pepper, thinly sliced
1 small onion, thinly sliced
1 (14-ounce) can artichoke hearts,
   drained
½ cup celery, diced
1 cucumber, unpeeled and thinly
   sliced
1 cup mozzarella cheese, cubed
½ pound fresh mushrooms, sliced
1 teaspoon pepper
¼ teaspoon dillweed
1 (14-ounce) can Hearts of Palm,
   drained
Lettuce
2 slices bacon, cooked and
   crumbled

MARINADE:
¾ cup oil
1 Tablespoon cider vinegar
¼ teaspoon garlic salt
1 Tablespoon Dijon mustard
1 Tablespoon Parmesan cheese,
   grated

SALAD: Combine salad ingredients except lettuce and bacon and toss with marinade. Chill several hours. Arrange on lettuce and garnish with bacon.

MARINADE: Combine all ingredients in a 1-pint jar; shake well.

HENNING SALAD

yield: 6 servings

DRESSING:
½ cup mayonnaise
⅓ cup sour cream or yogurt
1 teaspoon curry powder
1 teaspoon lemon juice
1 Tablespoon minced onion
6 tomatoes
6 artichoke hearts, halved
6 (or more) mushrooms, fresh or
   canned
Lettuce leaves
Paprika

Wedge tomatoes in ⅛-inches almost to the bottom. You may peel tomatoes if desired. Mix dressing ingredients. Place tomatoes on lettuce leaves and put artichoke halves in tomatoes. Mix mushrooms with dressing and spoon over tomatoes and artichokes. Sprinkle lightly with paprika.

BROCCOLI SALAD

yield: 8-12 servings

DRESSING:
⅓ cup sugar
¾ cup salad dressing
3 Tablespoons wine vinegar

SALAD:
1 head broccoli cut into flowerettes
½ head cauliflower, cut into
   flowerettes
1 cup cheese, grated
1 purple onion, thinly sliced
8 slices bacon, fried crisp and
   crumbled

About 1 hour before serving mix the dressing ingredients well.

SALAD: Combine the ingredients and shortly before serving add the dressing and toss.

MARINATED COLE SLAW

yield: 16-18 servings

1 medium head of cabbage
1 large onion
1 large green pepper
1 small carrot
1 cup sugar
¾ cup oil
1 cup cider vinegar
1 teaspoon dry mustard
1 teaspoon celery seed
1 Tablespoon salt

Shred, chop, or grate cabbage, onion, green pepper and carrot. Sprinkle sugar over top (DO NOT STIR.) Bring oil, vinegar, mustard, celery seed and salt to a rolling boil. While hot, pour over cabbage mixture. Cover and place in refrigerator immediately. Refrigerate at least 8 hours before serving. Stir well before serving. Keeps indefinitely.

BEAN SALAD

yield: 10-12 servings

1 Tablespoon salt
1 cup vinegar
1 Tablespoon water
1½ cups sugar
½ cup oil
1 purple onion, sliced
1 green pepper, sliced
2 cups green beans
1 (2-ounce) can pimiento, drained
1 (8½-ounce) can green peas
1 (15-ounce) can black-eyed peas

Mix and heat to dissolve salt, vinegar, sugar, oil. Cool. Pour solution over drained vegetables. Place in the refrigerator for 24 hours.

FRESH MUSHROOM SALAD

yield: 8 servings

DRESSING:
1 small bunch green onions, finely chopped
¼ cup parsley, chopped
1 Tablespoon Dijon mustard
¼ cup white wine vinegar
½ cup olive oil
1 Tablespoon brandy
Hot pepper sauce, to taste (1-2 drops)
Black pepper, to taste
Juice of 1 lemon
Pinch of salt

SALAD:
1½ pounds fresh mushrooms, sliced
16 hearts of lettuce leaves
4 ounces Blue cheese

Blend all ingredients for the dressing. Pour over the mushrooms and allow to marinate for several hours at room temperature.

Serve on lettuce leaves, crumbling Blue cheese on top. Serve at room temperature.

CUCUMBERS IN SOUR CREAM

yield: 2 servings

1 medium cucumber, peeled, thinly sliced
½ cup sour cream
¼ teaspoon salt
1½ Tablespoons onion, minced
Pepper, to taste

Place sliced cucumber in a small bowl. Add the remaining ingredients and gently toss. Chill thoroughly.

POTATOES à la PARSLEY

yield: 10-12 servings

8 medium potatoes
1½ cups mayonnaise
1 cup sour cream
1½ teaspoons prepared horseradish
1 teaspoon celery seed
½ teaspoon salt
1 cup *fresh* parsley, chopped
1 medium onion, finely chopped

Prepare the day before serving. Boil the whole potato until tender. Cool. Peel and slice into ⅛-inch thick slices.
Blend together mayonnaise, sour cream, horseradish, celery seed, and salt. Layer half of the potatoes in a shallow 9 x 13-inch pan. Spread half the mayonnaise mixture over the potatoes. Repeat with the remaining potatoes and mayonnaise mixture.
Combine parsley and onion. Sprinkle over the salad. Cover tightly and refrigerate overnight.

A very different potato salad — a must to slice the potatoes ⅛-inch thick.

SPINACH SALAD

yield: 6-8 servings

Spinach leaves, washed and dried
Onion, sliced into rings
Fresh mushrooms, sliced
Eggs, hard boiled and sliced
Bacon, cooked and crumbled
½ cup salad dressing
½ cup sugar
¼ cup milk
2 Tablespoons vinegar

Mix salad dressing, sugar, milk and vinegar; refrigerate for 1-2 hours before serving. To serve; assemble spinach, onion, mushrooms, eggs and bacon and pour dressing over the top.

SPINACH SALAD AND DRESSING

yield: 5-8 servings

2 bunches fresh spinach (8 cups)
⅔ cup oil
¼ cup wine vinegar
2 Tablespoons white wine
2 teaspoons soy sauce
1 teaspoon sugar
1 teaspoon dry mustard
½ teaspoon curry powder
½ teaspoon salt
1 teaspoon pepper
½ pound bacon, cooked crisp, crumbled
2 hard boiled eggs, coarsely grated

Combine oil, vinegar, wine, soy sauce, sugar and seasonings in a covered jar — chill — shake well. Wash the spinach and tear into pieces. Mix eggs and bacon with spinach. Pour dressing over this mixture and toss well. Delicious!!

CURRIED TOMATO SALAD

yield: 6-8 servings

2 large tomatoes; peeled, seeded and diced
½ large red onion, chopped
Salt, to taste
Pepper, to taste
¼ cup mayonnaise
¼ cup sour cream
2½ Tablespoons fresh parsley, minced
1 Tablespoon whipping cream
1 teaspoon curry powder
Lettuce

Combine tomatoes and red onion in small mixing bowl. Salt and pepper to taste. Cover and refrigerate until ready to serve. Combine mayonnaise, sour cream, parsley, whipped cream and curry and blend well. When ready to serve, spoon tomato and onion mixture into lettuce cups and top with dressing.

VEGETABLE SALAD

yield: 10-12 servings

1 (16-ounce) can of French green beans
1 (16-ounce) can Shoe Peg corn (whole white kernel)
1 (16-ounce) can small peas
1 cup celery, chopped
1 red onion, chopped
1 green pepper, chopped
1 (2-ounce) jar pimiento, chopped

DRESSING:
¾ cup sugar
½ cup cider vinegar
½ cup oil
½ teaspoon pepper
1 teaspoon salt

Drain all canned vegetables. Mix green beans, corn, peas, celery, red onions, green pepper and pimientos together in covered dish. Mix sugar, vinegar, oil, pepper and salt in saucepan. Bring to a boil while stirring. Let cool. Pour over vegetables and refrigerate overnight or for 8-10 hours.

Great for cookouts and picnics!

ORIENTAL SALAD

yield: 8-10 servings

1 (16-ounce) can French style green beans, drained
1 (16-ounce) can small English peas, drained
1 (14-ounce) can Fancy Chinese vegetables, drained
1 (3-ounce) jar pimiento, drained and chopped
1 (8-ounce) can water chestnuts, thinly sliced
1½ cups celery, thinly sliced
3 medium onions, thinly sliced
1 cup sugar
¾ cup cider vinegar
1 teaspoon salt
Pepper, to taste

Mix all ingredients in a large bowl; cover and refrigerate for several hours or overnight before serving. This will keep several weeks in the refrigerator if covered tightly.

OVERNIGHT LETTUCE SALAD

yield: 12 servings

1 head lettuce, shredded
½ cup celery, chopped
½ cup green pepper, diced
1 small onion, diced
1 (10-ounce) package frozen green peas, thawed
1 (8-ounce) can water chestnuts, sliced
1 cup mayonnaise
1 cup Parmesan cheese, grated
6 slices bacon, fried crisp, crumbled
1 cup radishes, sliced thinly

Layer vegetables in the following order: Lettuce, celery, green pepper, onion, peas and water chestnuts. Spread mayonnaise over top sealing the sides. Cover with plastic wrap and refrigerate for 24 hours. Sprinkle Parmesan cheese and bacon over the top. Toss from the bottom before serving. Garnish with radishes.

ARTICHOKE RICE SALAD

1 (6-ounce) package rice for chicken, French Style
¾ teaspoon curry powder
4 green onions, thinly sliced
½ green pepper, chopped
1 (14-ounce) can artichoke hearts, drained and chopped
⅓ cup mayonnaise
1 cup stuffed green olives, chopped

Cook rice according to directions. Add curry powder during cooking. Cool. Add green onion, green pepper, artichoke hearts, mayonnaise and green olives. Chill and serve.

COLD PASTA PRIMAVERA

yield: 6 luncheon size servings
12 side dish servings

2 cups spaghetti or linguini, tender-cooked
½ pound part-skim mozzarella cheese, cubed
1 cup broccoli or cauliflower, uncooked
1 cup cherry tomatoes
½ cup carrots, thinly sliced
Red onion rings, thinly sliced, to taste
8 stuffed green olives, thinly sliced
4 Tablespoons olive liquid (from jar of olives)
2 Tablespoons vinegar
1 Tablespoon olive oil
2 Tablespoons Parmesan cheese, freshly grated
½ teaspoon basil
½ teaspoon oregano
Salt or garlic salt, to taste
Pepper, coarsely ground, to taste

Rinse spaghetti in cold water, drain well. Combine with remaining ingredients and mix lightly. Chill until serving time.

GREEK PASTA SALAD

yield: 8 servings

DRESSING:

¼ cup oil
2 Tablespoons fresh lemon juice
2 Tablespoons wine vinegar
1 teaspoon dried oregano leaves
½ teaspoon salt
⅛ teaspoon cracked pepper

SALAD:

1 (8-ounce) package elbow
    macaroni, or other pasta
1 cup green pepper strips, ⅛-inch
    wide
½ cup green onion, sliced
½ pound feta cheese, cubed
½ cup pitted black olives, sliced
2 Tablespoons snipped fresh
    dillweed or 1 teaspoon dried
    dillweed
1 large tomato, thinly sliced

Make dressing and place in jar with tight fitting lid. Shake up. Cook macaroni as package directs; drain well and place in large bowl. Add dressing and toss until well mixed. Cool completely. To macaroni mixture add remaining ingredients in the order listed. Toss lightly to mix. Place in serving bowl; cover and refrigerate. Toss well before serving.

COLD FRENCH BEEF SALAD

yield: 4-6 servings

1½ pounds flank steak
1 (10-ounce) bottle Teriyaki
  marinade sauce
3 Tablespoons olive oil
1 pound fresh mushrooms, sliced
2 Tablespoons lemon juice
Salt, to taste
Pepper, to taste
¼ pound Swiss cheese, grated
1 Tablespoon parsley

DRESSING:
4 Tablespoons oil
4 teaspoons red wine vinegar
1 medium clove garlic, minced
¼ teaspoon dry mustard
Pinch of basil
Pinch of thyme

Cut flank steak into thin julienne strips; marinate in teriyaki sauce for 3-4 hours.

Heat olive oil in large skillet and sauté mushrooms; add lemon juice, salt and pepper. Drain marinade from skillet and immediately stir-fry steak strips. Combine beef strips, mushrooms, Swiss cheese and parsley in large bowl.

Combine all dressing ingredients and shake well.

Cover beef mixture with dressing and chill for several hours. Serve on a bed of lettuce with cherry tomatoes.

A whole lemon heated in water for 5 minutes will yield 1-2 tablespoons more juice.

CLASSICAL CHICKEN MOLD

yield: 12 servings

1 (4-pound) hen
1 large onion, chopped
2 celery ribs with leaves
2 teaspoons salt
¼ cup cold water
1 envelope gelatin, unflavored
1 cup chicken broth
1½ Tablespoons Worcestershire
  sauce
½ Tablespoon onion, scraped
1 dash red pepper
½ teaspoon salt
2 cups mayonnaise
1 cup whipping cream
¾ cup almonds, slivered
1½ cups celery, minced
3 pimientos, minced
1 Tablespoon lemon juice

In Dutch oven, cover the hen with cold water. Add the chopped onion, celery ribs, 2 teaspoons salt, and simmer covered, for 2 hours. Remove the chicken and chop it coarsely.

Strain and chill the broth, then remove the solidified grease. Heat 1 cup broth to boiling.

Sprinkle gelatin over the cold water. Pour the boiling broth over the gelatin. Add the Worcestershire sauce, scraped onion, red pepper and salt.

Chill this mixture until slightly thickened. Add mayonnaise and whipping cream. Add the chicken, almonds, minced celery, pimientos and lemon juice. Pour mixture into individual molds or a 3-quart mold. Chill until set. Serve unmolded on lettuce leaves.

CHICKEN SALAD TARRAGON

yield: 8-10 servings
oven temperature: 350 °F

3 pounds boneless chicken breasts
1 cup creme fraiche or heavy
  cream
½ cup dairy sour cream
½ cup mayonnaise
½ cup shelled walnuts
2 celery ribs, julienned
1 Tablespoon tarragon, dried and
  crumbled
Salt and pepper, freshly ground, to
  taste

Arrange chicken breasts in a single layer in a large jelly roll pan. Spread evenly with cream and bake at 350° for 25 minutes or until done to your taste. Remove and cool. Shred meat with hands into bite-size pieces, and transfer into bowl. Whisk mayonnaise and sour cream together in a small bowl and spread over chicken. Toss. Add celery, walnuts, tarragon, salt and pepper. Refrigerate covered at least 4 hours.

WILD TUNA SALAD

yield: 8-10 servings

1 (6-ounce) package wild and long
  grain rice with seasonings
1 cup mayonnaise
½ cup sour cream
1 cup celery, chopped
1 cup pecans, chopped
2 Tablespoons onion, chopped
⅛ teaspoon salt
⅛ teaspoon pepper
1 (14-ounce) can white tuna (water
  packed)
Green grapes, optional garnish
Apple, sliced, optional garnish

Cook rice as directed on package and cool. Add remaining ingredients and chill overnight. Keeps several days and gets better each day. Serve on lettuce cups. Garnish with green grapes and sliced pear or apple.

WILD RICE AND CRAB MEAT SALAD

yield: 6-8 servings

⅓ cup mayonnaise
⅓ cup sour cream
¼ cup chili sauce (tomato based)
1 Tablespoon lemon juice
1 teaspoon Dijon mustard
1 large tomato, peeled, seeded and
   diced
1 cup celery, thinly sliced
½ cup green onion, chopped
3 cups wild rice, cooked
7 ounce package frozen snow crab
   meat
Salt and pepper, to taste
Lettuce

Make a dressing by blending mayonnaise, sour cream, chili sauce, lemon juice and mustard. Refrigerate. Mix tomato, celery, green onion, wild rice, crab meat, salt and pepper. Place salad in lettuce cups and serve with dressing.

SHRIMP SALAD

yield: 6 servings

1 cup cooked rice, cooled
2 cups shrimp, boiled, cooled,
   peeled, chopped
½ teaspoon seasoned salt
2 Tablespoons lemon juice
¼ cup green pepper, chopped
4 scallions with tops, chopped
1 cup cauliflower, chopped
2 Tablespoons French dressing
⅓ cup mayonnaise
Black pepper freshly ground, to
   taste
Lettuce

Combine rice, shrimp, seasoned salt, lemon juice, green pepper, scallions and cauliflower in salad bowl; toss to mix well. Mix French dressing, mayonnaise and pepper; spoon over shrimp mixture. Toss gently. Chill in refrigerator. Serve on bed of lettuce.

CHINESE MELON

yield: 6 servings

1 large cantaloupe
2 stalks celery, finely chopped
1 large onion, finely chopped
8-12 ounces chicken, cooked
½ pound white seedless grapes, halved
8 ounces shrimp
1 (6-ounce) package crab meat
Mayonnaise, to moisten
Salt and pepper, to taste
2 ounces walnuts, (optional)
Lettuce leaves

Cut the top off the melon, serrating the edge. Make sure the melon will stand straight; if not taper the base. Using a melon scoop, hollow out inside of the melon, making small balls. Turn melon upside down to drain for 1 hour.

Cut cooked chicken into 1-inch cubes and add to onion, celery, grapes and cantaloupe. Add shrimp, crab meat, mayonnaise, salt, pepper and walnuts, gently tossing. Spoon mixture back into melon shell. Place melon on a bed of lettuce leaves. Top of melon may be replaced, if desired, for decoration.

FRUIT SALAD DRESSING

½ cup sugar
1 teaspoon dry mustard
1 teaspoon paprika
¼ teaspoon salt
1 teaspoon celery seed
⅓ cup honey
1 Tablespoon lemon juice
4 Tablespoons vinegar
1 cup oil

Mix dry ingredients. Add honey, lemon juice and vinegar. With mixer on medium speed, add oil slowly, beating constantly. Make 1¼ cups.

Serve over fresh fruit.

YOGURT DRESSING

yield: 1 cup

1 cup plain low-fat yogurt
½ teaspoon dill
⅛ teaspoon garlic powder
½ teaspoon caraway seeds
1 Tablespoon tarragon vinegar
¼ teaspoon onion powder
Salt, to taste

Mix and chill several hours.

LEMON LOW-CAL DRESSING

yield: 1 cup

1 cup low-fat yogurt
2-3 Tablespoons buttermilk
1-2 Tablespoons lemon juice
Sesame seeds, toasted, optional

Mix and chill several hours. Especially good sprinkled with toasted sesame seeds.

My family ate it and never knew what it was.

HOMECOMING SALAD DRESSING

yield: 2 cups

½ cup sugar
1 Tablespoon flour
1 egg, beaten
½ cup vinegar
½ cup water
1 Tablespoon butter

Mix sugar and flour together. Add remaining ingredients and mix well. Cook on medium heat until thickened stirring constantly.

Good on lettuce, onions and boiled eggs, as well as potato salad or slaw.

⧖ GARLIC SALAD DRESSING

yield: 4-6 servings

1 clove garlic, pressed
1 teaspoon salt (or less, to taste)
2 Tablespoons lemon juice
¼ teaspoon sugar
⅛ teaspoon pepper
⅛ teaspoon celery seed
½ teaspoon paprika
¾ teaspoon dry mustard
¼ teaspoon monosodium
   glutamate
5 Tablespoons oil

Blend garlic and salt until salt absorbs garlic (mash with back of a spoon). Add other ingredients. Blend well.

Toss with leafy salad or vegetable salad.

⧖ BLUE CHEESE SALAD DRESSING

yield: 1½ pints

½ teaspoon celery salt
½ teaspoon paprika
2 Tablespoons vinegar
2 cups sour cream
½ cup mayonnaise
Salt and pepper, to taste
½ pound Gorgonzola or another
   blue cheese

Mix all ingredients except blue cheese in small mixing bowl. Crumble the cheese and fold it into the mixture.

Refrigerate dressing to mellow. Thin with milk or buttermilk as needed.

SUGGESTED ACCOMPANIMENTS: Tomato aspic or green salad.

⌛ RELIABLE FRENCH DRESSING

yield: 3 cups

½ cup water
½ cup wine vinegar
½ teaspoon sugar
1 Tablespoon lemon juice
1 Tablespoon salt
1½ teaspoons black pepper, freshly ground
1½ teaspoons Worcestershire sauce
1½ teaspoons dry mustard
3 cloves garlic, minced
1½ cups salad oil
½ cup olive oil

Mix all ingredients in a 1-quart jar. Chill thoroughly. Shake well before using.

⌛ PAUL'S HONEY DRESSING

yield: 3½ cups

½ cup honey
2 cups mayonnaise
½ cup oil
½ cup prepared mustard
⅛ teaspoon onion salt
Dash red pepper
1½ teaspoons apple cider vinegar

Mix all ingredients in a blender until smooth. Refrigerate. Will keep 2-3 weeks. Discard when oil starts to separate.

SUGGESTED ACCOMPANIMENTS: Green salad.

ENTREES

UPPER CRUST CORNISH HENS

yield: 4 servings
oven temperature: 350°F

STUFFING:
2½ cups water, boiling
½ cup long grain rice
¼ cup wild rice
4 Tablespoons butter, melted
1½ cups blackberries
1 apple, chopped
¼ cup brown sugar
4 green onions, chopped
½ cup pecans, broken
½ teaspoon thyme
½ teaspoon marjoram
½ teaspoon white pepper
4 Cornish hens
Salt
Peppercorns, cracked
1½ cups dry white wine

SAUCE:
1 cup butter, melted
½ cup pecans, ground

Boil both rices for 15 minutes on high. (Cook longer if you do not want crunchy wild rice.) Combine the rice with the other stuffing ingredients.

Remove giblets and rinse hens. Sprinkle salt and peppercorns in the cavity of each hen and stuff each hen with the rice mixture. Close cavities, truss and secure with wooden picks. Place hens breast side-up in an uncovered roaster. Pour wine over each hen. Combine melted butter and pecans and spread on each hen coating completely. Bake at 350° for 1 hour, basting frequently with the drippings.

BROCCOLI STUFFED CORNISH HENS

yield: 4 servings

1 (10-ounce) package chopped
  frozen broccoli, cooked, drained
1 cup long grain rice, cooked
½ cup Swiss cheese, grated
2 Tablespoons butter, melted
¼ teaspoon salt
Dash of pepper
4 Cornish hens

Combine broccoli, rice, cheese, butter, salt and pepper. Rinse hens; pat dry and lightly salt the cavities. Stuff with broccoli mixture; tie legs to tail and secure neck skin to back. Mount hens crosswise on a spit; alternating front-back, back-front. DO NOT let them touch! Brush with additional butter. Cook on rotisserie. Roast hens over medium coals about 1¼-1½ hours; brushing with butter every ½ hour.

Can be baked in the oven without the rotisserie, at 375°F for 1¼-½ hours.

EXOTIC CHICKEN

yield: 4 servings
oven temperature: 350°F

½ cup oil
½ cup white wine
1 Tablespoon ginger, grated
1 clove garlic, minced
Salt and pepper, to taste
4 chicken breasts or 2 Cornish
  hens, halved
½ cup chutney, chopped
½ cup plum preserves
½ cup flaked coconut, toasted
1 Tablespooon brandy

Mix oil, wine, ginger, garlic, salt and pepper together to make a marinade. Place skinned pieces of chicken in mixture and marinate for 1-3 hours.
Bake chicken in 350° oven for 30-40 minutes in baking pan. Baste twice with marinade. Broil quickly to brown, if necessary. Serve with coconut chutney made from mixture of remaining 4 ingredients.

CUBAN CHICKEN

yield: 4 servings

½ cup butter or margarine
1 medium onion, chopped
1 red pepper, chopped
1 green pepper, chopped
4 cups tomatoes, canned or tomato
 juice
½-1 teaspoon pepper
½-1 teaspoon salt
1 (2-pound) chicken cut into pieces
1 cup rice, raw

Melt butter in Dutch oven or skillet; add onion and cook until clear. Add peppers, tomatoes, salt, pepper and chicken pieces. Bring to a boil; cover and reduce heat to low. Add rice and simmer 1 hour longer.

NORTH CAROLINA BARBEQUED CHICKEN

yield: 4-6 servings
oven temperature: 350°F

1 chicken fryer, cut up
½ cup butter
⅓ cup Worcestershire sauce
⅔ cup vinegar
¼ teaspoon salt
1 teaspoon black pepper
¼ teaspoon red pepper
2 Tablespoons lemon juice
2 teaspoons sugar

Bake chicken at 350° for 45 minutes. Meanwhile, melt butter and add remaining ingredients. Mix well. Transfer chicken to a grill and baste with sauce until chicken is brown. Then place chicken in a large pot with the spare sauce and steam it until it falls from the bone.
Well worth all the extra steps.

CHICKEN WITH SQUASH

yield: 6 servings
oven temperature: 350°F

2 cups yellow squash, sliced
2 cups chicken, cooked, skinned
  and boned
½ cup onion, chopped
½ cup celery, sliced
1 (10¾-ounce) can cream of
  mushroom soup
¼ cup pimiento, diced
½ cup water chestnuts, sliced
Salt and pepper, to taste
½ cup bread crumbs

Cook squash in boiling water for 5 minutes. Drain well.
In large buttered casserole mix squash, chicken and all other ingredients except bread crumbs. Top with bread crumbs.
Bake at 350° for 35 minutes.

CHICKEN ELÉGANT

yield: 8 servings
oven temperature: 350°F

2 large fryers
Water
½ cup sherry
¾ teaspoon curry powder
1 medium onion, sliced
2 (6-ounce) packages wild and long
  grain rice
½ cup butter
1 (10¾-ounce) can cream of
  mushroom soup
1 cup sour cream

Cover chicken with water, add sherry, curry powder and onion and cook. Reserve broth and cool chicken. Bone chicken. Cook rice in broth while sautéing mushrooms in butter.
Layer rice, chicken and mushrooms in a 13 x 9-inch casserole.
Blend sour cream and soup, and pour over top.
Refrigerate overnight. Bake at 350° for 1 hour.

CHICKEN SPECTACULAR

yield: 8 servings
oven temperature: 350°F

3 cups chicken, cooked and diced
1 (6-ounce) package rice, wild and
  long grain, cooked
1 (16-ounce) can French-style green
  beans, drained
1 onion, chopped
1 (10¾-ounce) can cream of celery
  soup
1 (4-ounce) jar pimientos, chopped
½ cup mayonnaise
½ cup water chestnuts, diced or
  sliced
Salt and pepper, to taste

Mix all ingredients in 13 x 9-inch baking dish. Cover and bake at 350° for 30-45 minutes. May be prepared ahead; freezes well.

POPPY SEED CHICKEN

yield: 6 servings
oven temperature: 350°F

1 (10¾-ounce) can cream of
  mushroom soup
1 (10¾-ounce) can cream of
  chicken soup
4 cups chicken, cooked and cut
  into pieces
1 cup sour cream
1 roll butter crackers, crushed
½ cup margarine, melted
2 Tablespoons poppyseeds

Mix together soups and sour cream. Add chicken pieces and stir well. Pour into ungreased 9 x 13-inch casserole; stir cracker crumbs into margarine and spread over casserole. Sprinkle with poppyseeds. Bake at 350°F for 30 minutes.

This seems to be better when frozen before cooking — what more can you ask for!?

103

CHICKEN ALMONDINE

yield: 4 servings
oven temperature: 350 °F

¾ cup rice, raw
1 (10¾-ounce) can cream of
  chicken soup
¾ cup mayonnaise
½ cup celery, diced
1 medium onion, diced
1 Tablespoon lemon juice
½ teaspoon salt
2 cups chicken, cooked, diced
1 cup cornflakes, crushed
¼ cup butter, melted
½ cup almonds

Cook rice according to package directions. Mix rice, soup, mayonnaise, celery, onion, lemon and salt together; fold in chicken. Place in a buttered 1½-quart casserole dish.

Mix cornflakes and butter; sprinkle over casserole. Top with almonds. Bake at 350° for 30 minutes.

CRESCENT ROLL CHICKEN

yield: 4 servings
oven temperature: 350 °F

4 ounces cream cheese
5 Tablespoons butter, melted,
  divided
2 cups chicken, cooked, cubed
¼ teaspoon salt
2 Tablespoons milk
¼ cup onion, chopped
1½ Tablespoons pimiento, chopped
1 (8-ounce) package of crescent
  rolls

In medium bowl blend cream cheese and 2 tablespoons butter. Add chicken, salt, milk, onion and pimiento; mix well. Separate rolls into 4 squares instead of 8 triangles. Pinch seams to secure. Spoon ½ cup of chicken mixture in middle of rolls and press the four corners together. Brush top with 3 tablespoons of butter and put on an ungreased cookie sheet. Bake at 350°F for 20-25 minutes.

CHICKEN TETRAZZINI

yield: 8-10 servings
oven temperature: 350°F

6 stalks celery, chopped
2 onions, chopped
3 Tablespoons butter
1 cup chicken stock
1 Tablespoon Worcestershire sauce
Salt and red pepper, to taste
1 (10¾-ounce) can cream of
   mushroom soup
½ pound sharp Cheddar cheese,
   grated
1 (8-ounce) package spaghetti,
   cooked and drained
1 large chicken, boiled and cut into
   small pieces
1 (4-ounce) bottle stuffed olives,
   chopped
1 cup walnuts, chopped

Sauté celery and onion in butter until tender. Add chicken stock, Worcestershire, salt and pepper; simmer 15 minutes. Stir in mushroom soup and cheese. Add spaghetti to this mixture and let stand 1 hour.

Fold in chicken and olives. Spoon mixture into a buttered 13 x 9-inch casserole. Sprinkle walnuts over all. Bake at 350° for 20 minutes or until heated thoroughly.

This casserole takes time to prepare so make 2 or 3, they freeze beautifully!

LEMON CHICKEN

yield: 4 servings

¾ cup oil
½ cup fresh lemon juice
½ teaspoon salt
½ teaspoon paprika
¼ teaspoon pepper
¼ teaspoon thyme
¼ teaspoon poultry seasoning
4 medium chicken breasts

Combine liquids and seasonings and pour over chicken breasts. Marinate chicken for several hours, turning occasionally. Grill chicken approximately 15 minutes on each side or until done.

⧗ ORIENTAL LIME CHICKEN

yield: 4 servings
oven temperature: 375°F

8 chicken thighs, no substitutions
Juice of a fresh lime
1 cup soy sauce
2 cloves garlic, minced
⅓ cup sweetened bottled lime juice
1 Tablespoon fresh ginger, grated, or more to taste
White pepper, to taste
Lime slices, optional

Wash chicken thighs leaving skin on one side. Squeeze juice of fresh lime over chicken. Mix soy sauce, garlic, lime juice, ginger and pepper; marinate chicken for 24 hours.

Place chicken skin side down in a baking dish; cover with marinade. Bake uncovered for 35 minutes. Turn chicken and continue baking for another 40 minutes.

Serve with rice. You may add a very thin slice of lime atop each piece of chicken. Skim fat off marinade and serve as a sauce to drizzle over rice or chicken.

This chicken has a wonderful distinctive flavor and turns a beautiful golden brown while cooking.

ORANGE CHICKEN

yield: 6 servings
oven temperature: 350 °F

6 chicken breast halves, skinned
  and boned
2 Tablespoons margarine, melted
1 teaspoon paprika
⅛ teaspoon pepper
1 (6-ounce) can frozen orange juice
  concentrate, thawed
1 teaspoon rosemary
½ teaspoon thyme, dried

Brush chicken with margarine; place on rack of broiler pan. Broil 3-5 minutes on each side or until golden brown. Remove from oven and place chicken in a 13 x 9-inch baking dish. Sprinkle with paprika and pepper. Pour orange juice concentrate over chicken; sprinkle with rosemary and thyme. Bake chicken, uncovered at 350° for 30 minutes.

⧗ BUSY DAY CHICKEN AND RICE

yield: 6 servings
oven temperature: 300 °F

Salt and pepper, to taste
6 chicken breasts, boned
½ cup butter, melted
1 (10¾-ounce) can golden
  mushroom soup
1 (10¾-ounce) can onion soup
1 (10¾-ounce) can cream of
  chicken soup
1½ cups rice, raw

Salt and pepper chicken and dip in melted butter. Pour excess butter in casserole. Mix soups and rice and pour in casserole. Place chicken breasts on top. Bake in 300° oven for 1 hour and 15 minutes. Cover with aluminum foil and bake an additional 45 minutes.

COMPANY CHICKEN N' BREAD

yield: 6-8 servings
oven temperature: 325 °F

1 large round loaf French bread
  (long may be substituted)
8-10 boneless chicken breasts
½ cup butter
2 (3-ounce) cans mushrooms,
  drained and sliced
1 large onion, chopped
½ teaspoon onion salt
½ teaspoon garlic salt
1 cup white wine
½-1 teaspoon of each:
  oregano
  basil
  thyme
  rosemary
  curry powder

Cut off the top of the bread and scoop out the inside. Lightly brown chicken in butter about 10 minutes on each side; remove from pan. Sauté mushrooms, onion, onion salt, garlic salt, wine, oregano, basil, thyme, rosemary and curry.

Place chicken in bread and top with mushroom mixture. Wrap bread in foil and bake at 325° for 2 hours.

Easy clean up since you eat pan and all!

CHICKEN MOZZARELLA

yield: 6 servings
oven temperature: 350 °F

6 chicken breasts, halved
¼ cup butter, melted
1 cup cornflake crumbs
1 teaspoon salt
½ teaspoon pepper
½ teaspoon Italian seasoning
½ pound mozzarella cheese,
  shredded

Skin chicken and dip in melted butter. Combine cornflake crumbs, salt, pepper and Italian seasoning in plastic bag. Shake chicken breasts in crumb mixture to coat evenly. Place in a single layer in greased baking pan. Bake at 350° for 1 hour. Top with cheese and return to oven until cheese melts and barely browns.

HERB-CHICKEN BAKE

yield: 6 servings
oven temperature: 350°F

1 (6-ounce) package long grain and wild rice mix
6 chicken breasts, skinned and boned
Salt and pepper, to taste
¼ cup butter
1 (10¾-ounce) can cream of chicken soup
¾ cup sauterne wine
½ cup celery, sliced
1 (3-ounce) can sliced mushrooms, drained
2 Tablespoons pimientos, chopped

Prepare rice using package directions.
Season chicken with salt and pepper. In a skillet, brown chicken in butter.
Spoon rice into 1½-quart casserole. Top with chicken. Add soup to the skillet and slowly add wine stirring until smooth. Add the remaining ingredients and bring to a boil. Pour mixture over the chicken.
Cover and bake at 350°F for 25 minutes. Uncover and bake 15-20 minutes longer or until tender.

CALIFORNIA CHICKEN

yield: 4 servings
oven temperature: 350°F

4 large chicken breasts, skinned
Oil
Garlic salt
Salt and pepper
¼ cup onion, chopped
¼ cup green pepper, chopped
1 (14-ounce) can artichoke hearts
1 (10¾-ounce) can Cheddar cheese soup
½ can milk

Brown chicken in small amount of oil. Place in a 10-inch square casserole. Season with garlic salt, salt and pepper to taste. Sprinkle chopped onion and peppers over chicken. Place halved artichoke hearts around chicken. Pour soup diluted with ½ can milk over all. Bake at 350° covered for 1½-2 hours. Uncover last 15 minutes.

ASPARAGUS CHICKEN

yield: 6 servings
oven temperature: 350°F

6 large chicken breasts, boned and skinned
⅓ cup water
2 (16-ounce) cans asparagus
1 cup mayonnaise
2 (10¾-ounce) cans cream of chicken soup
Rind of 1 lemon, grated
1 teaspoon lemon juice
¼ teaspoon curry powder
½ cup Cheddar cheese, grated

Simmer chicken breasts in water, with the skillet covered, for 30 minutes or until tender. Place drained chicken breasts in rectangular pan and top with remaining ingredients in the following order: asparagus, mayonnaise, soup, lemon rind, lemon juice, curry powder and cheese. Bake at 350° for 30 minutes.

⧗ MARINATED CHICKEN

yield: 6 servings

6 whole chicken breasts
2 cups water

MARINADE:
1 cup oil
½ cup tarragon vinegar
1 teaspoon salt
½ teaspoon garlic salt
½ teaspoon sesame seeds
¼ cup chives or green onions, chopped
¼ cup fresh parsley, chopped

Poach chicken with water in a skillet for 20 minutes. Bone chicken and cut into bite size pieces. Cool.

MARINADE: Mix all the marinade ingredients, pour over chicken and marinate in refrigerator for 6 hours.

Great as an appetizer, as a salad or as an accompaniment for a salad lunch.
Substitute for tarragon vinegar: a pinch of tarragon mixed with 1 cup wine vinegar.

CHICKEN BREASTS IN WINE SAUCE

yield: 6-12 servings
oven temperature: 350°F

6 whole chicken breasts, boned, skinned
Salt and pepper, to taste
½ teaspoon basil leaves, crushed
1 (10¾-ounce) can cream of chicken soup
1 (10¾-ounce) can cream of celery soup
½ cup sherry or dry white wine
5 Tablespoons almonds, blanched, and slivered

Place whole or split chicken breasts in 8 x 12-inch casserole, sprinkle with salt, pepper and basil.

Combine soup and wine; pour over chicken and top with almonds. Cover and bake at 350° for 1 hour.

This can be prepared the night before or early in the day and marinated in the refrigerator until baking time.

CHICKEN DIJON

yield: 6-8 servings
oven temperature: 400°F

2 cups sour cream
1 (8-ounce) jar Dijon mustard
6 whole chicken breasts, skinned and boned
1½ cups seasoned bread crumbs
¼ cup butter

Combine sour cream and mustard; dip chicken breasts in mixture. Heavily coat chicken by rolling breasts in seasoned bread crumbs. Place chicken in greased 3-quart casserole and dot with butter. Cover with foil and bake for 30 minutes at 400°; uncover and bake for about 15 minutes at 450° until chicken is browned.

ALMOND CHICKEN

yield: 6 servings

1½ pounds chicken breasts
1 teaspoon ginger
2 teaspoons honey
1 Tablespoon cornstarch
3 Tablespoons water
3 Tablespoons soy sauce
⅓ cup sherry
¼ cup oil
1 cup slivered almonds
1 (6-ounce) package frozen snow
    peas or ½ pound fresh snow peas
Rice

Cut chicken into ½-inch cubes. Mix ginger, honey, cornstarch, and blend in water, soy sauce and sherry. Thaw pea pods. Heat oil in a skillet over medium heat. Add almonds, stirring and cooking for about 3 minutes. Add chicken and cook just until meat turns white. Pour in sherry mixture and cook until sauce thickens. Add pea pods and stir-fry until hot and glazed. Serve over rice. VARIATION: May substitute 1 (10-ounce) package sliced green beans for snow peas.

CHICKEN PAPRIKA

yield: 4 servings

4 Tablespoons butter, divided
4 whole chicken breasts, skinned
    and boned
½ cup onion, minced
½ cup dry white wine
1 heaping Tablespoon paprika
1 teaspoon lemon juice
Salt and pepper, to taste
⅔ cup heavy cream

Sauté chicken in 2 tablespoons butter until golden brown. Remove and keep warm. Melt 2 tablespoons butter in same skillet and cook the onion for 10-15 minutes until the onion is limp and golden. Add wine and paprika. Cover and simmer 10 minutes. Add chicken, lemon juice, salt and pepper. Cover and simmer for 45 minutes. Slowly stir in the cream. Cover and heat thoroughly. To prevent curdling, DO NOT overheat cream.

POULET NORMANDE

yield: 4 servings
oven temperature: 350°F

4 chicken breasts or whole chicken, boned, skinned, and cut into smaller pieces
½ cup flour
½ cup olive oil
1 large onion, thinly sliced
Mushrooms, sliced
1¼ cups apple cider
2 apples, cored and sliced
1 teaspoon chives, chopped
Parsley, to taste
Salt and pepper, to taste

Dredge chicken pieces in flour, brown in ½ cup olive oil; set aside in a baking dish. In same skillet, sauté onion and mushrooms, cooking until barely tender and add to the chicken. Deglaze skillet with cider and pour over chicken. Add apples, chives, parsley, salt and pepper to the baking dish. Bake at 350°F for 1 hour.

CHICKEN MILANO

yield: 12 servings
oven temperature: 350°F

12 chicken breasts, boned and skinned
Salt and pepper, to taste
½ cup flour
4 cloves garlic, crushed
3 Tablespoons butter, melted
3 Tablespoons olive oil
1½ cups chicken broth
½ cup dry white wine
½ teaspoon tarragon
12 slices boiled ham
12 slices mozzarella cheese

Season chicken with salt, pepper and flour. Sprinkle with crushed garlic. In large skillet, sauté chicken in butter and oil until light brown. Place in shallow 9 x 13-inch casserole. Add broth to skillet and deglaze pan. Add wine and pour over chicken; sprinkle with tarragon. Cover and bake at 350° for 25-30 minutes. Uncover and bake for 15 minutes more. Remove from oven, and top each breast with one slice of ham and one slice of cheese. Continue baking until cheese melts, about 5 minutes.

TOMATO CHILI CASSEROLE

yield: 8-10 servings
oven temperature: 300 °F

6 chicken breasts
1 cup onion, chopped
1 cup celery, chopped
1 cup green pepper, chopped
2 Tablespoons butter
1 (12-ounce) package wide egg
noodles
1 (10-ounce) can tomatoes with
chilies, undrained
1 pound processed cheese food
with chili peppers, cubed
1 package butter crackers,
crumbled
Butter

Braise chicken until tender, about one hour. Reserve broth. Remove skin and bones and cube chicken. Sauté onions, celery and green peppers in butter. Cook egg noodles in the reserved broth, until tender. Mix noodles, tomatoes with chilies, onion, celery, green peppers and chicken. Place mixture in a 3-quart casserole or two smaller ones. Stir in cheese cubes and top with crackers. Dot with butter. Bake at 300° for about 15 minutes or until hot.

COUNTRY STYLE CHICKEN KIEV

yield: 4 servings
oven temperature: 375 °F

¼ cup bread crumbs
2 Tablespoons Parmesan cheese
1 teaspoon basil
1 teaspoon oregano
½ teaspoon garlic salt
¼ teaspoon salt
⅔ cup butter, melted
2 whole chicken breasts
¼ cup white wine
¼ cup green onion, chopped
¼ cup fresh parsley, chopped

Combine bread crumbs, Parmesan cheese, basil, oregano, garlic salt and salt. Dip chicken pieces in butter then roll in crumb mixture. Set remaining butter aside. Place chicken skin side up in 2-quart shallow casserole. Bake at 375° for 50-60 minutes.
To remaining butter add wine, green onions, and parsley. Pour over baked chicken and bake for 2-3 more minutes.

CHICKEN BREASTS

yield: 4-5 servings

2½ pounds chicken breasts, boned
3 Tablespoons plus 2 teaspoons
  butter, divided
½ cup dry white wine
½ cup chicken broth
Salt and pepper, to taste
2 sprigs parsley, chopped
2 (10-ounce) packages fresh
  spinach
2 cups water
⅛ teaspoon nutmeg
2 Tablespoons flour
1 cup heavy cream
1 egg yolk, slightly beaten
Parmesan cheese

Melt 2 teaspoons butter in skillet. Add chicken, wine, chicken broth, salt, pepper and parsley. Bring to a boil. Cover and simmer about 15-20 minutes, until breasts are cooked thoroughly. Remove from heat.

While chicken cooks, prepare spinach and cook 5 minutes in boiling water. Drain and coarsely chop. Melt 1 tablespoon butter in a skillet and add nutmeg and spinach. Cook, tossing and stirring just until heated.

Drain and reserve the liquid from the chicken (about 1½ cups), keep chicken covered.

Melt the remaining 2 tablespoons butter in a saucepan. Stir in the flour with a wire whisk until blended. Add the reserved liquid to the roux, stirring with a whisk. When roux is thick and smooth, simmer about 5 minutes. Add the heavy cream and cook 2 more minutes.

Remove from heat and add the egg yolk, stirring briskly.

Place the spinach in the center of a ovenproof serving dish. Add the chicken breasts. Spoon the sauce over the chicken and spinach. Sprinkle with cheese. Place under broiler until bubbly.

STIR-FRY SESAME CHICKEN

yield: 4-5 servings

1 pound chicken breasts, boned
   and skinned
1 Tablespoon sesame seeds
2 Tablespoons soy sauce
¼ teaspoon pepper
3 teaspoons oil
1 cup carrots, thinly sliced
½ cup snow peas
1-1½ cups broccoli flowerettes
½ cup mushrooms, sliced
1 Tablespoon cornstarch
½ cup water, cold

Slice chicken while partially frozen (across the grain, in thin strips). Toss with sesame seeds, soy sauce, pepper and 2 teaspoons oil in small bowl. Let stand 5-25 minutes.

Parboil carrots until slightly tender. Drain. Heat a wok over moderately high heat. When hot, add chicken mixture and stir constantly, about 5-7 minutes, until chicken is lightly cooked. Remove to a bowl. Add carrots, broccoli, snow peas, mushrooms and remaining teaspoon of oil to skillet. Stir 2-3 minutes. Reduce heat, add broth, cover and simmer 3 minutes, until vegetables are tender, but still crisp. Stir in chicken and cornstarch mixed in water; stir until boiling. Cover and simmer 2 minutes.

Less than 250 calories per serving.

STIR FRY CHICKEN

yield: 4 servings

2 whole chicken breasts, boned,
  skinned, halved
2 Tablespoons oil
1 cup celery, thinly sliced
1 medium green pepper, sliced into
  strips
1 small onion, sliced
1 teaspoon salt
½ teaspoon ginger
1 (16-ounce) can bean sprouts,
  drained
1 (5-ounce) can water chestnuts,
  drained, sliced
1 teaspoon chicken bouillon or 1
  cube
½ cup water
2 teaspoons cornstarch
2 Tablespoons soy sauce
3 cups rice, optional

Slice chicken crosswise into
¼-inch strips. In a large skillet,
over high heat; heat oil and sauté
celery, green pepper, onion, salt
and ginger, stirring quickly and
frequently about 3 minutes.
Remove vegetables to warm platter and keep warm. In remaining
oil (if there is none add more)
sauté chicken until it turns white,
about 3 minutes. Return vegetables to pan add bean sprouts,
water chestnuts, bouillon and
water. Blend cornstarch and soy
sauce until smooth; gradually stir
into hot chicken mixture and cook
stirring constantly until mixture
thickens. Serve over hot rice or
warm noodles.

▨ HOLIDAY TURKEY CASSEROLE

yield: 4-6 servings
oven temperature: 350°F

¾ cup rice, cooked
1 (10¾-ounce) can cream of
  chicken mushroom soup
1 cup celery, diced
½ cup onion, diced
1 (2-ounce) jar pimiento, chopped
½ cup water chestnuts, sliced
½ cup milk
2 cups turkey, diced
1 (6-ounce) package chicken
  flavored stuffing mix

Mix together all ingredients except the stuffing. Pour into a
greased 2-quart casserole dish.
Mix stuffing according to directions. Spoon over turkey mixture.
Bake at 350° for 30-45 minutes or
until bubbly.

TURKEY FLORENTINE

yield: 8 servings
oven temperature: 350°F

2 (10-ounce) packages frozen
  spinach, chopped
¾ cup chicken broth, divided
1 cup sour cream
¼ cup dry white wine
1 garlic clove, crushed
¼ teaspoon thyme
¼ teaspoon nutmeg
⅛ teaspoon cayenne pepper
2 (14-ounce) cans artichoke hearts,
  drained, halved
8 slices of turkey breast
2 cups Parmesan cheese, grated

In a saucepan, cook spinach in ½ cup broth until barely cooked. Drain and set aside.
Combine sour cream, remaining broth, wine, garlic, thyme, nutmeg and pepper; mix until well blended.

Lightly grease 8 ramekins or a 13 x 9-inch casserole; place 2 artichoke halves in each ramekin and top with spinach mixture or layer in 13 x 9-inch with spinach on top. Place a slice of turkey over the spinach; pour sour cream sauce over the turkey. Sprinkle with cheese and bake at 350° for 20 minutes or until bubbly.

DELUXE CRANBERRY SAUCE

yield: 2-3 cups

2 cups sugar
1 cup water
1 pound fresh cranberries, washed
1 envelope gelatin
Juice of 2 lemons
¾ cup almonds, blanched
¼ cup crystallized ginger, chopped

Boil sugar and water for 5 minutes; add cranberries. Cook berries until they pop and look clear. Dissolve gelatin in lemon juice and add to cranberries. Stir in almonds and ginger. The ginger may be increased according to taste.

SPINACH AND HAM STUFFED TURKEY

yield: 8-12 servings
oven temperature: 325 °F

1 pound mushrooms, fresh, sliced
1 medium onion, finely chopped
½ cup butter or margarine
2 (10-ounce) packages frozen
   spinach, chopped, thawed and
   drained
1 (15-ounce) carton ricotta cheese,
   drained
1 cup Parmesan cheese, grated
2 (8-ounce) packages herb-
   seasoned stuffing mix
3 cups ham, cooked
3 eggs, beaten
½ cup fresh parsley, snipped or
   equivalent dried parsley
Salt and pepper, to taste
1 (10½-ounce) can chicken broth
1 (12-pound) turkey, whole or
   boned
(turkey breast can be substituted)

Cook mushrooms and onion in butter. Then mix together spinach, cheese, stuffing, ham, eggs and parsley; add mushrooms, onion, salt and pepper.

Add broth to make mixture moist enough to stuff the turkey, about ½ cup. Stuff the turkey and roast at 325° for 4-4½ hours.

Add extra broth to remaining stuffing mixture. Bake in separate casserole for about 1 hour.

DOVES

yield: 6-8 servings
oven temperature: 350 °F

8 whole doves or double breasts
Salt and pepper, to taste
Sherry
Margarine

Soak doves in salt and soda water before cooking. Place doves in cast iron skillet. Season with salt and pepper. Dot generously with margarine. Pour enough sherry over doves to fill bottom of skillet ¼-inch. Cook in 350° oven for 60 minutes. Baste frequently.

EASY WILD GOOSE IN A BAG

yield: 6 servings
oven temperature: 400 °F

Goose
Salt and pepper, to taste

SAUCE:
3 Tablespoons flour
1 teaspoon salt
1 (6-ounce) can frozen orange juice
   concentrate
2 cups water
2 Tablespoons orange marmalade
   or currant jelly
2 medium onions, finely chopped
¼ cup wine, optional

Wash and clean the goose thoroughly; lightly salt and pepper inside and out.

SAUCE: Combine sauce ingredients in a saucepan; heat and stir until smooth.

Put goose in a large browning bag with the breast up. Tilt bag and pour sauce over goose; tie the end of the bag tightly and punch 3 holes in the top to allow steam to escape. Try and keep the bag from touching the goose except on the bottom.

Cook at 400 °F for 10 minutes, reduce heat to 325 °F and continue cooking for 1 hour and 50 minutes.

Serve the sauce with the goose.

You may want to soak your game in salt water overnight before preparing. This recipe does not need the extra soaking though.

STUFFING OR DRESSING

yield: 8-10 servings
oven temperature: 375 °F

1 cup onion, chopped
1 cup celery, chopped
1 clove garlic
4 cups chicken or turkey stock
4 cups cornbread, dried and
  crumbled
2 cups dry bread crumbs
3 eggs, slightly beaten
1 cup milk
2 teaspoons salt
½ teaspoon pepper

Simmer onion, celery and garlic in stock until celery is soft. Discard garlic. In a bowl, mix cornbread and bread crumbs; pour stock over mixture. Add remaining ingredients, mix well. Bake in a well greased 9 x 13-inch casserole for 30-40 minutes.

Cornbread made with white cornmeal is best. May be prepared the day before and baked before serving.
May be served as an appetizer, cut into small squares and serve with toothpicks.

⧗ VERY SIMPLE COATING MIX

6-8 slices bread, fresh, dry, OR 4
  cups commercial bread crumbs
1 small package Italian salad
  dressing mix

Grind bread slices in blender or food processor. Stir salad dressing mix into ground crumbs and pour into quart size bag.
Coats 4-5 pieces of chicken or fish. Leftover mix keeps best if frozen.
TO USE: Coat chicken or fish with milk and/or egg. Drop chicken into bag and shake to cover.
Bake as desired.

RARE ROAST BEEF

yield: 6-8 servings
oven temperature: 375 °F

6-8 pounds standing rib roast, at room temperature
Salt, to taste
Pepper, to taste

Rub roast with salt and pepper. Place on a rack in a roasting pan, rib side down. Roast uncovered 1 hour. Turn oven off, DO NOT OPEN OVEN DOOR. Keep roast in the oven 3-5 hours, not longer than 5. Before serving turn the oven back on to 375° and roast 30 minutes for rare; 45 minutes for medium rare. DO NOT OPEN DOOR UNTIL THE END OF ROASTING TIME! At the end of the cooking time, remove the roast from the oven and let stand 15 minutes before carving.

YORKSHIRE PUDDING

yield: 6-8 servings
oven temperature: 450 °F

¼ teaspoon salt
1 cup flour
⅛ teaspoon baking powder
1 cup milk
2 eggs
¼ cup roast beef drippings
(use oil to supplement if needed)

Mix salt, flour and baking powder; add milk gradually to form a smooth paste. Add eggs and beat with mixer for 2 minutes. Cover bottom of 8-inch square pan with meat drippings. Pour mixture into pan. Bake at 450° for 15 minutes. Reduce heat to 350° and bake 10-15 miuntes longer. Cut into squares and serve.

Serve with Fluffy Horseradish Sauce.

⧗ FLUFFY HORSERADISH SAUCE

yield: 1½ cups

1 cup sour cream
¼ cup horseradish, drained
1 Tablespoon lemon juice
1 Tablespoon sugar
1 Tablespoon chives, minced

Mix all the ingredients; cover and chill several hours.

⧗ MICROWAVE PRIME RIB

yield: 4 servings

3 pounds prime rib roast
Browning and seasoning sauce

Brush roast with browning and seasoning sauce and broil in conventional oven until brown. Microwave on medium until thermometer registers 135° for medium rare, 140° or more for well done.
Let stand 15 minutes before carving.

MILLIES'S MARINATED BEEF

yield: 16 servings
oven temperature: 350°F

4 pounds filet, eye of round or
  sirloin tip roast
1 cup soy sauce
½ cup dry sherry
⅓ cup oil
3 cloves garlic, minced
2 teaspoons ground ginger

Combine soy sauce, sherry, oil, and spices. Refrigerate roast in marinade for 4 hours or overnight. Remove from refrigerator 1 hour before cooking. Roast, basting several times, at 350° for 45-50 minutes (or 120° rare or 140° medium rare on meat thermometer).

Slice, pour juice over top and serve cold. Marinade may be saved in refrigerator for another use.

SUGGESTED ACCOMPANIMENTS: Horseradish sauce.
Also excellent marinade for steaks to be grilled.

MARINATED FLANK STEAK

yield: 6-8 servings

3 (1½-pound) flank steaks
1 (10-ounce) bottle soy sauce
1 (16-ounce) bottle French salad
  dressing
1 ounce liquid smoke

Marinate steaks in a mixture of soy sauce, dressing and liquid smoke in refrigerator for 48 hours. Turn steaks to keep meat well coated. Grill 10 minutes on each side. DO NOT OVERCOOK!
Slice thinly across the grain and serve.

GRILLED EYE OF ROUND

yield: 6-8 servings

½ cup lemon juice
¼ cup Worcestershire sauce
1 cup oil
¾ cup soy sauce
¼ cup prepared mustard
2 cloves garlic, minced
3-4 pound eye of round roast

Combine all ingredients except roast and stir well. Pour over roast and marinate in refrigerator 12-24 hours; turning meat occasionally. Remove meat from marinade, reserving marinade. Grill over drip pan surrounded by medium coals in covered charcoal grill for 15 minutes per pound. Baste occasionally with reserved marinade. Follow manufacturer's directions if using gas grill.

Marinade is also good for shish-kabobs.

BEEF MIROTON

yield: 4-6 servings
oven temperature: 400°F

Butter
2 medium onions, thinly sliced
2 cups sliced roast beef, cooked
1 Tablespoon flour
1 cup beef broth
¼ cup dry white wine
¼ cup fresh bread crumbs
Parsley

Sauté the onions in butter until limp and golden. Place half the onions in a 9 x 9-inch casserole. Place beef on top of onions. Combine with remaining onion, flour, beef broth and wine. Pour sauce over beef. Scatter bread crumbs on top. Bake at 400° for 15-20 minutes. Garnish with fresh chopped parsley.

Great gourmet leftovers!

Beef

STEAK WITH BURGUNDY

yield: 4-5 servings

1 pound round steak, sliced into
   1-inch strips
1½ Tablespoons oil
2 cups onions, sliced
2 cups carrots, sliced
1 (10¾-ounce) can beef broth
1 (4-ounce) can mushrooms,
   undrained
⅓-¾ cup dry white wine
2 Tablespoons Worcestershire
   sauce
2 teaspoons seasoned salt
2 cups celery, sliced diagonally
2 Tablespoons cornstarch
¼ cup water

Sauté meat in oil. Add onions and cook 2 minutes. Stir in carrots, broth, mushrooms and wine. Bring to a boil and simmer for 10 minutes. Add Worcestershire sauce, salt and celery. Cook 10 minutes longer. Dissolve cornstarch in water, add to meat mixture and cook until clear. Serve with rice.

BARBECUE STEAK MARINADE

yield: 8-10 servings

3 pounds steak, very thinly sliced
½ cup soy sauce
¼ cup sugar
2 Tablespoons sesame oil
1 teaspoon garlic powder
1 teaspoon black pepper
3 green onions, finely chopped

Combine all ingredients with steak, and mix thoroughly. Cover and refrigerate 6-10 hours. Broil in oven or grill to desired doneness.

Could be stir-fried with peppers, onions and mushrooms. Rice and/or oriental vegetables would be good with this steak recipe.

PEPPER STEAK

yield: 4-5 servings

1 pound sirloin steak, thinly sliced
Salt and pepper, to taste
2 Tablespoons oil
1 medium onion, chopped
1 clove garlic, minced
2 green peppers, diced
1 cup bouillon
1 cup canned tomatoes with juice
2 Tablespoons cornstarch
2 Tablespoon soy sauce
¼ cup water

Sprinkle steak strips with salt and pepper. In large frying pan heat oil; add steak, onion, garlic and sauté until meat is browned. Add green peppers and bouillon; cover and simmer 15 minutes. Stir in tomatoes and cook 5 additional minutes. Mix cornstarch with soy sauce and water and stir into meat mixture. Cook until thickened. Serve with rice.

CORNISH PASTIES

yield: 6 servings
oven temperature: 325 °F

1½ pounds beef round steak, raw and cut into ½-inch cubes
3 medium potatoes, peeled and cubed
½ cup carrots, grated
½ cup onion, finely chopped
1 egg, well beaten
1 teaspoon salt
¼ teaspoon pepper
1 Tablespoon margarine, cut-up
3 9-inch pre-prepared crusts or 3 homemade crusts

In large bowl combine meat, vegetables, and seasonings; mix well. Grease a large cookie sheet. Lay out the 3 pastry rounds and cut each one in half. Divide the filling mixture among the six pieces placing filling only on one half so the other half can be folded over the filling. Seal the edges with water and press with a fork dipped in flour. Make 4 slits in the top of the pastry. Bake 1 hour or until slightly browned.

JIFFY STROGANOFF

yield: 6 servings

1 pound ground beef
½ cup onion, chopped
1 small clove garlic, minced
1 (4-ounce) can mushrooms,
    drained
1 (10¾-ounce) can cream of
    mushroom soup
¼ cup Cheddar cheese, grated
¼ cup pimiento, chopped
2 Tablespoons flour
1 teaspoon salt
¼ teaspoon black pepper
1 cup sour cream
½ teaspoon brown seasoning sauce
3 cups rice or noodles, cooked

Brown meat, drain off fat; add onions, garlic, mushrooms, soup, cheese, pimiento, flour, salt and pepper. Mix well and cover skillet. Cook on low for 25 minutes. Stir in sour cream and brown seasoning sauce, deglazing the skillet while stirring. Serve over rice or noodles.

BEFF STROGANOFF

yield: 4-6 servings

2 pounds sirloin steak, cut in
    2-inch strips
½ cup margarine
4 Tablespoons green onion, sliced
5 Tablespoons flour
1 (10¾-ounce) can beef broth
2 teaspoons Dijon mustard
1 (4-ounce) can sliced mushrooms,
    drained
⅓ cup sherry
½ cup sour cream

Brown beef in margarine. Remove from pan with slotted spoon. Sauté onion until soft. Add flour stirring until thick paste forms; add broth stir until thickened. Add mustard and mushrooms. Return meat to pan, simmer 15-20 minutes until tender. Prior to serving add sherry and simmer 2 minutes. Stir in sour cream. Serve over hot buttered egg noodles.

BRAISED SIRLOIN TIPS

yield: 6-8 servings
oven temperature: 275 °F

1½ pounds fresh mushrooms, sliced
¼ cup butter, melted
1 Tablespoon oil
3 pounds sirloin steak, cut into
    1-inch cubes
¾ cup beef bouillon
¾ cup red wine
2 Tablespoons soy sauce
2 cloves garlic, minced
½ medium onion, grated
2 Tablespoons cornstarch
¼ cup beef bouillon
5 ounces cream of mushroom soup
Salt, to taste
6-8 cups rice, cooked

In a large skillet, sauté mushrooms in 2 tablespoons of the butter, until lightly browned. Spoon into 3-quart, oven-proof casserole. Add remaining butter and oil to skillet; brown the steak on all sides. Spoon meat over mushrooms in casserole. Combine ¾ cup bouillon, red wine, soy sauce, garlic and onion; add to the skillet. Deglaze the skillet.

Blend the cornstarch with ¼ cup bouillon; stir into the wine mixture. Cook on medium heat stirring constantly until mixture is smooth and thick. Spoon mixture over meat in the casserole and stir to blend. Cover the casserole and bake at 275° for 1 hour. Then add the mushroom soup to the casserole; stirring to blend. Add salt, to taste, and bake 10-15 minutes more.

Serve over rice.

CORNED BEEF BBQ

yield: 4-6 servings

1 cup celery, chopped
1 cup onion, chopped
1 cup ketchup
¼ cup Worcestershire sauce
2½ Tablespoons brown sugar
1 Tablespoon vinegar
¾ cup water
1½ teaspoons chili powder
1 (12-ounce) can corned beef,
  broken up with a fork

Combine all ingredients in heavy pan. Simmer 1 hour on medium-low heat. Serve on hot buns.

NEVER FAIL BEEF STEW

yield: 8 servings
oven temperature: 250°F

2-3 pounds stew beef
Flour
Oil or shortening
3 stalks celery, sliced
4 large carrots, sliced
2-3 medium onions, quartered
3 large potatoes, cubed
2 teaspoons sugar
1 Tablespoon cornstarch
2 teaspoons salt
1½ cups tomato juice

Salt and pepper beef to taste and roll in flour. Brown in a skillet with oil or shortening; drain. Place beef in a casserole with the vegetables. Mix sugar, cornstarch, salt and tomato juice together; pour over beef and vegetable mixture. Stir to blend. Bake at 250° for 4 hours.

ORIENTAL BEEF WITH BROCCOLI

yield: 4 servings

2 (10-ounce) packages broccoli spears, frozen or 1 large bunch fresh broccoli
1 pound flank steak, partially frozen, thinly sliced across the grain
2 teaspoons cornstarch, divided
1 Tablespoon soy sauce
3 Tablespoons water and 1½ teaspoons water
1 teaspoon sugar, divided
1 clove garlic, crushed
5 Tablespoons oil, divided
1 (8-ounce) can water chestnuts
½ cup mushrooms, fresh, sliced
1½ teaspoons salt
4 servings rice, hot, cooked

Cut broccoli into flowerets. Cut steak into 1 x 2-inch pieces. In a small bowl combine: 1 teaspoon cornstarch, soy sauce, 1½ teaspoons water, and ¼ teaspoon sugar and blend well. Stir in beef and set aside.

Preheat a large skillet and pour in 2 tablespoons oil. Add beef mixture and cook 1 minute, stirring frequently; return beef to bowl. Heat 3 tablespoons oil in the skillet and stir in broccoli flowerets, water chestnuts and the mushrooms. Stir-fry for 3 minutes. Add salt, ¾ teaspoon sugar, 2 tablespoons water and mix well. Cook for 1 minute. Add the meat and stir-fry for 1 minute.

Blend together 1 teaspoon cornstarch and 1 tablespoon water. Add to skillet, cooking until thick.

Serve over hot rice.

Beef

STIR-FRIED BEEF AND BROCCOLI

yield: 4-6 servings

1 pound sirloin steak, partially
  frozen, sliced thin or cubed bite
  size
½ cup water, divided
⅓ cup soy sauce
2 Tablespoons brown sugar
3 Tablespoons sherry
1 Tablespoon cornstarch
1 teaspoon garlic salt, or 1 clove
  garlic, minced
1 teaspoon ginger
⅛ cup olive or peanut oil
1 bunch broccoli, cut in flowerets
1 large onion, sliced

Marinate steak in mixture of ¼ cup water, soy sauce, sugar, sherry, cornstarch, garlic and ginger for 10 minutes. Drain well, reserving marinade. Heat oil in wok or large skillet. Add steak and fry over high heat until browned. Remove and set aside. Add broccoli and onion to hot wok or skillet and stir-fry 1 minute. Add remaining ¼ cup water; cover and steam 3 minutes or until broccoli is crisp-tender. Return meat and marinade to skillet and heat thoroughly. Serve over rice.

A tester's children even liked it — she is going to make it again.

FLAVORFUL HAMBURGERS

yield: 6 servings

1 slice bread
2 Tablespoons tomato juice
2 pounds ground chuck or round
1 onion, finely chopped
1 green pepper, finely chopped
1 egg
¼ cup sour cream
1 teaspoon garlic powder
Salt and pepper, to taste
Seasoned salt, to taste

Moisten bread with tomato juice. Combine all ingredients. Refrigerate for several hours. Pat into hamburgers and grill, fry or broil.

SUPREME BEEF AND RICE

yield: 8 servings
oven temperature: 325 °F

1 pound ground beef, extra lean
1 medium onion, chopped
⅓ cup green pepper, chopped
¼ cup margarine, melted
1 cup rice, uncooked
1 (10½-ounce) can beef consomme
1 (2.5-ounce) jar whole
  mushrooms
2 cups water
1 Tablespoon beef bouillon,
  granules
1 cup almonds, slivered
Salt, pepper and garlic salt, to taste
Paprika

Brown ground beef slightly, then add onions and green pepper and cook until tender. Drain well. Combine all other ingredients. Bake at 325° covered for 1 hour in a 9 x 9-inch casserole dish. Sprinkle paprika on top for color. Slow cooking is the secret of the taste. Best if it stands about ½ hour before serving.

Can be prepared ahead if rice is added just before baking.

BEEF N' BISCUITS

yield: 4-5 servings
oven temperature: 375 °F

1 pound lean ground beef
1 medium onion, chopped
1 medium green pepper, chopped
2 cups Cheddar cheese, grated
½ cup sour cream
1 egg
1 (8-ounce) can tomato sauce
Dash garlic salt
Dash black pepper
3 teaspoons chili powder
1 small can (5) biscuits, split in
  half

Brown meat, onion, and green pepper. Drain well. Mix ½ cup cheese, sour cream and egg with browned meat mixture. Add tomato sauce and seasonings. Lay biscuits in the bottom of casserole; pour meat mixture over biscuits and cover with remaining biscuits. Top with remaining cheese. Bake at 375° for 25-30 minutes.

JIMMY'S MEAT LOAF

yield: 6 servings
oven temperature: 350°F

1 pound ground round
¼ pound sausage
2 medium onions, minced
2 cloves garlic, chopped
2 celery stalks, chopped
1 egg, beaten
¼ cup milk
½ cup ketchup
2 teaspoons salt
½ teaspoon black pepper
1½ cups bread crumbs

TOPPING:
1 (8-ounce) can tomato sauce

Mix all ingredients except tomato sauce and shape into a loaf. Top with tomato sauce. Place in baking dish; bake at 350° for 1 hour.

BURRITOS

yield: 6 servings

1 pound ground beef
1 onion, chopped
1 teaspoon cumin or to taste
1 (10-ounce) can tomatoes and
    green chilies
1 (16-ounce) can refried beans
8 ounces Cheddar cheese, shredded
6 flour tortillas
Taco sauce, if desired
Sour cream, if desired

Brown meat and onions together and drain. Add cumin, garlic powder, tomatoes and refried beans. Simmer for 5 minutes. Place a heaping tablespoon (or more) into tortilla and sprinkle with cheese. Roll up. The burritos may be placed on a cookie sheet and kept in a warm oven until serving time. Taco sauce and/or sour cream are good served over the burritos.

HAWAIIAN MEATBALLS

yield: 6-8 servings

1½ pounds ground beef
⅔ cup cracker crumbs
⅓ cup onion, minced
1 egg
1 teaspoon salt
¼ teaspoon ginger
¼ cup milk
1 Tablespoon shortening
2 Tablespoons cornstarch
¼ cup sugar
⅓ cup vinegar
1½ Tablespoons soy sauce
⅓ cup green pepper, chopped
1 (13½-ounce) can pineapple
   tidbits, drained, liquid reserved

Mix thoroughly beef, crumbs, onion, egg, salt, ginger and milk. Shape mixture by rounded table-spoons into balls. Melt shortening in large skillet; brown and cook meatballs. Pour fat from skillet. Drain pineapple, reserving juice. Mix cornstarch and sugar; stir with reserved pineapple liquid, vinegar and soy sauce until smooth. Pour into skillet. Cook over medium heat, stirring con-stantly until mixture thickens and boils. Boil and stir 1 minute. Add pineapple tidbits, green pepper and meatballs. Heat thoroughly. May be prepared ahead. Freezes well.

SUGGESTED ACCOMPANIMENTS: Rice. Very rich; can be used as an appetizer.

STUFFED ITALIAN MEATLOAF

yield: 4-6 servings
oven temperature: 350 °F

1 pound lean ground beef
2 eggs, beaten
1 teaspoon salt
Garlic powder, to taste
⅓ cup Parmesan cheese
½ teaspoon dried parsley
5 slices bread, soaked in water and squeezed
3 eggs, scrambled
½ cup ham, chopped
½ cup American or mozzarella cheese, diced
Bread crumbs
Slice of bacon, uncooked

Mix beef, eggs, salt, garlic powder, cheese, parsley and bread together. Spread meat mixture on aluminum foil to form a rectangle about ¼-inch thick. Spread eggs, ham and cheese over the meat. Roll the meat like a jelly roll, pulling off foil as you roll. Fold in sides so filling stays inside. Sprinkle top of meatloaf with bread crumbs and lay the bacon on top. Bake in an 11 x 13-inch dish at 350° for 1 hour.

Meatloaf good enough for company!

SWEET AND SOUR MEATLOAF

yield: 4-6 servings
oven temperature: 350°F

1½ pounds lean ground beef
1 cup bread crumbs
1 egg
1½ teaspoons salt
¼ teaspoon pepper
1 medium onion, chopped
1 (8-ounce) can tomato sauce with
  mushrooms
1 (8-ounce) can tomato sauce with
  cheese

SAUCE:
3 Tablespoons brown sugar
1 teaspoon vinegar
1 Tablespoon Worcestershire sauce
2 Tablespoons prepared mustard

Mix all the meatloaf ingredients well and make into 2 loaves. Place in a rectangular baking dish.

SAUCE: Mix ingredients for sauce and spoon over loaves, reserving some for basting. Bake at 350° for 1 hour and 15 minutes, start basting after the first 30 minutes and use the remaining sauce. It if begins to brown too fast, turn heat to 325°.

Serve with rice; it's delicious! Delightful oriental flavor!

TACO CASSEROLE

yield: 6 servings

1 pound ground beef, cooked and
  drained
½ cup onion, chopped
1 (.85-ounce) package taco
  seasoning mix
1 (8-ounce) can tomato sauce
¼ cup green pepper, chopped
1 (16-ounce) can tomatoes
1 (10¾-ounce) can bean with bacon
  soup
½ teaspoon chili powder
Corn chips
Lettuce, shredded
Tomatoes, chopped
Onion, chopped
Cheddar cheese, grated
Sour cream, optional
Picante sauce

Combine ground beef, onion, taco seasoning, tomato sauce, green pepper, tomatoes, soup and chili powder; heat thoroughly. Serve over corn chips and let everyone build his own taco with lettuce, tomatoes, onions, cheese, sour cream and picante sauce.

VERSATILE MEAT SAUCE

yield: 6 servings

1 large onion, chopped
1 large green pepper, chopped
1 pound mushrooms, coarsely
   chopped
6 cloves garlic, finely chopped
2 Tablespoons olive oil
1½ pounds ground chuck or
   ground round
2 cups carrots, grated
3 (16-ounce) cans whole tomatoes,
   drained and coarsely chopped
24 ounces tomato paste
2 teaspoons each: basil, parsley,
   oregano, white pepper, garlic
   salt
1 teaspoon allspice
1 teaspoon red pepper, crushed
½ cup brown sugar
½ cup Parmesan cheese, grated
½ cup dry red wine

Sauté onion, green pepper, mushrooms and garlic in olive oil. Brown the ground chuck in a large skillet with the carrots and drain. To the meat mixture, add the sautéed onion mixture, tomatoes, tomato paste, and spices, brown sugar and Parmesan cheese. Simmer uncovered for 1 hour. Adjust the seasonings and add wine. Simmer 20 minutes longer.

This sauce may be served over spaghetti, used in lasagne or with the Stuffed Shells on page 168.

VEAL AND PEPPERS

yield: 6 servings

1½ pounds stewing veal
5 Tablespoons butter
1 (20-ounce) can whole tomatoes, chopped
Salt, to taste
Pepper, to taste
1 large onion, thinly sliced
4 large green peppers, cut into 1-inch strips
4 Tablespoons oil
¼ pound mushrooms, sliced
⅔ cup dry white wine
Cooked rice

Cut veal into 1½-inch cubes. Melt butter in skillet. Brown veal and cook for about 10 minutes. Add tomatoes, salt and pepper. Cover and simmer for 30 minutes. In another skillet sauté the onion and green peppers in oil until tender, stirring often. Combine with veal mixture. Add mushrooms and wine. Cover and simmer for another 15 minutes. Serve over rice.

VEAL WITH HERBS

yield: 4 servings

¾-1 pound veal scallops, pounded flat
3 Tablespoons oil
3 Tablespoons butter
Salt, to taste
Pepper, to taste
1 Tablespoon chicken stock or a sprinkle of instant bouillon
½ cup dry white wine
1 Tablespoon fresh parsley
1 Tablespoon herb mixture
Juice of lemon
4 Tablespoons shallots, minced

Sauté the veal in hot oil and butter until golden on both sides. Season with salt and pepper. Add chicken broth and wine and simmer for 5 minutes. Add parsley, 1 tablespoon herb mixture, lemon juice and shallots. Simmer 2 more minutes. Place veal on a platter; pour sauce over top.

HERB MIXTURE:
1½ teaspoons basil
½ teaspoon marjoram

½ teaspoon thyme
¼ teaspoon tarragon
¼ teaspoon rosemary

HOLLYHOCK HOUSE ROAST LAMB

yield: 6-8 servings
oven temperature: 500 °F

1 leg of lamb
1 clove garlic
1 teaspoon salt
1 teaspoon celery salt
½ teaspoon pepper
¼ teaspoon paprika
1 Tablespoon parsley, minced
¼ cup butter, melted
2 Tablespoons flour
½ bay leaf
¼ cup carrots, finely minced
1 Tablespoon onion, finely minced

Rub leg of lamb with garlic. Combine salt, celery salt, pepper, paprika and parsley. Rub into lamb. Sear lamb for 20 minutes at 500°. While lamb is searing, blend butter and flour; add bay leaf, carrot and onion. After lamb sears 20 minutes reduce heat to 375°, spread with butter mixture and roast 20 minutes per pound.

PLUM JELLY SAUCE

¾ cup plum jelly
2 Tablespoons orange juice
Dash mace
1 teaspoon flour
¼ teaspoon dry mustard
3 Tablespoons pineapple juice

Melt jelly, add orange juice and mace. Blend flour, mustard and pineapple juice. Add to jelly. Simmer 5 minutes. Serve with sliced lamb.

⧗ BROILED LAMB CHOPS

yield: 4 servings

8 loin lamb chops, ¾-inch thick
1 Tablespoon oil
1 Tablespoon butter
1 clove garlic, minced
Salt, to taste
Pepper, to taste
¼ cup dry white wine
¼ cup margarine
1 Tablespoon Worcestershire sauce
2 Tablespoons parsley, finely
    chopped

Remove fat from chops. In a skillet heat oil and butter; add garlic and sauté. Add the chops and sear, turning often over medium high heat. Remove and season with salt and pepper, keep chops warm. Pour off cooking fat; add wine. Deglaze by scraping brown bits from the bottom and sides of the pan. Add the remaining ingredients, stir until well blended. Pour over chops and serve.

BAKED PORK CHOPS WITH APRICOT RICE

yield: 6 servings
oven temperature: 350°F

¾ cup apricot brandy
1½ cups chicken broth
½ cup rice, uncooked
1 medium onion, chopped
¼ teaspoon salt
1 cup American cheese, grated
3 Tablespoons parsley, minced
½ cup sour cream
½ cup dried apricots, chopped
6 center-cut trimmed pork chops

In medium saucepan combine ½ cup brandy, 1 cup broth, rice, onion and the salt. Bring to boil. Simmer covered 25 minutes until rice is tender. Remove from heat. Mix in cheese, parsley, sour cream and apricots. Arrange chops in single layer in pan. Spoon rice over the chops. Combine remaining brandy and broth. Pour over chops. Bake covered at 350° for 1 hour, or longer, depending on thickness of chops.

LUAU RIBS I

yield: 4-6 servings
oven temperature: 450 °F

2 (4½-ounce) jars strained baby peaches
⅓ cup ketchup
⅓ cup vinegar
2 Tablespoons soy sauce
½ cup brown sugar
2 cloves garlic, minced
1 teaspoon salt
2 teaspoons salt
2 teaspoons ginger
Dash pepper
4 pounds meaty spareribs

Combine the ingredients for the sauce and set aside.

Separate ribs and sprinkle with salt and pepper. Place ribs in a single layer in the pan and cook in hot (450°) oven for 15 minutes. Remove from oven and drain off fat. Reduce oven to 350°. Cover ribs with sauce, reserving some for basting. Continue cooking until tender, basting occasionally.

LUAU RIBS II

yield: 4-6 servings
oven temperature: 375 °F

4 pounds meaty spareribs
⅓ cup onion, chopped
½ cup water
1 cup ketchup
½ cup crushed pineapple
¼ cup lemon juice or vinegar
¼ cup brown sugar
1 Tablespoon Worcestershire sauce
4 dashes hot sauce
4 slices pineapple
Green grapes

Bake ribs on rack in covered roasting pan at 375° for 1 hour. Meanwhile, cook onion in water until tender. Add remaining ingredients except pineapple slices and grapes.

Uncover ribs and continue baking 45 minutes; brushing with sauce every 5 minutes. During last 20 minutes of cooking garnish with pineapple slices and grapes.

MANDARIN PORK ROAST

yield: 12 servings
oven temperature: 325°F

1 (4-pound) boneless pork loin
  roast
½ teaspoon salt
¼ teaspoon pepper
½ teaspoon garlic powder
2 Tablespoons Dijon mustard
1 (11-ounce)can mandarin oranges,
  drain and reserve liquid
¼ cup light brown sugar
¼ cup cider vinegar
1 chicken flavored bouillon cube
1 Tablespoon soy sauce
2 Tablespoons cornstarch
½ cup water
1 large onion, chopped
⅓ cup green pepper, chopped

Trim the fat from the roast, sprinkle with salt, pepper and garlic powder. Spread mustard over the roast. Cover and bake at 325° for 2½ hours. Combine orange liquid, sugar, vinegar, bouillon cube, soy sauce, cornstarch and water. Cook over medium heat, stirring constantly until smooth and thickened; remove from heat. Stir in onion, green pepper and oranges. Spoon sauce over roast and bake uncovered at 400° for 30 minutes, basting occasionally. Slice the pork and serve with the pan drippings.

⧗ CHARCOAL-GRILLED HAM STEAK

yield: 2 servings

1 cup brown sugar
¼ teaspoon dry mustard
⅛ teaspoon ground cloves
¼ cup vinegar
1 ham steak, at least ½-inch thick

Mix together sugar, mustard and cloves; slowly add vinegar until glaze is consistency of thick paste. Spread half of the glaze over ham steak; turn over and use the remaining glaze on the other side. Let stand at least 10 minutes before grilling over hot coals.

Leftover ham is great reheated in the morning and served with eggs.

PORK CHOPS

yield: 1-2 chops per person

Pork chops, center cut or pork loin (as many as needed for number to be served)
Prepared mustard
Worcestershire sauce

Brush both sides of each chop with mustard. Sprinkle both sides with Worcestershire sauce. Cook over medium heat in large covered skillet. Turn chops after 20 minutes. DO NOT OVER-COOK or Worcestershire sauce will burn.

HAM AND SPINACH ROLL-UPS

yield: 6 servings
oven temperature: 350°F

1 (10-ounce) package frozen spinach, cooked and drained
1 cup packaged corn bread stuffing mix
1 cup sour cream
12 ham slices, cooked and thinly sliced
3 Tablespoons butter
3 Tablespoons flour
1½ cups milk
½ cup Cheddar cheese, shredded
2 Tablespoons Parmesan cheese

Combine spinach, stuffing mix and sour cream in a medium bowl. Divide evenly and place in log-shape in center of ham slices. Fold ham slices over as for crepes and place seam side down in one layer in a shallow baking dish. Melt butter in a small saucepan. Stir in flour and cook 1 minute. Add milk slowly and continue to cook, stirring constantly until sauce thickens and bubbles. Add Cheddar cheese; remove from heat and continue stirring until cheese is melted. Pour over the ham rolls; sprinkle top with Parmesan cheese. Bake, covered at 350° for 15 minutes. Uncover and bake 15 additional minutes.

Good for brunches and lunches with fruit or vegetable salads and rolls.

AGED COUNTRY CURED HAM

yield: 25 servings
oven temperature: 500°F

1 (12 - 13 pound) ham
7 cups water
1 cup brown sugar
½ cup orange juice
2 teaspoons dry mustard
¼ cup vinegar

Soak ham overnight. Place ham in deep covered roasting pan. Add 7 cups water and bake at 500° for 20 minutes, then turn oven off. Leave oven door closed for 3 hours. Turn heat to 500° and cook for 20 minutes more. Turn heat off and leave ham in oven overnight or 8-10 hours. When ham is removed from oven, cut off the skin and score the fat. Glaze ham with a mixture of the sugar, mustard, orange juice and vinegar. Brown the glazed ham in a 350° oven for 15 minutes.

An easy and less messy way to cook country ham.

HAM AND SWISS FILLING FOR CRÊPES

yield: 6-8 servings
oven temperature: 350°F

½ cup sour cream
3 green onions, white part only, chopped
¼ teaspoon Dijon mustard
¼ teaspoon salt
Dash of pepper
12 crêpes
1½ cups Swiss cheese, grated
12 ounces ham, thinly sliced
⅓ cup dried bread crumbs
3 Tablespoons butter, melted

Mix together sour cream, onions, mustard, salt and pepper. Sprinkle cheese on crêpes; top with ham and spread heaping tablespoon of sour cream mixture over the ham. Roll crêpes and place seam side down in 3-quart casserole. Combine bread crumbs and melted butter; sprinkle over crêpes. Bake at 350° for 12 minutes. Serve hot.

Sour cream filling may be doubled if a creamier crepe is desired.

SPENCER'S BAR-B-QUE

oven temperature: 325°F

5-6 pound pork loin roast
3 onions, chopped
½ cup vinegar
½ cup brown sugar
2 (16-ounce) cans tomatoes
4 Tablespoons soy sauce
6 Tablespoons Worcestershire sauce
3 cloves garlic
Salt, to taste
Hot sauce, to taste

Place pork roast, onions, vinegar, brown sugar, tomatoes, soy sauce, Worcestershire sauce, garlic, salt and hot sauce in a 5-quart Dutch oven. Cover and bake at 325° for 5 hours. Remove from the oven, and let stand until cool enough to handle. Remove bones and fat. If necessary, simmer uncovered on top of the stove until juice is reduced.

HAM LOAF WITH MUSTARD SAUCE

yield: 6-8 servings
oven temperature: 350°F

1 pound ham
1 pound pork
1 cup tomato juice
1 cup bread crumbs
¾ cup milk
2 eggs, beaten

MUSTARD SAUCE:
2 eggs
1 Tablespoon flour
2 Tablespoons dry mustard
¼ cup sugar
1 cup milk scalded
½ cup vinegar, warmed
Salt, to taste

Grind ham and pork together. Mix ham and pork with tomato juice, bread crumbs, milk, and eggs. Bake in loaf pan at 350° for 2 hours. Pour off any fat before removing from pan. Serve with mustard sauce.

MUSTARD SAUCE: Beat eggs with dry ingredients. Over low heat add milk slowly, stirring constantly. Add vinegar slowly until thickened.

Sauce may be made ahead and reheated. It is also good served on cold ham loaf sandwiches.

POLISH SAUSAGE AND CABBAGE

yield: 4 servings

½ medium head cabbage, sliced
½ cup green pepper, chopped
Salt, to taste
Pepper, to taste
¼ cup water
1½ pounds Polish sausage, 1-inch slices

In a medium saucepan combine cabbage, green pepper, salt and pepper. Add water and bring to a boil, reduce heat and place sausage on top. Cover and simmer about 15 minutes.

SALMON STEAK

yield: 4 servings

¾ cup water
¾ cup dry white wine
1 teaspoon thyme
1 bay leaf
¼ teaspoon hot sauce
1 large carrot, julienne strips
1 zucchini, julienne strips
1 red pepper, julienne strips
1 leek, white part only, julienne
  strips
1½ pounds salmon steaks (4)
1 egg yolk

In a large skillet combine water, wine, thyme, bay leaf and hot sauce; bring to a boil. Add carrot, zucchini, red pepper and leek; arrange steaks on top. Reduce heat; cover and simmer 10-12 minutes until fish flakes easily with a fork. Place steaks and vegetables on a heated platter. Raise heat and reduce poaching liquid to ¾ cup and strain.

In electric blender, blend liquid, 1 cup of the vegetables and egg yolk until smooth. Spoon over fish and vegetables on platter. Serve.

POACHED FISH

yield: 4-6 servings
oven temperature: 350°F

¾ cup dry white wine
¾ cup chicken stock
½ pound fresh mushrooms, sliced
1 Tablespoon lemon juice
2 Tablespoons shallots or scallions,
  minced
2 Tablespoons each:
  parsley, minced
  chives, minced
  tarragon, minced
Pepper
1½ pounds fish

Mix all the ingredients except fish in a stove and oven proof pan. Simmer for 5 minutes. Add fish. Cover pan with waxed paper and place in lower middle of oven and bake at 350° until fish is opaque and flaky.

FLOUNDER ON SPINACH

yield: 4-6 servings
oven temperature: 375°F

2 (10-ounce) packages frozen
  spinach, chopped
1 cup sour cream
1 medium onion, chopped
3 Tablespoons lemon juice
1½ Tablespoons flour
2 teaspoons salt
¼ pound fresh mushrooms, sliced
  or 4-ounce can, drained
1½ pounds flounder fillets
Paprika

Cook and drain spinach. Mix together sour cream, onion, lemon juice, flour and salt. Add ½ of this mixture to spinach. Put in bottom of a 13 x 9-inch baking dish. Arrange flounder fillets on top. Place mushrooms around the fish. Spread remaining sour cream mixture on top of flounder. Sprinkle with paprika. Bake at 375° for 20 minutes.

Season the spinach with a little nutmeg for a different taste.

STUFFED FLOUNDER FILLETS

yield: 6 servings
oven temperature: 375°F

5 cups bread, cubed
1¾ cups carrots, grated
2 Tablespoons pimiento, chopped
½ cup onion, chopped
Salt, to taste
⅛ teaspoon pepper
¼ cup butter or margarine
2 pounds flounder fillets
2 Tablespoons butter or margarine,
  melted

To make stuffing, combine bread, carrots, pimiento, onion, salt and pepper. Add butter and toss until well combined.
Grease 2-quart baking dish and line bottom of dish with half of the fish fillets. Arrange stuffing mixture evenly over fish and place remaining fillets on top of stuffing. Brush with 2 Tablespoons melted butter. Bake at 375° for 30 minutes or until fish is done.

SHRIMP CASSEROLE

yield: 6-8 servings
oven temperature: 375 °F

1 pound mushrooms, sliced
9½ Tablespoons butter, divided
2 pounds shrimp, cooked, peeled
and cleaned
1 (14-ounce) can artichoke hearts,
quartered
4½ Tablespoons flour
¾ cup milk
¾ cup heavy cream
½ cup dry cream sherry
1 Tablespoon Worcestershire sauce
Salt and pepper, to taste
½ cup Parmesan cheese, grated
Paprika

Sauté mushrooms in 5 tablespoons butter. Layer shrimp,
mushrooms and artichokes in a
2-quart casserole. Melt 4½ tablespoons butter; add flour, milk
and cream. Cook until thick and
add sherry, Worcestershire, salt
and pepper. Pour over casserole
and refrigerate overnight. Top
with Parmesan and sprinkle with
paprika. Bake at 375° for 30
minutes.

SHRIMP SCAMPI

yield: 4-5 servings

1 cup butter
2 cloves garlic, finely chopped or 1
teaspoon garlic powder
2 Tablespoons parsley, finely
chopped
¼ cup dry white wine or vermouth
Fresh lemon juice, to taste
Salt and pepper, to taste
2 pounds raw shrimp, peeled and
cleaned
5 cups rice, cooked

Melt butter in pan; add garlic,
parsley, wine, lemon juice, salt
and pepper. Simmer for about 3
minutes, add shrimp and cook 4
more minutes. Serve over hot
rice.

*Suggested accompaniments: Avocado with grapefruit sections on bibb
lettuce. Baked whole tomato with buttered herbed breadcrumbs and
grated Parmesan cheese.*

PEKING SHRIMP

yield: 4 servings

¼ cup light corn syrup
¼ cup water
2 Tablespoons soy sauce
2 Tablespoons sherry (optional)
1 Tablespoon cornstarch
1 clove garlic, minced
¼ teaspoon ginger
2 Tablespoons oil
1 pound medium shrimp, peeled
   and cleaned
1 medium tomato, cut into wedges
1 small green pepper, cut in chunks

Combine corn syrup, water, soy sauce, sherry, cornstarch, garlic and ginger. Heat oil in skillet. Add shrimp; cook 3 minutes stirring occasionally. Add the combined ingredients, tomato and green pepper to the skillet. Gently boil about 2 minutes.

Serve over rice.

MICROWAVE SHRIMP IN GARLIC BUTTER

yield: 4 servings

¼ cup butter
2 teaspoons parsley
½ teaspoon garlic powder or garlic
   salt
1 (12-ounce) package frozen or
   fresh shrimp, peeled and cleaned

Melt butter in microwave. Add garlic and parsley. Separate shrimp and place in 10-inch dish. Pour butter mixture over shrimp. Microwave shrimp at high power, stirring every 2 minutes, until shrimp are done (4-8 minutes, depending on microwave). Let stand a minute or two before serving.

SHRIMP BOILED IN BEER

yield: 6-8 servings

1 (12-ounce) can beer
1¾ cups water
1 Tablespoon salt
1 Tablespoon celery seed
⅓ cup onion, chopped
3 whole peppercorns
½ bay leaf
2 pounds shrimp, in the shell

SAUCE:
1 (12-ounce) bottle chili sauce
1 teaspoon horseradish
2 teaspoons lemon juice
1 Tablespoon grated onion
Dash hot sauce

Bring to a boil: beer, water, salt, celery seed, onion, peppercorns and bay leaf. Boil for 5 minutes. Add shrimp and cook for 10-15 minutes. Remove from the liquid. Chill until serving time. Serve with cocktail sauce.

CHARCOALED GARLIC SHRIMP

yield: 4 servings

½ cup butter
4 cloves garlic, sliced
¼ cup fresh lemon juice
1 Tablespoon parsley flakes
½ teaspoon seasoned salt
½ teaspoon lemon-pepper
    seasoning
12-16 ounces shrimp, freshly
    boiled, peeled and cleaned
Green pepper, if desired
Fresh mushrooms, if desired
Onion, if desired
Cherry tomatoes, if desired

Sauté garlic in butter for 2-3 minutes; add lemon juice, parsley, seasoned salt and lemon-pepper seasoning. Heat until blended. Place shrimp in a shallow dish; pour marinade over shrimp and let stand 1 hour. Thread shrimp on skewers and cook for 3-5 minutes per side. Baste occasionally. May alternate shrimp on the skewers with green pepper, mushrooms, onion and tomatoes.

SHRIMP CREOLE

yield: 6 servings

3 Tablespoons bacon drippings
3 Tablespoons flour
1 medium onion, chopped
4 stalks celery, sliced
1 green pepper, diced
1 (16-ounce) can tomatoes
2 teaspoons salt
Pepper, to taste
2 pounds raw shrimp, peeled and
  cleaned

Heat bacon drippings in large skillet. Add flour and cook until brown. Add onion, celery and green pepper. Chop tomatoes and add with salt and pepper to skillet mixture. Simmer for 45 minutes. Add the raw, cleaned shrimp and cook slowly for 20 minutes more. Serve over cooked white rice.

SPICY SHRIMP

yield: 8 servings

3 pounds shrimp, peeled and
  cleaned
Water
¾ cup celery tops, chopped
  coarsley
½ cup mixed pickling spices
1 teaspoon salt
2½ cups onion, sliced
10 bay leaves
10 lemon slices
2 cups oil
1 cup white vinegar
4 Tablespoons capers
3 teaspoons celery seed
Salt, to taste
Hot sauce, to taste

Boil shrimp in water seasoned with celery tops, pickling spices, salt, onions, bay leaves and lemon slices until shrimp is done. Drain water saving seasonings; place onions, shrimp and spices in a large bowl and cover with a mixture of oil, vinegar, capers, celery seed, salt and hot sauce. Refrigerate.

You may like to put the spices in 2 cheesecloth bags.

May be served as an appetizer.

HOT CRAB AND SHRIMP

yield: 6 servings
oven temperature: 350 °F

2 cups celery, sliced
½ cup onion, chopped
1 medium green pepper, finely
   chopped
1 (8-ounce) can sliced water
   chestnuts, drained
1 (6½-ounce) can crab meat
1 (6-ounce) package small frozen
   shrimp, rinsed
¾ cup fresh mushrooms, sliced
1 cup mayonnaise
½ teaspoon salt
½ teaspoon paprika
4 eggs, hard boiled and sliced
½ cup bread crumbs, buttered or
   dressing mix buttered

In a large bowl combine celery, onion, green pepper, water chestnuts, crab meat, shrimp, mushrooms, mayonnaise, salt, paprika and eggs, and mix gently. Pour into a greased 2-quart casserole and cover with the bread crumbs. Bake at 350° for 30 minutes or until hot.

BACK FIN CRAB

yield: 8 servings
oven temperature: 325 °F

1 (8-ounce) package cream cheese
1 cup sour cream
1 cup mayonnaise
½ cup celery, chopped
Juice of ½ lemon
1 teaspoon dry mustard
⅛ teaspoon garlic salt
¼ teaspoon paprika
Dash Worcestershire sauce
1¼ pounds back fin crab or canned
   crab meat
1 cup sharp Cheddar cheese,
   grated

Mix all ingredients, except crab and cheese, together. Add crab, rinsed and drained, and half of the Cheddar cheese. Pour into a buttered 2-quart casserole and top with remaining Cheddar cheese. Bake at 325° for 45 minutes.

BOLTON'S DEVILED CRAB

yield: 6-8 servings
oven temperature: 350°F

1 pound fresh crab meat or
2 (6½-ounce) cans crab meat,
  cleaned
4 eggs, hard-boiled, finely mashed
2 Tablespoons Worcestershire
  sauce
2 teaspoons dry mustard
1 teaspoon mace (optional)
3 Tablespoons butter
3 Tablespoons flour
1 cup light cream or milk
1 Tablespoon lemon juice
1 cup cracker crumbs
2 Tablespoons butter
Paprika

Mix crab meat, eggs and seasonings and set aside.

To prepare cream sauce, melt butter in small saucepan. Whisk in flour and stir until smooth and golden, about 1 minute. Gradually add cream and lemon juice, stirring constantly until thickened.

Remove cream sauce from heat and add crab mixture; mix thoroughly.

Pack mixture into cleaned crab shells or individual serving dishes. Press cracker crumbs on top; dot with butter and sprinkle with paprika. Bake at 350° until slightly brown, 10-20 minutes. To freeze: before baking wrap each serving in plastic wrap and store in freezer bags. If baking unthawed, bake 20-30 minutes. To prepare fresh crab shells: Boil backs in baking soda and water. When cool, scrub with brush.

REMOULADE SAUCE WITH SCALLOPS

yield: 6-8 servings

4 egg yolks
3 Tablespoons lemon juice
1 teaspoon salt
½ teaspoon white pepper
1½ cups oil
1 Tablespoon Dijon mustard
½ clove garlic
½ teaspoon anchovy paste
1 teaspoon tarragon, dried
1 teaspoon basil, dried
1 teaspoon parsley, dried
2 Tablespoons capers
1-2 pounds scallops
Water
½ cup vermouth

In a food processor or blender, blend egg yolks, lemon juice, salt and white pepper. With the machine running, add the oil very slowly. Then add mustard, garlic, anchovy paste, tarragon, basil and parsley. Fold in the capers. Chill. Mixture will be thick, if it is too thick it can be thinned with heavy cream for a lighter consistency. Poach the scallops in water mixed with the vermouth for 1 minute or until cracks appear. DO NOT OVERCOOK! Chill. Serve the chilled scallops with sauce.

An easy, elegant way to serve scallops.

QUICK SCALLOPS

yield: 2 servings

2 Tablespoons butter
½ cup mushrooms, sliced
½ cup green pepper, chopped
½ cup tomatoes, peeled and
  chopped
¾ pound scallops
Salt and pepper, to taste
¼ cup white wine
Lemon wedges

Melt butter in large skillet. Sauté mushrooms and green pepper until tender. Add tomatoes and continue to sauté 3-5 minutes. Stir in scallops, seasonings and wine. Simmer stirring occasionally for 5 minutes, or until scallops are done. DO NOT OVERCOOK. Garnish with lemon wedges.

MINCED OYSTERS

yield: 12 servings
oven temperature: 400°F

1 quart oysters, finely minced
2 cups bread crumbs, toasted
2 eggs, beaten
¼ cup butter, melted
1 teaspoon onion, chopped
4 Tablespoons celery, chopped
Salt and pepper, to taste
Butter

Mix all ingredients except additional butter. Cook on top of stove, stirring constantly, for about 5 minutes, or until thoroughly cooked. Put in baking dish or shells. Dot with butter. Bake at 400° until brown.

SHRIMP AND HAM IN PATTY SHELLS

yield: 6 servings

1 cup ham, cut into julienne strips
½ pound fresh mushrooms, sliced
1 medium clove garlic, minced
¼ cup butter
2 (10¾-ounce) cans cream of
   chicken soup
½ cup light cream
2 cups shrimp, cooked
¼ cup parsley, chopped
6 patty shells

In a skillet, sauté ham, mushrooms and garlic in butter. Stir in soup and cream. Add shrimp and parsley. Heat slowly over low heat, stirring occasionally.

Serve in patty shells which have been prepared according to package directions.

SEAFOOD LASAGNE

yield: 8-10 servings
oven temperature: 350°F

6 lasagne noodles
½ cup onion, diced
2 Tablespoons butter
1 (8-ounce) package cream cheese, softened
1 (12-ounce) carton cottage cheese
1 egg, beaten
2 teaspoons oregano
½ teaspoon salt
½ teaspoon pepper
½ teaspoon garlic powder
2 (10¾-ounce) cans cream of mushroom soup
¼ cup milk
⅓ cup dry white wine
Dash hot sauce
1 pound small or medium shrimp, raw, peeled and cleaned
¾ pound crab meat, cleaned
¼ cup Parmesan cheese, grated
¾ cup Cheddar cheese, grated (optional)

Cook noodles according to package directions and arrange 3 in the bottom of a greased 9 x 13-inch casserole dish.

Cook onion in butter until tender and blend in cream cheese, cottage cheese, egg, salt, pepper and garlic powder. Spread ½ of this mixture over noodles.

Combine soup, milk, wine and hot sauce and heat thoroughly. Add the shrimp and crab meat. Layer ½ of this mixture in the casserole.

Repeat the noodle, cheese and seafood layers. Sprinkle entire casserole with Parmesan cheese and bake at 350° for 45 minutes. Top with Cheddar cheese and bake for 3-5 more minutes. Let stand for 15 minutes before serving.

Very good and very rich!

EGG ROLLS

yield: 12-14 egg rolls
oven temperature: 250°F

2 Tablespoons oil
2-3 cups raw cabbage, finely
   shredded
1 large celery stalk, finely minced
2 scallions, finely minced
1 cup chicken, cooked and finely
   shredded
2 cups shrimp, cooked and finely
   chopped
1 teaspoon salt
⅛ teaspoon pepper
2½ teaspoons sugar
12-14 egg roll wrappers
1 egg, slightly beaten
3 cups peanut oil
Sweet and sour sauce
Hot mustard sauce

Prepare and measure all the ingredients. Put wok over high heat for 30 seconds and swirl in 2 tablespoons oil. Count to 20; add cabbage, celery and scallions. Stir fry together for 2 minutes. Remove wok from heat; add chicken, shrimp, salt, pepper and sugar; toss well.

Fill egg roll wrappers using 2 tablespoons of mixture per wrapper; roll and seal with egg. Let rolls stand for 1 hour.

Cook 3-5 rolls in peanut oil in the wok or deep fat fryer at 375° for 4-5 minutes or until golden brown, turning often. Drain and keep warm in a 250° oven until ready to serve.

Serve with sweet and sour sauce and hot mustard.

These are worth the little extra effort and really are a meal with rice and a salad.
A food processor makes chopping easy!

SEAFOOD STUFFING

yield: 5 cups
oven temperature: 350°F

4 cups bread cubes
¼ cup parsley
½ teaspoon sage
¼ teaspoon thyme, crushed
¼ teaspoon pepper
½-¾ cup celery, chopped
½ cup onion, chopped
2-3 Tablespoons margarine
1 (10¾-ounce) can cream of shrimp
  soup
1 (7½-ounce) can crab meat,
  drained and cleaned
½-1 cup shrimp, chopped
  (optional)
¼ cup milk
2 eggs, beaten

Combine bread cubes, parsley, sage, thyme and pepper in a large bowl. Cook celery and onion in margarine until tender but not brown. Pour over the bread. Combine soup, crab meat, shrimp, milk and eggs. Add to stuffing mixture and toss lightly until they are well mixed. Bake in a casserole at 350° for 20-25 minutes.

EGG OMELET CASSEROLE
FOR AN ARMY

yield: 20 servings
oven temperature: 350°F

2½ pounds ham, cooked and
  chopped
2 (10½-ounce) cans stewed
  tomatoes, drained
3 green peppers, chopped
2 pounds processed pasteurized
  cheese, chopped or cubed
½ cup butter, melted
24 eggs
1 cup sour cream

Combine all the ingredients and mix well. Pour into two 13 x 9-inch buttered pans. DO NOT use cooking spray.

Bake at 350° for 1 hour or until knife inserted comes out clean.

CHEESE STRATA

yield: 8-10 servings
oven temperature: 325°F

12 slices white bread
¾ pound sharp cheese, grated
1 (10-ounce) package frozen
  broccoli, cooked and drained
2 cups cooked ham, finely diced
6 eggs, slightly beaten
3½ cups milk
½ teaspoon salt
¼ teaspoon dry mustard
2 Tablespoons instant minced
  onion
Cheddar cheese

Cube 6 slices of bread and place in a greased 9 x 13-inch pan. Layer cheese over bread, then broccoli, then ham. Arrange remaining 6 slices of bread on top. Combine eggs, milk, salt and dry mustard; mix well; add onions and pour over all. Cover and refrigerate for at least 6 hours or overnight. Bake, uncovered, at 325° for 55 minutes. Top with additional Cheddar cheese for last 5-10 minutes of cooking. Let stand 10 minutes before cutting into squares.

This says Christmas morning to our family.

ARTICHOKE CASSEROLE

yield: 6-8 servings
oven temperature: 350°F

2 (6-ounce) jars marinated
  artichoke hearts, drained;
  reserve liquid
¾ cup green onion, chopped
1 garlic clove, minced
4 eggs, beaten
8 ounces Cheddar cheese, grated
6 saltine crackers, crushed
Dash hot sauce

Grease a 9 x 9-inch pan with marinade liquid. Sauté onion and garlic in remaining marinade. Slice artichoke hearts into thirds and combine with onions, garlic, eggs, cheese, crackers and hot sauce; pour into baking dish. Bake at 350° for 40 minutes.

CHEESE SOUFFLE

yield: 4 servings
oven temperature: 375 °F

3 Tablespoons butter, melted
3 Tablespoons flour
1 cup milk, scalded
1 teaspoon salt
½ cup sharp Cheddar cheese,
 grated
4 eggs, separated

Combine butter and flour over heat; remove from heat and gradually stir in the milk. Return to heat, stir constantly until mixture is smooth and thickened. Add salt and cheese. Beat egg yolks and pour milk mixture over them; beat egg whites stiff and stir ½ of them into mixture. Gently fold in the remaining ½ of the egg whites. Pour into a greased 1½-quart souffle dish; bake at 375° for 35 minutes.

SPINACH AND EGG CASSEROLE

yield: 10 servings
oven temperature: 350 °F

2 (10-ounce) packages chopped
 spinach
4 Tablespoons butter
¼ cup flour
⅛ teaspoon pepper
1½ cups milk
1½ cups bread crumbs (3 slices)
4 eggs, hard boiled and sliced
1 cup Cheddar cheese, shredded
12 ounces bacon, fried crisp

Cook the spinach and drain well. Melt butter in saucepan, blend in flour and pepper. Add milk slowly, stirring constantly. Cook until sauce thickens and is bubbly, about 3 minutes.
Butter a 6 cup baking dish. Layer the following ingredients in order: bread crumbs, spinach, egg, bacon, sauce and cheese. Repeat the layers, ending with an additional layer of sauce. Crumble remaining bacon on top.
Bake uncovered for 40 minutes at 350°.

EGG PIE

yield: 6 servings
oven temperature: 350°F

4 eggs, beaten
1½ cups milk
½ teaspoon seasoned salt
Dash of cayenne
2 cups sharp Cheddar cheese, grated
2 Tablespoons flour

Combine eggs, milk, salt and cayenne; and mix well. Toss cheese with flour; add to egg mixture. Pour into a well greased and floured 9-inch pie plate. Bake at 350° for 45-55 minutes. Let stand 10 minutes before serving. VARIATIONS: May also add ½ cup onion, diced; 1 cup mushrooms, diced; 1 cup ham, diced; or ½ cup zucchini, diced.

BRUNCH

yield: 6-8 servings
oven temperature: 350°F

½ pound mushrooms, sliced
2 cups sweet onion, thinly sliced
¼ cup butter, melted
Salt and pepper, to taste
1½ pounds bulk sausage
12 slices white bread
¾ pound Cheddar cheese, grated
5 eggs
2½ cups milk
1 Tablespoon Dijon mustard
1 teaspoon dry mustard
1 teaspoon nutmeg, ground
2 Tablespoons fresh parsley, chopped

Sauté mushrooms and onion in butter about 5-8 minutes; add salt and pepper. Cook sausage; drain well and break into bite size pieces.
Remove crusts from bread; butter one side; layer half the bread, buttered side down in a buttered 2-quart casserole.
Layer half the mushroom onion mixture, half the sausage and half the cheese; repeat layers. Mix eggs, milk, Dijon mustard, dry mustard, nutmeg and parsley. Pour over the casserole; let stand at room temperature for 1 hour. Bake at 350° for 1 hour and garnish with fresh parsley.

DELICIOUS SOUR CREAM ENCHILADAS

yield: 6 servings
oven temperature:350 °F

1 cup sour cream
2 (10¾-ounce) cans cream of
   mushroom soup
1 (2-ounce) can green chili peppers,
   chopped
¼ teaspoon pepper
½ teaspoon garlic powder
2-2½ cups Cheddar cheese,
   shredded
½-¾ cups onion, chopped
12 corn tortillas
Hot oil, to cover bottom of skillet
Jalapeno pepper, sliced (optional)

Combine sour cream, soup, chilies, pepper and garlic powder in a medium saucepan, stirring often until heated. Combine cheese and onion, in a separate bowl, mixing well. Heat each tortilla in hot oil for a few seconds on each side until softened; drain well on paper towels. Immediately spoon about 1½ tablespoons cheese mixture and 2 tablespoons soup mixture in center of each tortilla. Roll up and place in a greased 9 x 13-inch pan, seam-side down. Spoon remaining soup mixture over enchiladas and top with remaining cheese mixture. Bake at 350° for 20-30 minutes.

Garnish with sliced jalapeno peppers before serving.

BREAKFAST PIZZA

yield: 6-8 servings
oven temperature: 325°F

1 package of 8 crescent rolls
1 pound sausage, cooked
2 cups frozen tater tots
1 cup Cheddar cheese, grated
5 eggs, beaten
¼ cup milk
Salt, to taste
Pepper, to taste
¼ cup Parmesan cheese

Press unrolled crescent rolls into 9 x 13-inch pan to make crust. Crumble sausage over crust, sprinkle tater tots over sausage; top with Cheddar cheese. Beat eggs, salt and pepper. Pour egg mixture over entire casserole. Bake 325° for 30 minutes. Sprinkle Parmesan cheese over top and serve.

FETTUCCINI

yield: 12 servings

½ pound bacon or ham, cooked
    and drained
1 pound fettuccini
2 Tablespoons olive oil
Salt
1 gallon water, boiling
6-12 Tablespoons butter
4 Tablespoons parsley, finely
    chopped
3 garlic cloves, finely chopped
½ pound mushrooms, sliced
¾ cup onions, chopped
3 egg yolks, beaten lightly
1 cup heavy cream
6 ounces Parmesan cheese
Pepper, freshly ground

Cook pasta in water with olive oil and salt for 5 minutes. Drain. Melt butter over low heat in a large skillet. Sauté parsley, garlic, mushrooms and onions over medium heat until tender. Add pasta and toss for one minute; reduce heat. To avoid scrambling the egg yolks, quickly add the egg yolks and cream. Add ½ cup cheese and pepper and toss for 30 seconds. Stir in bacon.

Serve at once with remaining cheese sprinkled on top.

SPINACH LASAGNE ROLL-UPS

yield: 6 servings
oven temperature: 350°F

12 lasagne noodles, cooked and
    cooled
1 cup onion, chopped
2 Tablespoons butter
2 (10-ounce) packages frozen
    spinach, thawed and drained
1¾ cups mozzarella cheese, grated
½ cup sour cream
1 egg, slightly beaten

SAUCE:
¼ cup butter
¼ cup flour
1½ teaspoons chicken bouillon
    granules
⅛ teaspoon pepper
1 cup light cream
1 cup milk
½ cup Parmesan cheese

Sauté onion in butter until tender. Combine spinach, onion, mozzarella cheese, sour cream and egg, set aside.

Melt ¼ cup butter in a saucepan; stir in flour, bouillon, pepper, cream and milk; bring to a boil, stirring constantly. Boil and stir for 1 minute.

Dry noodles; spread about ¼ cup spinach mixture over each noodle and roll up like a jelly roll. Spread a small amount of sauce in bottom of buttered 2-quart casserole. Place rolled noodles on top of sauce and spoon remaining sauce on top. Sprinkle with Parmesan cheese. Bake at 350° for 30-35 minutes.

LASAGNE

yield: 8 servings
oven temperature: 375°F

1 pound ground beef
1 clove garlic, pressed
1 Tablespoon parsley flakes
1 Tablespoon basil
1½ teaspoons salt
1 (16-ounce) can tomatoes,
  undrained
2 (6-ounce) cans tomato paste
10 ounces lasagne noodles
3 cups cottage cheese
2 eggs, beaten
1 cup Parmesan cheese, grated
1 pound mozzarella cheese

Brown meat and drain. Add seasonings, tomatoes, and tomato paste. Simmer uncovered for 30 minutes, stirring occasionally. Cook noodles according to package directions; drain and rinse. Combine cottage cheese with eggs and Parmesan cheese. Put half of noodles in 9 x 13-inch pan. Spread with half cottage cheese mixture, half mozzarella and half meat sauce. Repeat layers. Bake for 30 minutes.

STUFFED SHELLS

yield: 8 servings
oven temperature: 350°F

30 pasta shells
2 pounds ricotta cheese
2 eggs
1 (10-ounce) package frozen
  spinach
1 teaspoon garlic powder, optional
¼ teaspoon nutmeg, optional
½ teaspoon oregano, optional
¼ pound mozzarella cheese, grated
Spaghetti sauce

Parboil pasta 9 minutes. Drain, rinse with cold water and dry on paper towels. Combine ricotta cheese, eggs and spinach and optional spices; mix. Add mozzarella cheese. Stuff the shells with this mixture and freeze or bake. Cover the bottom of a 9 x 13-inch pan with spaghetti sauce and arrange shells in a single layer. Pour additional sauce over the shells. Bake at 350° for 20 minutes.

PANSIT

yield: 4-5 servings

1 teaspoon salt
3 or 4 (2½-ounce) packages beef flavored noodles, reserve flavor packets
¼ cup oil
4 cloves garlic, minced
1 medium onion, diced
1½ cups chicken, beef or pork, sliced in ¼-inch strip
½ cup shrimp, peeled and cleaned (optional)
1½ cups celery, thinly sliced
1½ cups carrots, thinly sliced lengthwise
1 small head cabbage, shredded

Bring 2 quarts water, with salt, to a boil and add the noodles; stir to separate the noodles. As soon as the noodles are separated remove from heat and drain well. This does not take long!

Heat the oil in a skillet or wok; add garlic; stir until brown. Saute onions until transparent but firm; add meat and 2 flavor packets, cooking until meat is done; remove from skillet to a warm platter. Cook celery and carrots with remaining flavor packets for 2 minutes; add cabbage and stir well. DO NOT OVERCOOK: vegetables should be crunchy. Return meat mixture to the pan and mix well, heat. DO NOT COOK!

Serve over noodles.

LASAGNE FLORENTINE

yield: 16 servings
oven temperature: 375 °F

2 (10-ounce) packages frozen
spinach, chopped, thawed and
well drained
2 cups onions, finely chopped
4 cloves garlic, crushed
2 teaspoons dried basil leaves
1½ teaspoons dried oregano leaves
1 bay leaf
3 (28-ounce) cans Italian tomatoes,
with basil
2 (8-ounce) cans tomato sauce
¼ teaspoon freshly ground pepper
4 Tablespoons parsley, chopped
2 (8-ounce) packages whole wheat
lasagne noodles, cooked
4 cups low-fat cottage cheese
6 Tablespoons Parmesan cheese,
freshly grated or more to taste

Drain spinach well; squeeze out remaining moisture. In large pan, heat onion, garlic, basil, oregano, bay leaf, tomatoes, tomato sauce, pepper and parsley. Mix well, mashing tomatoes with a fork. Bring to a boil; reduce heat and simmer, uncovered, stirring occasionally, for 1 hour. Remove from heat.

Spoon 1 cup sauce in bottoms of two 3-quart shallow baking dishes (13 x 9-inches). Layer each casserole with 5 lasagne noodles, overlapping to cover, ¼ of the spinach, 1 cup cottage cheese and 1 cup tomato sauce. Repeat layers; top with remaining tomato sauce. Sprinkle each casserole with 3 tablespoons or more Parmesan cheese. Bake at 375° for 50 minutes or until bubbly and browned. Cool 10 minutes before serving.

Approximately 210 calories per serving.

HOMEMADE PASTA

yield: 1 pound of pasta

2⅓ cups flour
½ teaspoon salt
2 beaten eggs
⅓ cup water
1 teaspoon olive oil or other oil

HAND MIX — Combine 2 cups flour and salt in a mixing bowl; make a well in the center. Combine eggs, water and oil; add to flour. Mix well. Sprinkle kneading surface with flour. Turn dough out and knead until smooth and elastic, about 8-10 minutes. Cover and let rest 10 minutes. Use pasta machine or rolling pin to roll out dough. Cut as desired. Dough can be refrigerated for 3 days or frozen.

FOOD PROCESSOR — Place steel blade in dry work bowl. Add flour, salt and eggs; process until consistency of corn meal. With the machine running slowly pour water through feed tube and process until a ball forms. Add oil and process until smooth. Divide dough and roll, using rolling pin or pasta machine.

WHOLE WHEAT — Substitute whole wheat flour.

SPINACH PASTA — Increase flour to 3¼ cups and substitute for the water, one (10-ounce) package frozen chopped spinach, cooked and drained.

BEET PASTA — Increase flour to 3¼ cups and substitute for the water, one (16 ounce) can beets, drained and mashed.

CARROT PASTA — Increase flour to 3¼ cups and substitute for the water, one (16-ounce) can carrots, drained and mashed.

TO FREEZE — Let pasta dry for 1 hour — seal in moisture proof container. Freeze up to 8 months.

BLUE CHEESE STEAK SAUCE

yield: 4 servings

½ cup butter
4 ounces blue cheese
2 Tablespoons chives or shallots,
  chopped
Pepper, freshly ground

Blend all the ingredients together in a saucepan over low heat. DO NOT BOIL. Cover the steaks with pepper.

Grill steaks on one side and brush with sauce after turning. Serve extra sauce with the steaks.

BEARNAISE SAUCE

yield: 6-8 servings

¼ cup tarragon vinegar
¼ cup white wine
1 Tablespoon shallots or green
  onions, chopped
1 teaspoon tarragon
¼ teaspoon thyme
2 Tablespoons parsley, fresh,
  chopped
1 Tablespoon chives
¼ teaspoon basil
¼ teaspoon marjoram
3 egg yolks, well beaten
½ cup butter

Combine vinegar, wine, shallots and herbs in a saucepan; boil, reducing the liquid to ¼ cup, about 8-10 minutes. Strain mixture into top of non-aluminum double boiler and heat. Slowly beat in egg yolks, stirring constantly. When the mixture is thick, whisk in butter, 1 tablespoon at a time and beat well. Do not overcook. Serve hot.

CURRY SAUCE

yield: 2 cups

2 Tablespoons butter or margarine
2 teaspoons oil
2 large onions, finely chopped
1 garlic clove, finely chopped
2 Tablespoons curry powder
1 Tablespoon flour
1 teaspoon cloves
1 (8-ounce) can tomato sauce
¼ teaspoon ground ginger
¼ teaspoon ground cinnamon
2 Tablespoons sweet pickles, chopped
1 Tablespoon lemon juice
1 Tablespoon sugar
1 cup water or chicken stock
½ teaspoon salt

Heat butter and oil in a medium saucepan to the sizzling point; add onions and garlic. Sauté gently until the onions are golden; stir in curry powder and flour; add cloves, tomato sauce, ginger, cinnamon, sweet pickles, lemon juice and sugar. Gradually blend in water. Slowly bring to a boil, stirring constantly. Lower heat and season with salt. Cover and simmer slowly for 45-60 minutes.
Sauce may be strained and reheated before serving. If combining with meat, the meat should be added during simmering.

BARBECUE SAUCE FOR PORK

yield: sauce for 3-4 pounds ribs

3 cups ketchup
½ cup brown sugar
½ cup molasses
3 Tablespoons liquid smoke
3 Tablespoons Worcestershire sauce
2 Tablespoons vinegar
1 teaspoon garlic powder
1 teaspoon hot sauce
½ teaspoon pepper

Combine all the ingredients and marinate ribs in sauce overnight. If charcoal grilling ribs, grill 30-40 minutes, turning and basting frequently.
When using country style ribs, parboil 20 minutes before marinating.

BARBECUE SAUCE

yield: 2 cups

1 cup onion, finely chopped
1 cup ketchup
¼ - ⅓ cup brown sugar
¼ cup vinegar
¼ cup Worcestershire sauce
1 teaspoon dry mustard
¼ teaspoon hot sauce
2 teaspoons salt
Pepper, to taste
1 teaspoon lemon juice

Mix all the ingredients. Keeps for a month in the refrigerator.

Good basic recipe for chicken. For pork, substitute 1 cup peach preserves for the ketchup.

HOT SWEET MUSTARD

yield: 2½ cups

1 cup white vinegar
1 cup dry mustard
2 eggs, beaten
¾ cup honey
¼ teaspoon salt
1½ teaspoons unsalted butter

Combine vinegar and mustard; let stand overnight at room temperature. Mix eggs, honey and salt well; add to mustard mixture.
Melt butter; add mixture, and bring to a boil over medium heat. Stir constantly until mixture coats a spoon. Good on cold cuts, sausages or in deviled eggs.

HUNT SAUCE

yield: 2½ cups

1 (10-ounce) jar red currant jelly
1 cup ketchup
1 cup Burgundy wine

Mix ingredients in a double boiler and stir constantly over low heat until smooth. Serve warm.

BREADS

WHOLE WHEAT BREAD

yield: 2 loaves
oven temperature: 375 °F

2 packages dry yeast
2 teaspoons sugar
¼ cup warm water
½ cup brown sugar, firmly packed
2 teaspoons salt
2½ cups hot water
¼ cup oil
5 cups whole wheat flour
2 eggs
2½-3½ cups flour

In a small bowl dissolve sugar and yeast in warm water (105° - 115°F). In large bowl combine brown sugar, salt, hot water and oil. Cool slightly. To cooled mixture, add 3 cups whole wheat flour. Blend at low speed of mixer until moistened; add remaining whole wheat flour and dissolved yeast mixture. Beat 2 eggs and add. Stir in enough all-purpose flour to form a soft dough. On floured surface knead until smooth. Place dough in greased bowl — turning dough to grease all sides. Cover with plastic wrap and towel. Let rise until doubled in bulk (45-60 minutes). Punch dough down. Divide dough into 2 parts and shape into loaves. Place in 9 x 5-inch pans, cover, let rise until light and doubled in bulk. Bake at 375° for 30 minutes. Reduce oven heat to 350° and bake an additional 15 minutes. Remove bread from pans and let cool on racks.

Dough may be made into rolls; and baked on a cookie sheet. Let rise and bake at 375° for 15 minutes. Freezes well after baking.

HARRIET'S BREAD

yield: 2-3 loaves
oven temperature: 350°F

3 Tablespoons vegetable shortening
2 teaspoons salt
½ cup sugar
2 cups milk, scalded
1 package dry yeast
¼ cup warm water
4-6 cups flour

Put shortening, salt and sugar in large bowl. Pour scalded milk over dry ingredients and stir until dissolved. Cool to lukewarm temperature. Dissolve yeast in warm water and add to first mixture. Add enough flour to make a spongy dough; ¾-1 cup. Cover and let rise 2 hours. Work in enough flour so it won't stick to your hands. KNEAD 100 TIMES. Put in greased bowl, turning so top is greased. Cover and let rise 2 more hours. Punch down and put in loaf pans. Let rise 1 hour. Bake at 350° for 1 hour.

This recipe was shared many years ago by a friend. It is time consuming but makes 3 loaves of luscious bread and worth every minute.

CHEESE BREAD

yield: 2 loaves
oven temperature: 375°F

1½ cups milk, scalded
⅓ cup sugar
¼ cup butter
1 Tablespoon salt (or less, to taste)
2 packages dry yeast
½ cup lukewarm water
1 egg, well beaten
1½ cups sharp cheese, grated
6 cups flour

In large bowl, combine sugar, butter and salt with scalded milk; cool to lukewarm. Dissolve 2 packages yeast in ½ cup lukewarm water; combine with sugar and butter mixture. Add egg and cheese and beat until smooth. Beat in 3 cups flour and mix well. Add remaining flour and continue beating until mixture forms a ball. Knead well. Form 2 loaves in loaf pans. Let rise until doubled in bulk. Bake at 375° for 30 minutes.

Let cool before slicing. Freezes well after baking.

Great with leftover turkey at Christmas.

CELERY LOAF

1 loaf French bread, unsliced
½ cup butter
1 teaspoon celery seed
¼ teaspoon salt
¼ teaspoon paprika
Dash cayenne pepper

Combine ingredients. Trim crusts from top, sides, and ends of the loaf. Cuts are made almost to the bottom crust. Slit the loaf in the center once lengthwise and crosswise at 1-inch intervals. Spread mixture over entire surface of the cuts! Cover, refrigerate. When chilled, bake at 400° for 15-20 minutes.

RYE BREAD

yield: 2 loaves
oven temperature: 350 °F

2 packages yeast
2¼ cups tap water, very warm
⅓ cup molasses
2 teaspoons salt
1 Tablespoon caraway seeds
3 cups rye flour
3 cups whole wheat flour

Dissolve yeast in water. Stir in molasses. Allow yeast to proof. Stir in salt, caraway seeds and 5 cups flour. Knead in last cup of flour. Cover and allow dough to rise until double in bulk. Punch down and shape into 2 loaves. Place in greased loaf pans. Cover loosely and allow to double again. Put a cup of water in oven. Bake bread for 30 minutes at 350°. Remove from pans and wrap tightly in foil.

ICE BOX ROLLS

yield: 2 dozen
oven temperature: 350 °F

1 package dry yeast
1 cup warm water
½ cup shortening
¼ cup sugar
1 egg
1 teaspoon salt
3-4 cups flour

Dissolve yeast in warm water. Cream shortening with sugar and beat in egg. Beat in yeast mixture until well mixed. Add salt and flour working until a smooth dough is formed. Cover bowl with plastic wrap and refrigerate until ready to use. Roll and form rolls. Let rise in pan 1½ hours. Bake at 350° for 15 minutes. Refrigerated dough will keep for 2-3 weeks.

ORANGE ROLLS

yield: 24 rolls
oven temperature: 350°F

ROLLS:
1 package yeast
¼ cup warm water
¼ cup sugar
1 teaspoon salt
2 eggs
½ cup sour cream
6 Tablespoons butter, melted
3½ cups flour

FILLING:
¾ cup sugar
2 Tablespoons orange rind
2 Tablespoons butter, melted

GLAZE:
¾ cup sugar
½ cup sour cream
2 Tablespoons orange juice
½ cup butter, melted

Dissolve yeast in water; beat in sugar, salt, eggs, sour cream and 6 tablespoons butter. Gradually add 2 cups flour; knead remaining flour into dough. Let rise until doubled, about 2 hours. Knead dough again on a well floured surface about 15 times. Divide the dough in half and roll into 12-inch circles.

FILLING: Combine sugar and orange rind. Brush circles with butter and sprinkle with half the orange mixture. Cut into 12 wedges and roll each wedge up starting at the wide end. Place point down in a greased 9 x 13-inch pan. Cover and let rise about 1 hour. Bake at 350° for 20 minutes.

GLAZE: Combine all the ingredients and boil 3 minutes, stirring constantly. Pour on rolls just after removing from oven.

CINNAMON ROLLS

yield: 3 dozen
oven temperature: 350°F

ROLLS:
4¼ cups flour, unsifted
⅓ cup sugar
1 teaspoon salt
2 packages yeast
¾ cup milk
½ cup water
½ cup butter
2 eggs

FILLING:
Butter, melted
1 cup sugar
1 Tablespoon cinnamon

TOPPING:
1 cup powdered sugar
½ teaspoon rum flavoring
2 Tablespoons cream

ROLLS: In a large mixer bowl combine 1 cup flour, sugar, salt and yeast. Heat milk, water and butter over low heat to 120° - 130°. Use a candy thermometer. Add to dry ingredients; beat 2 minutes at medium speed. Add ½ cup flour and eggs, beat at high speed for 2 minutes. Then add enough flour to make a stiff dough. Cover tightly and refrigerate for 2 hours or up to 2 days. Turn on floured board; divide dough into 3 equal parts. Roll each into a 9 x 13-inch rectangle.

FILLING: Brush with melted butter and sprinkle with combined sugar and cinnamon. Roll up starting with the short end, seal seams and cut into 1-inch slices. Place all the rolls on a cookie sheet or 9 rolls in each 9-inch round pan. Cover with a damp cloth and let rise 45 minutes. Bake at 350° for 20 minutes. Remove from pans; cool on a wire rack.

TOPPING: Mix topping ingredients together and frost, if desired.

Freezes well after baking.

MRS HOLMES' CINNAMON RING ROLL

oven temperature: 350°F

1 package yeast
¼ cup lukewarm water
¾ cup milk
4 Tablespoons shortening
2 Tablespoons sugar
2 eggs, beaten
½ teaspoon salt
3¼ cups flour, sifted
1 cup sugar
4 teaspoons cinnamon
½-¾ cup butter or margarine,
  melted
1 cup nuts, finely chopped
  (optional)

Dissolve yeast in ¼ cup lukewarm water. Scald milk, cool and add yeast to it. Cream shortening and sugar; add eggs, milk mixture, salt and flour, and mix well. Let rise, covered with a damp cloth in a warm place until doubled in bulk. Punch down. Pinch off walnut sized bits of the dough. Don't attempt to roll the dough into balls; it will be too sticky. Mix the sugar and cinnamon in a bowl. Dip the bits of dough in the melted butter, then in the sugar mixture. Place the balls in layers in a greased 10-inch tube pan. If desired, chopped nuts may be sprinkled between layers. Let rise about 1 hour, or until nearly doubled in bulk. Bake at 350° for 35-45 minutes.

VARIATION:

1 package frozen dough

Partially thaw rolls and cut in half. Dip each piece in melted butter, then in mixture of cinnamon and sugar. Place in layers in greased 10-inch tube pan. Sprinkle nuts between layers as filling pan, if desired. Bake 35-45 minutes at 350°.

CREAM CHEESE BRAID

yield: 4 loaves
oven temperature: 375 °F

1 cup sour cream, scalded
½ cup butter or margarine, melted
½ cup sugar
1 teaspoon salt
2 packages dry yeast
½ cup warm water
2 eggs, beaten
4 cups flour

FILLING:
2 (8-ounce) packages cream cheese,
   softened
¾ cup sugar
1 egg, beaten
⅛ teaspoon salt
2 teaspoons vanilla

GLAZE:
2 cups powdered sugar, sifted
¼ cup milk
2 teaspoons vanilla extract

Combine hot sour cream, butter, sugar and salt; cool to lukewarm. Dissolve yeast in warm water and add to lukewarm mixture; stir in eggs. Gradually add 4 cups flour; mix well, cover tightly and chill overnight.

FILLING: Combine the ingredients for the filling and mix well.

ASSEMBLY: Divide dough into 4 equal portions. Knead each portion on a heavily floured surface (4-5 times). Roll each into a 12 x 18-inch rectangle. Spread ¼ of the filling over each leaving a ½-inch margin at edges. Roll up jelly roll fashion beginning at long side. Firmly pinch edges to seal. Place rolls seam side down on greased baking sheets. Make equally spaced "x" marks across the top with sharp knife. Cover and let rise until doubled, about 1 hour. Bake at 375° for 15-20 minutes.

GLAZE: Combine the ingredients for the glaze and mix well. Spread the braid with glaze while warm.

CHRISTMAS STOLLEN

yield: 12-16 servings
oven temperature: 350 °F

1 cup milk
1 cup butter, melted
½ cup water
5¼ cups bread flour
6 Tablespoons sugar
1 teaspoon salt
2 packages dry yeast
2 eggs, beaten
½ teaspoon lemon rind
½ teaspoon orange rind
1 cup seedless raisins
1 cup candied fruit, chopped
½ cup nuts, chopped
4 Tablespoons butter, softened

FILLING:
½ cup sugar
½ cup brown sugar
2 Tablespoons ground cinnamon

TOPPING:
2 cups powdered sugar
5 Tablespoons milk
½ teaspoon almond extract
Candied cherry halves, if desired

Combine milk, butter and water in a small saucepan, place over low heat until lukewarm. In a large bowl combine flour, sugar, salt and yeast; stir in warm milk mixture and eggs, mix well. Add lemon rind, orange rind, raisins, fruit and nuts; mix well. Cover dough and refrigerate overnight. Place chilled dough on a floured surface, roll into an 18 x 12-inch rectangle and spread with 4 tablespoons soft butter.

FILLING: Combine sugar, brown sugar and cinnamon and sprinkle over buttered dough.

Beginning with long edge, roll dough up jelly-roll fashion, pinching edges to seal. Place roll on a large greased cookie sheet and shape into a ring, (should resemble a large donut). Brush ends of roll with cold water, pinch and seal.

Using kitchen shears, make cuts in dough every inch around ring, cutting ⅔ of the way through roll at each cut. Gently turn each piece of dough on its side slightly overlapping the previous piece.
Let rise in warm place, uncovered for 1 hour. Bake at 350° for 25-30 minutes or until golden brown.

TOPPING: Combine powdered sugar, milk and almond extract. Drizzle over hot ring. Decorate with candied cherry halves.

MONKEY BREAD

yield: 8 servings
oven temperature: 375 °F

1 cup butter, no substitutions,
  divided
1 cup milk
1 package dry yeast
⅓ cup warm water
2 eggs
½ cup sugar
½ teaspoon salt
3 cups flour

Melt half of the butter in a saucepan. Add milk and scald. Remove from heat and cool. Dissolve yeast in warm water and add to milk mixture. Beat together eggs, sugar and salt, and add to yeast mixture. Stir in 1½ cups flour and mix well by hand. Place in large bowl and add remaining flour. Mix well and form a ball of dough. Cover and let rise for one hour. Melt ¼ cup butter. Cut remaining ¼ cup butter into cubes and place around bottom of tube or bundt pan. Spoon bread dough into pan and pour melted butter over it. Bake at 375° for 30 minutes.

⌛ SOUR CREAM QUICK BREAD

yield: 1 loaf
oven temperature: 325 °F

1 package dry yeast
¼ cup warm water
⅛ cup sugar
1½ cups self-rising flour
1 egg, beaten
1 cup sour cream

Soften yeast in warm water. Mix sugar and flour. Beat egg into sour cream. Mix all the above ingredients together and turn into a well-greased loaf pan. Bake at 325° for about 1 hour.

VARIATION: Sugar may be omitted if desired.

NO-KNEAD OATMEAL BREAD

yield: 2 loaves
oven temperature: 350°F

2 cups water, boiling
1 cup quick oats
½ cup molasses
⅓ cup shortening
4 teaspoons salt
2 packages yeast
2 eggs, beaten
5½ cups flour

Combine water, oats, molasses, shortening and salt. When mixture cools to lukewarm, add yeast and eggs. Then add flour, mixing well. Place dough in large greased bowl. Cover with clean tea towel and refrigerate for 2 hours. Place dough on floured board and pat out flat. Start at the back and roll up. Cut in half to form 2 loaves and place each loaf in a buttered loaf pan. Cover and let rise 2 hours. Bake at 350° for 40 minutes.

This loaf freezes well.

QUICK WHOLE WHEAT RAISIN BREAD

yield: 2 loaves
oven temperature: 325°F

6 cups whole wheat flour
4 teaspoons baking soda
½ teaspoon salt
½ cup molasses
½ cup water
4 cups non-fat buttermilk
2 cups raisins

Mix flour, baking soda and salt. Blend in molasses (you may use less according to taste), water and buttermilk. Stir in raisins. Pour into 2 non-stick bread pans. Let stand 1 hour. Bake at 325° for 1 hour.

⌛ BUSY DAY HIGH-RISE BISCUITS

yield: 18 biscuits
oven temperature: 425°F

2 cups self-rising flour
½ cup shortening
1 teaspoon baking powder
½ - ¾ cup buttermilk

Combine flour and baking powder. Cut in shortening until mixture resembles coarse meal. Add buttermilk and mix well. Turn dough out on floured surface and knead lightly 10-12 times. Roll dough to ½-inch thickness and cut with 3-inch biscuit cutter. Place on a lightly greased baking sheet. Bake at 425° for 15 to 20 minutes or until biscuits are lightly brown.

CRANBERRY BREAD

yield: 1 loaf
oven temperature: 350°F

1½ cups fresh cranberries
2 cups flour
1 cup sugar
1½ teaspoons baking powder
½ teaspoon baking soda
1 teaspoon salt
¼ cup butter
1 egg
1 teaspoon orange rind, grated
¾ cup orange juice
1½ cups golden raisins

Grease and flour 9 x 5-inch loaf pan. Wash cranberries and chop coarsely in blender. Combine dry ingredients. Cut in butter until mixture resembles coarse corn meal. Add egg, orange rind and juice. Blend well. Stir in raisins and cranberries.

Pour into pan and bake at 350° for 1 hour.

BLUEBERRY LEMON LOAF

yield: 1 loaf
oven temperature: 350° F

2 eggs
1 cup sugar
1 cup milk
3 Tablespoons oil
1 teaspoon vanilla
2 teaspoons lemon rind
3 cups flour
4 teaspoons baking powder
1½ teaspoons salt
1 (10-ounce) package frozen
   blueberries, thawed and
   drained, or 1 cup fresh
½ cup walnuts, chopped (optional)

SAUCE:
¼ cup sugar
2 teaspoons cornstarch
¼ cup water
2 Tablespoons lemon juice
½ teaspoon lemon peel
1 cup fresh or frozen blueberries

In a large bowl, beat eggs well while gradually adding sugar. Add in order milk, oil, vanilla, lemon rind, flour, baking powder and salt, mixing well. Fold in blueberries and walnuts. Pour into a greased 8 x 5-inch pan and bake at 350° for 1 hour or until done. Cool.

SAUCE: Blend sugar and cornstarch in saucepan. Stir in remaining ingredients, except blueberries. Cook, stirring constantly until mixture boils. Reduce heat, simmer 5 minutes, stirring occasionally. Add blueberries and heat until they are thoroughly heated. Pour over warm loaf or serve on individual slices.

EASY PUMPKIN BREAD

yield: 2 loaves
oven temperature: 350°F

3⅓ cups flour
3 cups sugar
2 teaspoons baking soda
1¼ teaspoons salt
3 teaspoons nutmeg
3 teaspoons cinnamon
1 cup oil
4 eggs, slightly beaten
⅔ cup water
1 (16-ounce) can pumpkin
2 cups nuts, chopped, optional

Sift dry ingredients together in a large mixing bowl. Make a well in the dry mixture and add the remaining ingredients. Mix until smooth. Pour into greased and floured loaf pans. Bake at 350° for 45-60 minutes. A toothpick inserted in the center should come out clean.

ORANGE DATE LOAF

yield: 1 loaf
oven temperature: 350°F

2 cups flour, sifted
2 teaspoons baking powder
½ teaspoon baking soda
½ teaspoon salt
½ cup water, hot
⅔ cup pitted dates
1 orange, seeded and sectioned
1 egg
2 Tablespoons butter, softened
¾ cup sugar
½ cup nuts

In a mixing bowl, combine flour, baking powder, baking soda and salt. Combine water and dates in a blender, cover and press low, as soon as full speed is reached press high, blend for 5 seconds. Continue blending and add orange, egg, butter, sugar and nuts. Turn off when nuts are chopped. Pour mixture over the dry ingredients, mix just to moisten.

Bake in a greased 9 x 5-inch loaf pan at 350° for 50-60 minutes.

APPLESAUCE MUFFINS

yield: 3 dozen
oven temperature: 400 °F

1 cup margarine
2 cups sugar
2 eggs
3 teaspoons vanilla
4 cups flour
1 teaspoon ground cloves
2 teaspoons ground allspice
3 teaspoons ground cinnamon
2 teaspoons baking soda
1 (16-ounce) can applesauce

Cream margarine, sugar, eggs and vanilla. Add flour and spices. Combine baking soda with applesauce and add to batter. Stir until well mixed. Fill muffin tins half full and bake at 400° for 12 minutes.

BLUEBERRY MUFFINS

yield: 1 dozen
oven temperature: 350 °F

1 cup sugar
¼ cup butter
1 egg
1⅓ cups flour
2 teaspoons baking powder
¾ teaspoon cinnamon
1 teaspoon vanilla
½ teaspoon salt
1 cup blueberries
1 cup milk

Grease and flour muffin pan. Set aside.

Cream butter and sugar, add egg. Combine flour, baking powder, cinnamon, vanilla and salt. Add to creamed mixture alternately with milk. Add blueberries and fill muffin cups ¾ full. Bake at 350° for 30 minutes.

BLAIRDY'S BANANA BREAD

yield: 3 large loaves
oven temperature: 325 °F

1 cup shortening
3 cups sugar
4 eggs
2 teaspoons salt
5 cups flour
1 teaspoon baking powder
1¼ teaspoons baking soda
½ cup buttermilk
2 cups bananas, mashed

Cream shortening and sugar. Add eggs one at a time, beating well after each addition. Sift together salt, flour, baking powder and baking soda.
Alternately add buttermilk and dry ingredients to creamed sugar mixture. Fold in mashed bananas. Bake in 3 greased and floured loaf pans at 325° for 60-75 minutes.

SUNSHINE MUFFINS

yield: 1 dozen
oven temperature: 400 °F

1 cup flour
¾ cup whole wheat flour
½ cup oatmeal
1 cup sugar
1½ teaspoons baking powder
½ teaspoon baking soda
1 teaspoon salt
½ cup raisins, optional
1 Tablespoon orange rind, grated
1 cup carrots, grated
1 egg, beaten
¼ cup oil
¾ cup orange juice

Blend flour, whole wheat flour, oatmeal, sugar, baking powder, baking soda and salt together. Add raisins and mix so they are well coated. Combine grated carrots and orange rind, then add to flour mixture.
Combine beaten egg, oil and orange juice; stir into dry ingredients until well mixed. Fill lined muffin pan ⅔ full. Bake at 400° for 20 minutes.

SWEET POTATO MUFFINS

yield: 18 muffins
oven temperature: 400°F

1¼ cups oatmeal
1 cup flour
⅓ cup pecans, chopped
1 teaspoon baking powder
1 teaspoon ground cinnamon
½ teaspoon baking soda
½ teaspoon salt
½ teaspoon nutmeg
1 cup canned sweet potatoes,
   mashed
¾ cup brown sugar, firmly packed
½ cup oil
¼ cup milk
1 egg
1 teaspoon vanilla

TOPPING:
¼ cup oatmeal
¼ cup flour
¼ cup brown sugar, firmly packed
¼ cup pecans, chopped
1 teaspoon ground cinnamon
¼ cup butter, softened

Combine oatmeal, flour, pecans, baking powder, cinnamon, baking soda, salt and nutmeg; add sweet potatoes, brown sugar, oil, milk, egg and vanilla; stir until moistened. Fill muffin tins ¾ full.

TOPPING: Combine all ingredients for topping until crumbly. Sprinkle over muffins and bake at 400° for 15-20 minutes. Serve warm.

VIRGINIA SPOON BREAD

oven temperature: 350°F

2 cups water
1 cup corn meal
1 teaspoon salt
¾ cup butter
2 teaspoons baking powder
2 cups milk
4 eggs, beaten

Boil water; add corn meal and salt. Cook until mush. Remove from heat; add butter and let cool. Mix baking powder, milk and eggs in a small bowl; add to mush mixture. Bake in a greased 2-quart casserole for about an hour at 350°. Serve warm.

PERFECT CORNBREAD

oven temperature: 425°F

1 cup flour, sifted
¼ cup sugar
4 teaspoons baking powder
¾ teaspoon salt
1 cup yellow corn meal
2 eggs
1 cup milk
¼ cup corn oil

Sift flour with sugar, baking powder and salt. Stir in corn meal then add eggs, milk and oil. Beat one minute or until smooth. Pour into greased 9 x 9-inch pan. Bake at 425° for 20-25 minutes.

Cornstick molds may also be used. Bake until firm and golden.

One tester has never been able to make good cornbread — she succeeded so she said it was perfectly named — it is truly perfect!

HUSHPUPPIES

yield: 6 servings

1½ cups self-rising corn meal
½ cup self-rising flour
1 large bell pepper, chopped
1 large onion, chopped
1 egg
3 Tablespoons sugar
½ cup instant mashed potatoes
   prepared with 3 Tablespoons
   margarine
Dash salt
Dash onion salt

Blend all ingredients well. Drop by rounded teaspoonfuls into hot oil. Cook until golden brown.

Great for that Saturday afternoon fish-fry!

BLUEBERRY COFFEE CAKE

oven temperature 375 °F

¾ cup sugar
¼ cup shortening
1 egg
2 cups flour
2 teaspoons baking powder
½ teaspoon salt
½ cup milk
2 cups blueberries

Cream sugar and shortening; add egg and mix until light and fluffy. Sift together flour, baking powder and salt. Alternately add flour mixture and milk to creamed mixture. Fold in blueberries. Spread in a greased 9 x 9-inch pan or 2 greased pie pans.

TOPPING:
½ cup sugar
⅓ cup flour
1 teaspoon cinnamon
¼ cup margarine, softened

TOPPING: Mix dry ingredients and cut in margarine. Sprinkle topping over blueberry mixture and bake for 40 minutes. Bake 15-20 minutes if using pie pans.

CRULLERS

yield: 18 servings

1¾ cups flour
2 teaspoons baking powder
½ teaspoon nutmeg
½ teaspoon salt
1 egg
½ cup milk
2 cups sugar
1 Tablespoon margarine, melted
1 (48-ounce) bottle oil, for frying

COATING:
1 cup sugar
1 teaspoon nutmeg

Sift flour, baking powder, nutmeg and salt into a bowl. Add milk, egg, sugar and margarine; mix well. Dough will be very soft. DO NOT add more flour or crullers will be tough. Chill dough 2-3 hours. Roll ⅓ of dough on well floured, cloth-covered board. Dough should be ⅓ - ¼-inch thick. With floured cutter, cut into donut shapes. Fry in hot oil (380° on frying thermometer), turning once, until golden brown. Drain on absorbent paper. Roll in sugar and spice mixture. Store in airtight container after donuts cool. If desired powdered sugar can be used in place of granulated in the dough to make a stiffer batter. Dough may be kept several days in the refrigerator before frying.

This recipe was translated by a school friend from his German grandmother — they've used it the last 50 years at Christmas.

ALMOND DANISH

yield: 2 pastries
oven temperature: 350°F

FIRST LAYER:
½ cup butter
2 Tablespoons water
1 cup flour

SECOND LAYER:
½ cup butter
1 cup water
1 teaspoon almond extract
1 cup flour
3 eggs

THIRD LAYER:
Icing:
3 ounces cream cheese
½ teaspoon vanilla
2 cups powdered sugar
Almonds, blanched, slivered and
     toasted

Glaze:
2 cups powdered sugar
2-2½ Tablespoons milk
½ teaspoon almond extract
Sliced almonds
Maraschino cherries

FIRST LAYER: Soften or melt butter with water in small saucepan. (DO NOT BOIL!) Add flour all at once and stir until smooth. Pat dough into 2 strips on a greased cookie sheet. Each strip should be 5 x 12 inches.
SECOND LAYER: Bring butter and water to a boil in saucepan used above (no washing necessary). Remove from heat and add almond extract. Working very quickly, beat in flour with a wooden spoon; then beat in eggs, one at a time, until thoroughly mixed. Spread batter over 2 pastry strips. Bake at 350° for 50-60 minutes. Cool and top with icing or glaze.
THIRD LAYER: Icing: Beat cream cheese until creamy. Beat in vanilla and powdered sugar. Spread icing over cooled pastries and sprinkle with almonds. Glaze: Beat powdered sugar, 2 tablespoons milk and almond extract until smooth. Add more milk a few drops at a time, if necessary, to make spreadable consistency. Frost pastries and sprinkle with almonds and cherries.

Store in refrigerator. Warm before serving. Freezes well after baking.

GENUINE NEW ENGLAND BREAD DONUTS

yield: 2 dozen

1 egg, slightly beaten
3 egg yolks
1 Tablespoon butter or margarine, melted
1 cup buttermilk
Vanilla extract, (a few drops)
½ teaspoon nutmeg
½ teaspoon ginger
1 cup sugar
1 teaspoon salt
1 heaping teaspoon baking soda
1 teaspoon cream of tartar
2 cups flour
Oil for frying
1 large grocery bag
1 medium grocery bag
1 cup sugar
1 teaspoon cinnamon

Slightly beat together egg, yolks, butter, buttermilk and vanilla. Sift together nutmeg, ginger, sugar, salt, baking soda, cream of tartar and one cup flour. Make a nest of flour mixture in a large bowl, pour liquid in center and fold together with a wooden spoon. If necessary, fold in just enough flour so you can handle it. The softer the dough, the more tender the donuts. Put dough onto a floured surface, working in just enough flour in order to cut. Follow the directions for your cooker for frying donuts. Roll out only enough donuts to fry at one time. Fry, flipping over to brown both sides. Lift out when brown. Drain on brown paper. Repeat, pinching off just enough dough to add to donut holes and scraps to make next batch. Punch together, DO NOT KNEAD. Repeat process until all dough is fried. When cool, shake donuts in a paper bag with 1 teaspoon cinnamon and 1 cup sugar. May freeze, but best when served fresh.

The secret of good New England donuts is to have dough as soft as you can handle. Pinch off enough dough for as many donuts as you can make at one time. Use as little flour as you can to prevent sticking when you roll them out. Have fat ready for cooking when you cut the donuts. Donuts sink and then rise as they brown. This is the 150 year old recipe of my husbands' grandmother. Abbie Turbush Dyer continued to make a dozen of these every morning for breakfast after her 90th birthday. She fired one live-in nurse who believed donuts were not good for a 90 year old woman. She shared her donuts with passing school children and neighbors until she was 100 years old.

BUBBLE BREAD

yield: 6-8 servings
oven temperature: 350 °F

¾ cup pecans, chopped
1 (25-ounce) package frozen dinner rolls, thawed
2 teaspoons cinnamon
½ cup butter
½ cup brown sugar, firmly packed
1 (3¾-ounce) package butterscotch pudding and pie filling (not instant)

Put pecans in the bottom of buttered tube pan and arrange 20 dinner rolls on end over the pecans. Sprinkle with cinnamon. Melt butter and brown sugar together and spoon over the rolls. Sprinkle pudding mix on the top. Cover with plastic wrap; let stand at room temperature overnight. Uncover and bake at 350° for 30 minutes. Let bread stand for 5 minutes before turning onto a serving plate.

CINNAMON NIBBLES

yield: 72 pieces
oven temperature: 350 °F

1 loaf thin sliced sandwich bread, white
1 egg yolk
1 (8-ounce) package cream cheese
¼ cup sugar
¾ cup butter, melted
¾ cup brown sugar
2-3 teaspoons cinnamon

Trim crusts from the bread and roll very thin. Cream together the egg yolk, cream cheese and sugar. Spread mixture on bread and roll up. In a separate bowl mix the brown sugar and cinnamon. Dip rolls in butter, then in cinnamon mixture. Place rolls on a cookie sheet. Freeze for 5 minutes. Cut into thirds. Refreeze in plastic bags until ready to use. Put on a greased cookie sheet. Bake at 350° for 15-20 minutes.

GRANOLA CEREAL

yield: 5 pounds of cereal
oven temperature: 250°F

2 pounds rolled oats
2 cups shredded coconut
2 cups nuts (almonds, chopped are preferred)
2 cups wheat germ
1½ cups oil
⅔ cup water
3 Tablespoons vanilla
1½ cups honey
3 cups raisins, chopped dried apricots, dates, or other similar dried fruit in any combination

Combine oats, coconut, nuts and wheat germ in large container. Combine oil, water, vanilla and honey in a separate bowl then mix with cereal mixture until well coated. Divide into two 9 x 13-inch pans. Bake at 250° for 1-1½ hours, stirring every 15 minutes. When cool, add dried fruits and store in airtight container.

MAMA'S WAFFLES

yield: 8 waffles

2 cups flour
4 teaspoons baking powder
½ teaspoon salt
2 teaspoons sugar
2 eggs, beaten
1¾ cups milk
½ cup butter or margarine, melted

Sift dry ingredients together. Add milk, eggs and butter. Beat until all lumps have disappeared and mixture is smooth and creamy. Pour into preheated waffle iron. Bake 2-3 minutes until steam stops.

These light and crispy waffles are wonderful topped with fresh fruit and whipped cream.

GRANDMA'S PANCAKES

yield: 12-14 (4-inch) pancakes

1 cup flour
¾ teaspoon baking soda
¾ teaspoon salt
2 Tablespoons oil
1 egg
1 cup buttermilk

Mix all ingredients together well. Fry on a hot griddle with plenty of fat. Serve with syrup or honey.

FRENCH WAFFLE TOAST

yield: 12 servings

6 eggs, beaten
1 cup light cream
¼ cup butter, melted
Pinch salt and pepper
2 drops Worcestershire sauce
2 drops hot sauce
2 Tablespoons sugar
½ cup maple-flavored syrup
Pinch of cinnamon
½ teaspoon ground nutmeg
1 (16-ounce) loaf Frech bread,
   sliced thick

Combine all ingredients except bread in a large mixing bowl, beat well, about 2 minutes. Dip slices of bread one at a time in the batter. Coat well and let drain. Place on waffle iron preheated to 375°F. Cook 2 minutes or until golden brown.

Leftover batter may be stored in refrigerator 10 days.

ORANGE BUTTER

yield: 2 cups

1 cup butter, softened
2 Tablespoons powdered sugar
1 orange rind, grated
1 lemon rind, grated
Juice of 1 orange

Combine all ingredients and beat well with an electric mixer until all orange juice is absorbed. Use as a spread on biscuits, muffins or pancakes.

VARIATION: Mix butter, honey, and lemon juice to suit personal taste.

CREAM CHEESE AND MARMALADE SPREAD

1 (8-ounce) package cream cheese, softened
½ cup marmalade

Blend cream cheese and marmalade in food processor or mixer until well mixed.

Adds an extra spark to almost any fruit bread or muffin. Keeps in the refrigerator a long time!

LOW CAL "BUTTER"

1 pound margarine sticks (no substitutions)
1 cup corn oil
1 cup buttermilk

Bring all ingredients to room temperature. Combine and whip until light and fluffy. Makes 2 pounds. Store in refrigerator.

Tastes like real butter!

VEGETABLES & ACCOMPANIMENTS

ASPARAGUS CASSEROLE

yield: 6-8 servings
oven temperature: 400 °F

2 Tablespoons celery, chopped
1 Tablespoon onion, chopped
4 Tablespoons margarine
½ teaspoon salt
¼ teaspoon paprika
3 Tablespoons flour
1½ cups milk
1 (10¾-ounce) can cream of
  mushroom soup
1 (8-ounce) package Swiss cheese,
  cubed
1 (2-ounce) jar pimiento, chopped,
  drained
2 (16-ounce) cans asparagus spears
2 eggs, hard-boiled and chopped
1 cup buttered bread crumbs

Sauté celery and onion in margarine; remove celery and onion. In the same margarine, mix salt, paprika and flour; blend well. Add milk and cook, stirring constantly until smooth and thick. Stir in soup and cheese, stirring until cheese is melted. Add celery, onion and pimiento. Place well drained asparagus spears in a buttered 7 x 11-inch dish. Sprinkle chopped eggs over the asparagus; top with cheese mixture. Sprinkle with bread crumbs. Bake at 400° for 25 minutes — or until bubbly and thoroughly heated.

BROCCOLI

¼ cup vinegar
½ cup oil
Lemon juice, to taste
½ teaspoon salt
Pepper, to taste
Garlic, to taste
1 teaspoon oregano
Broccoli head, cut in pieces

Combine vinegar, oil, lemon juice, salt, pepper, garlic and oregano in a jar with a tight lid and shake well.

In a saucepan with ¼-inch boiling salted water, cook broccoli, covered, for 3 minutes. Drain and toss in vinaigrette. Serve hot.

BROCCOLI AND RICE CASSEROLE

yield: 6-8 servings
oven temperature: 300°F

¼ cup margarine, melted
1 medium onion, chopped
1 (10-ounce) package chopped
  broccoli, thawed
1 (10¾-ounce) can cream of celery
  or mushroom soup
1 (8-ounce) jar processed cheese
2 cups rice, cooked

Sauté onion in margarine until clear; add broccoli and soup. Simmer 5 minutes. Add cheese and rice; mix well. Pour into a 1½-quart baking dish and bake at 300° for 20 minutes. Casserole can be made ahead of serving and refrigerated. Increase baking time if the casserole is not at room temperature.

CARROT RING

yield: 8-10 servings
oven temperature: 350°F

2 pounds carrots, sliced
2 Tablespoons sugar
Salt and pepper, to taste
3 Tablespoons onion, chopped
1 green pepper, chopped
½ cup celery, chopped
3 Tablespoons butter
1 egg, beaten
4 saltines, crumbled
Peas, cooked, buttered

Cook carrots until tender; mash (preferably by hand) and add sugar, salt and pepper. Sauté onion, green pepper and celery in butter. Stir into mashed carrot mixture. Add beaten egg and crumbled crackers. Put into a buttered 2-quart ring mold and place mold in a shallow pan of water. Bake at 350° for 30 minutes or until firm. Invert mold on a serving platter. Fill center with buttered peas.

HORSERADISH CARROTS

yield: 8 servings
oven temperature: 375 °F

2 pounds carrots, sliced in 3-inch
 strips
½ cup mayonnaise
1 Tablespoon onion, chopped
1 Tablespoon prepared horseradish
1 Tablespoon parsley
¼ cup cracker crumbs
2 Tablespoons butter
Paprika

Boil the carrots tender crisp in salted water. Drain; reserve ½ cup water. Place carrots in a buttered casserole. Blend mayonnaise, onion, horseradish and parsley with reserved water and pour over carrots. Combine cracker crumbs and butter; top casserole with mixture. Sprinkle with paprika. Bake at 375° for 20 minutes.

My family really liked this — they couldn't believe it had horseradish in it!!

CELERY ALMONDINE

yield: 4-6 servings

½ cup slivered almonds
4 Tablespoons butter, divided
4 cups celery, diagonally sliced
1 Tablespoon onion, minced
Salt, pepper and seasoned salt, to
 taste
2 Tablespoons dry white wine

Sauté almonds in 1 tablespoon butter. Remove and reserve almonds. Melt remaining butter; add celery, onion and seasonings. Cook over low heat, stirring occasionally for about 10 minutes. Add almonds and wine. Cook until almonds are reheated. This can be made ahead, except for adding almonds and wine.

Children like it too!!

SWEET AND SOUR CABBAGE

yield: 6-8 servings

1 small red cabbage
3 slices bacon
3 Tablespoons onion, chopped
¼ teaspoon salt
1 Tablespoon flour
4 Tablespoons brown sugar
2 Tablespoons vinegar

Soak cabbage covered in water for 30 minutes. Drain and chop coarsely. Fry bacon crisp. Remove bacon and sauté onions in bacon drippings. Add cabbage, (chopped fairly small), salt and bacon. Cover and cook until cabbage is crisp-tender. Add flour, brown sugar and vinegar. Cover and simmer 10 minutes.

SKILLET CABBAGE

yield: 6 servings

4-6 slices bacon, cooked
¼ cup bacon drippings
2 teaspoons sugar
1 teaspoon salt, or to taste
2 teaspoons vinegar
4 cups cabbage, finely shredded
  with a knife
1 green pepper, chopped
2 onions, very thinly sliced
2 tomatoes, diced

Cook bacon until crisp. Remove from skillet, drain well, crumble and set aside.

Measure bacon fat into large skillet and add sugar, salt and vinegar. Add the vegetables and toss to mix well. Cover and cook over medium heat for 5 minutes, stirring once or twice. DO NOT OVERCOOK. Add the crumbled bacon and serve immediately.

GRINGO CABBAGE

yield: 6-8 servings
oven temperature: 350°F

1 medium head cabbage, coarsely chopped
1 teaspoon salt

WHITE SAUCE:
⅓ cup butter
3 Tablespoons flour
1½ cups milk
½ teaspoon salt
⅛ teaspoon cayenne pepper
1 cup Parmesan cheese, freshly grated
1 cup buttered cracker crumbs

Place chopped cabbage in a large saucepan. Sprinkle with salt and cover with boiling water; boil 7 minutes. Drain well.
WHITE SAUCE: Melt butter in medium saucepan; add flour, stirring constantly. Slowly stir in milk and cook, stirring constantly until thickened. Season with salt and cayenne.
Place half of cabbage in greased 13 x 9-inch casserole. Pour half the white sauce over cabbage. Sprinkle with ½ cup cheese and ½ cup crumbs. Repeat layers with remaining ingredients. Bake at 350° for 30 minutes.

FRESH CORN PUDDING

yield: 4-6 servings
oven temperature: 350°F

3 large ears of corn
1½ Tablespoons flour
1 Tablespoon sugar
½ teaspoon salt
Dash cayenne
3 eggs, well beaten
1 cup light cream
¼ cup butter, melted

Slit kernels on each ear of corn with a sharp knife. Cut the kernels off the cob and scrape the pulp from each ear of corn. Mix all ingredients together and pour into a buttered baking dish. Set the dish in the oven in a pan containing about 1-inch of water. Bake at 350° for 30-40 minutes until custard is set.

FRIED EGGPLANT

yield: 4-6 servings

1 eggplant, peeled
1 cup flour
1 cup flat beer, cold
1 egg, beaten
1 Tablespoon oil
1 Tablespoon sugar
½ teaspoon salt
Oil

Cut eggplant into ½ x ½ x 3-inch slices and dredge in flour to coat. Combine beer, egg, oil and sugar; mix well. Dip eggplant into batter and fry until light brown in oil. Drain and salt before serving.

⌛ CRISPY EGGPLANT

yield: 4-6 servings
oven temperature: 425°F

½ cup mayonnaise
1 Tablespoon instant onion
¼ teaspoon salt
⅓ cup bread crumbs or herbed stuffing mix
⅓ cup Parmesan cheese, grated
½ teaspoon Italian seasoning
1 medium (1-pound) eggplant

In a small mixing bowl, mix mayonnaise, onion and salt. Combine bread crumbs and seasonings on a sheet of wax paper. Peel and slice the eggplant into 1½-inch slices. Brush edges and sides of eggplant with mayonnaise mixture; coat with bread crumb mixture. Place on foil-lined baking sheet so eggplant pieces do not touch each other. Bake at 425° for 15-17 minutes.

RATATOUILLE

yield: 6-8 servings

4 Tablespoons oil
2 large onions, chopped
2 large green peppers, sliced into strips
2 medium zucchini, unpeeled, cut into ½ x 2-inch pieces
2 small eggplants, peeled, cut into ½ x 2-inch pieces
1 (28-ounce) can tomatoes, or 4 fresh tomatoes, coarsely chopped
Salt and pepper, to taste
¼ cup fresh parsley, chopped
¼ teaspoon each: dried basil, thyme, rosemary and marjoram, or any spice to taste
½ teaspoon sugar
Parmesan cheese

Sauté celery and onions in oil in large skillet until limp. Add green peppers, zucchini and eggplants and sauté for couple of minutes. Stir in tomatoes, herbs and seasonings. Bring mixture to a boil, reduce heat, and simmer covered, for 30-40 minutes. Sprinkle with Parmesan cheese, if desired.

This recipe may be prepared ahead and reheated or served cold. If using fresh herbs use 3 times the amount of dried.
Omit eggplant for zucchini Provencal.

SWISS GREEN BEANS

yield: 6 servings
oven temperature: 400 °F

¼ cup butter, divided
½ cup corn flakes, crushed
2 Tablespoons flour
1 teaspoon salt
¼ teaspoon pepper
¼ teaspoon dehydrated minced
  onion
1 teaspoon sugar
1 cup sour cream
2 (16-ounce) cans French-style
  green beans, drained
2 cups Swiss cheese, shredded

Melt 2 tablespoons butter in small saucepan. Remove from heat and add crushed corn flakes. Mix well and set aside.

Melt the remaining 2 tablespoons butter in large saucepan over low heat. Stir in flour, salt, pepper, onion and sugar. Add sour cream and stir until smooth. Increase the heat to medium and cook until bubbly and thick, stirring constantly. Remove from heat; fold in the green beans.

Spread mixture into greased 1½-quart baking dish. Sprinkle with cheese and top with corn flake crumbs. Bake at 400° for 20 minutes until heated thoroughly.

FANCY CANNED GREEN BEANS

yield: 6 servings

8 slices bacon
½ cup vinegar
½ cup sugar
2 (16-ounce) cans green beans,
  drained

Fry bacon crisp; set aside. Into bacon drippings stir sugar, vinegar and green beans. Cover and simmer 10 minutes. Serve topped with crumbled bacon.

GREEN BEANS IN TOMATO SAUCE

yield: 6 servings

¼ cup olive oil
1½ cups onion, thinly sliced
2 cups tomatoes, fresh or canned, chopped
1½ teaspoons salt
½ teaspoon black pepper
¼ teaspoon oregano
1½ pounds green beans, cut or 2 (10-ounce) packages frozen green beans, thawed

Heat the oil in a saucepan and sauté the onion for 5 minutes. Mix in the tomatoes, salt, pepper, oregano and beans. Bring to a boil; cover and cook over low heat for 1 hour, removing the cover for the last 10 minutes. Serve hot or cold.

CHEESY BAKED BEANS

yield: 6-8 servings
oven temperature: 350°F

4 slices bacon
1 medium onion, chopped
1 (16-ounce) can baked beans in tomato sauce
1 (16-ounce) can kidney beans, drained
1 (16-ounce) can lima beans, drained
½ cup brown sugar
⅓ cup ketchup
2 teaspoons Worcestershire sauce
1 teaspoon chili powder
¼ pound Cheddar cheese, cubed
½ cup Parmesan cheese, grated

Fry the bacon crisp. Crumble and set aside. Sauté onion in bacon drippings. Combine all the beans, brown sugar and seasonings. Stir in onion, crumbled bacon and Cheddar cheese. Sprinkle with Parmesan cheese. Bake at 350° for 20-30 minutes, or until bubbly, in a 2-quart casserole.

Great for cookouts!!

BAKED LIMA BEANS

yield: 20 servings
oven temperature: 350 °F

2 pounds dried lima beans, large
1 pound bacon, diced
2 cups brown sugar
2 Tablespoons dry mustard
2 (16-ounce)cans tomatoes
Salt and pepper, to taste

Soak lima beans overnight in enough water to cover. Next day, place bacon in a large Dutch oven and fry until crisp. Add soaked beans and soaking water; cook for 1 hour on low heat (adding extra water, if necessary). Add remaining ingredients. Pour mixture into a large casserole and bake at 350° for 2 hours, uncovered.

These beans are good for a picnic or a barbeque. Serve with ham, green salad and cornbread.

MUSHROOMS IN WINE SAUCE

yield: 8 servings

⅔ cup butter
1 pound whole mushrooms, fresh
¼ teaspoon seasoned salt
⅛ teaspoon garlic powder
½ cup dry white wine

Melt butter in large skillet; add mushrooms and stir gently. Sprinkle with seasoned salt and garlic powder. Cover and cook over low heat for 5 minutes or until tender, stirring occasionally. Add wine; cover and simmer for 5 more minutes.

Great on steak or roast beef!

OKRA AND TOMATO MEDLEY

yield: 12 servings

2 green peppers, chopped
1 cup onion, chopped
6 Tablespoons bacon fat or butter, or combination
4 cups fresh okra or 5 cups frozen okra
2 (16-ounce)cans stewed tomatoes (4 cups)
2 cups cut corn kernels, fresh or frozen
¼ teaspoon basil leaves
Salt and pepper, to taste

Sauté pepper and onion in bacon fat until soft but not brown. Add fresh okra and cook 5 minutes, 10 minutes if using frozen. Add corn, tomatoes and basil. Simmer 20 minutes. Salt and pepper to taste.

FRENCH FRIED ONION RINGS

yield: 6 servings

¾ cup flour, sifted
½ teaspoon sugar
¼ teaspoon salt
½ cup milk
2 Tablespoons oil
3 drops hot sauce
1 egg, unbeaten
Oil, for frying
3 onions, peeled
Salt, to taste

Sift dry ingredients together. Add milk, oil, hot sauce and egg. Beat until smooth.
Heat vegetable oil in deep fat fryer to 375°.
Cut onions into ¼-inch rings and separate. Dip each ring into batter; drain over paper towel. Drop a few rings at a time into hot fat. Fry until golden brown, turning occasionally. Drain on paper towel. Sprinkle with salt and serve hot.

RED ONION TART

yield: 8 servings
oven temperature: 400 °F

8 medium red onions, thinly sliced
6 Tablespoons butter
¼ cup sugar
½ cup red wine vinegar
¾ cup red wine
¼ cup cassis
Salt and pepper, to taste
1 tart shell, unbaked
¼ cup Parmesan cheese, grated

Sauté the onion in the butter for 10 minutes. Add the sugar, vinegar, wine and cassis. Cook 10 minutes, stirring frequently. Cover and cook for 5 additional minutes. Season with the salt and pepper, and cook longer, reducing the amount of liquid. Cover and refrigerate overnight, allowing the flavors to blend.

About 10 minutes before serving, pour onion mixture in prepared tart shell. Sprinkle with cheese and bake at 400° for 5 minutes. Place under broiler for 1 minute until brown. Serve hot.

VARIATION: Phyllo pastry can be used to make individual tart shells.

SOUTHERN MEDLEY

yield: 8-12 servings
oven temperature: 400°F

1 cup onion, finely chopped
1½ cups celery, finely chopped
4 Tablespoons butter
2½ cups rice, cooked
2 (16-ounce) cans French-style green beans, drained
½ teaspoon celery salt
2 (16-ounce) cans stewed tomatoes
1½ teaspoons sugar
Salt and pepper, to taste
1 cup sharp Cheddar cheese, grated
6 Tablespoons bread crumbs, buttered

Sauté onions and celery in butter. Add green beans, rice, celery salt, tomatoes, sugar, salt, pepper and ¾ cup cheese. Place in a 3-quart casserole.

Mix 4 tablespoons cheese and bread crumbs and sprinkle on top of the casserole. Place casserole in a pan of hot water and bake at 400° for 30-45 minutes.

Great for a buffet!

SPINACH POTATO CASSEROLE

yield: 8 servings
oven temperature: 350°F

3 pounds large potatoes, peeled and cooked
¾ cup light cream
1 teaspoon sugar
½ cup butter
2 teaspoons salt
¼ teaspoon pepper
2 Tablespoons chives, chopped
1½ teaspoons dried dill, chopped
1 (10-ounce) package frozen chopped spinach

Mash potatoes. Add cream, sugar, butter, salt, pepper, chives and dill. Cook spinach only until done and squeeze out extra water. Add to potatoes. Place mixture in buttered casserole. Bake at 350° for approximately 20 minutes. Dot top with a little more butter before serving.

NEW POTATOES WITH SAUCE

yield: 4-6 servings
oven temperature: 350°F

½ cup butter, melted
3 Tablespoons flour
1 teaspoon salt
2 cups water
1 Tablespoon lemon juice, fresh
½ pound bacon, cooked crisp and
   crumbled
1 teaspoon dill, fresh
1 teaspoon chives, fresh or 1
   teaspoon parsley, fresh
2½ pounds new potatoes, one size

In a medium saucepan, combine the flour and butter. Add the salt, water and lemon juice; cook as you would for a medium white sauce. When creamy; add bacon, dill, chives or parsley. Pick potatoes that are one size if possible and boil. Place potatoes in a casserole and pour the sauce over them. Bake 20 minutes at 350°.

LUNCHEON POTATO

yield: 1 serving
oven temperature: 400°F

1 large red or Irish potato, baked
1 Tablespoon Parmesan cheese,
   grated
⅓ cup light cottage cheese
⅛ - ¼ cup water
1 teaspoon chicken bouillon
   granules
1 teaspoon dried minced onions
1 teaspoon chives, optional

Bake potato in oven at 400° for 1 hour or in the microwave according to your microwave directions. Slice top off baked potato. Scoop out contents, reserving shell. Mix potato with Parmesan cheese and cottage cheese. In small skillet, heat water, bouillon, onion and chives. Add potato mixture. Stir until cheese melts. Restuff potato shell and serve.

This is a very satisfying lunch for only 225-245 calories! May be prepared ahead and reheated in the microwave. Also great as a side dish.

JALAPENO POTATOES

yield: 6-8 servings
oven temperature: 350°F

4 medium potatoes
1 small green pepper, thinly sliced
1 (2-ounce) jar pimientos, drained
Salt and pepper, to taste
¼ cup butter
1 Tablespoon flour
1 cup milk
1 (4-ounce) garlic cheese roll, cubed
1 (4-ounce) jalapeno cheese roll, cubed

Boil potatoes until tender. Peel, slice and layer potatoes in a buttered 9 x 13-inch baking dish with the green pepper and pimiento. Salt and pepper each layer. Melt the butter in a saucepan, add the flour and stir until well blended. Gradually add milk, stirring constantly. Add the cheeses and cook until cheeses are melted.
Pour cheese sauce over the potatoes. Bake for 45-60 minutes at 350°.

A whole roll of either cheese could be used but the combination is delicious!

PARMESAN POTATOES

yield: 4 servings
oven temperature: 350°F

½ cup margarine
½ cup flour
½ cup Parmesan cheese, grated
Salt and pepper, to taste
8-10 small potatoes, peeled and sliced

Melt margarine in 8-inch square dish. Combine flour, cheese and seasonings in a plastic bag. Place sliced potatoes in the bag and shake. Lay coated potatoes in melted margarine. Bake at 350° for 1 hour, turning potatoes once.

POTATOES ANNA

yield: 4 servings
oven temperature: 375 °F

1½ pounds potatoes, peeled
3 Tablespoons butter or margarine, melted
Salt, to taste
Pepper, to taste

Slice potatoes thinly and dry thoroughly in a clean towel. Brush pie plate with butter; layer potato slices in overlapping circles in the plate. Brush each layer with butter and sprinkle with salt and pepper. Cover dish with foil. Bake at 375° for 1¼ hours. Turn onto warm heat-proof plate (potatoes should stay moulded in pie-dish shape). Return to oven for 20-30 minutes or until outside is golden brown.

MAKE AHEAD MASHED POTATOES

yield: 12 servings
oven temperature: 350 °F

11 medium-sized potatoes, peeled and sliced
3 Tablespoons butter
1 (8-ounce) package cream cheese, softened
1 cup sour cream
¾ cup milk
1 teaspoon onion salt
1 teaspoon garlic salt
¾ cup sharp Cheddar cheese, grated

Cook potatoes and drain, add butter and beat well. Add cream cheese, sour cream, milk and seasonings; beat until fluffy. Pour into well-buttered 9 x 13-inch baking dish and top with grated cheese. Refrigerate overnight. Bake at 350° for 30-40 minutes.

DUCHESSES POTATOES

yield: 4-5 servings
oven temperature: 425°F

1 pound potatoes (peeled and
  washed)
2 Tablespoons butter
2 yolks of small eggs
1 teaspoon hot milk
Egg white
Salt

Cook potatoes in boiling salted water until tender, drain. Mash with fork. Rub through fine sieve and return to saucepan. Place over low heat and add butter, egg yolks and milk. Beat until smooth. Transfer to piping bag fitted with large star-shaped icing tip. Pipe fairly small mounds or whirls onto buttered baking tray. Leave until cold. Brush with egg white. Bake in hot oven at 425° for 15 minutes or until golden. Serve hot.

PRALINE SWEET POTATO CASSEROLE

yield: 4-6 servings

1 (16-ounce) can sweet potatoes or
  yams
2 Tablespoons butter, melted
3 Tablespoons orange juice
6 Tablespoons brown sugar,
  packed
5 Tablespoons nuts, chopped
¼ teaspoon ground cinnamon

Lightly grease a 1-quart glass casserole suitable for microwave oven. Set aside. Mash sweet potatoes. Add melted butter and orange juice; blend thoroughly. Spoon into casserole. Combine brown sugar, nuts and cinnamon; mix well. Sprinkle over the sweet potato mixture. Cover with filmwrap. Microwave 6½ minutes at 80% power. Let stand 3 minutes before serving.

Perfect quick-to-fix side dish for those busy days.

HASHBROWNS

yield: 8-10 servings
oven temperature: 350°F

2 (10-ounce) packages frozen hash
 brown potatoes, thawed
½ cup butter, melted
1 teaspoon salt
¼ teaspoon pepper
½ cup onion, chopped
1 (10¾-ounce) can cream of
 chicken soup, undiluted
2 cups sour cream
2 cups sharp Cheddar cheese,
 grated
TOPPING:
2 cups crushed cornflakes
½ cup butter, melted

Combine potatoes with melted butter. Add remaining ingredients except topping. Blend thoroughly and pour into greased 8 x 12-inch casserole.
TOPPING: Mix cornflakes with butter. Cover casserole with buttered cornflakes. Bake at 350°F for 45 minutes.

HERB SPINACH BAKE

yield: 6 servings
oven temperature: 350°F

1 (10-ounce) frozen chopped
 spinach, cooked, drained
1 cup rice, cooked (⅓ cup raw)
2 Tablespoons butter
2 Tablespoons onion
2 eggs, beaten
1 cup Cheddar cheese, grated
¾ teaspoon Worcestershire sauce
¼ teaspoon rosemary, crushed
3 dashes hot sauce
⅓ cup milk
Salt, to taste
Nutmeg, to taste

Sauté onions in butter; add to rice and spinach. Add the rest of the ingredients and mix. Pour into 9 x 9-inch baking dish. Bake at 350° for 20-25 minutes. Cut into squares to serve.

MICROWAVE SPINACH AND TOMATOES

yield: 6 servings

1 (10-ounce) package frozen
 spinach, chopped
¾ cup ricotta cheese, drained
½ teaspoon garlic powder
¼ teaspoon nutmeg
Salt and pepper, to taste
2 tomatoes, thinly sliced
½-¾ cup mozzarella cheese, grated
Parmesan cheese

Defrost spinach and drain to
remove all liquid. Mix with
ricotta cheese, garlic, nutmeg, salt
and pepper. Spread half of mixture in bottom of 1-quart
casserole. Cover with half of
tomato slices and sprinkle with
half of mozzarella cheese. Repeat
layers; sprinkle top with
Parmesan cheese. Cover with wax
paper and cook on medium
power in microwave until cheese
is melted is heated thoroughly,
approximately 8-10 minutes.

May be baked in conventional oven at 350°F for 20 minutes.

SPINACH CHEESE BAKE

yield: 6 servings
oven temperature: 350°F

1 (10-ounce) package frozen
 spinach, chopped, cooked and
 drained
2 Tablespoons flour
2 eggs, beaten
1 (3-ounce) package cream cheese,
 cubed
¾ cup American cheese, cubed
¼ cup butter, cubed
1½ teaspoons instant minced onion
½ teaspoon salt
½ cup fine bread crumbs
¼ cup butter
¼ cup Parmesan cheese, grated

Stir flour into spinach and fold in
eggs, cream cheese, butter, onion
and salt. Place in 1½-quart
casserole. Mix bread crumbs, butter and Parmesan cheese; sprinkle
on casserole. Bake at 350° for 30
minutes.

SNAPPY SPINACH CASSEROLE

yield: 10-12 servings
oven temperature: 350°F

3 (10-ounce) packages frozen
  spinach, chopped
½ onion, chopped
2 Tablespoons butter
2 Tablespoons flour
1 cup milk
1 (9-ounce) roll hot pepper cheese,
  cubed
½ cup cracker crumbs
3 Tablespoons Parmesan cheese,
  grated

Cook spinach as directed on package for 3 minutes; drain well. Set spinach aside.
Sauté the onions in butter; stir in flour and milk to make a cream sauce. Add the cheese and stir until melted.
Combine the cheese sauce and spinach. Pour into 1½-2-quart casserole. Top with cracker crumbs and Parmesan cheese just before baking.
Bake 20 minutes at 350°. This recipe can be prepared ahead of time and refrigerated before baking. Bake an additional 10 minutes if it is not at room temperature.

For a milder taste: use ½ Gouda cheese and ½ hot peppercheese.

TURNIPS IN CREAM

yield: 6-8 servings
oven temperature: 375°F

6 medium turnips, peeled and
  sliced
2 cups onion, sliced
Nutmeg, to taste
3 cups heavy cream

Layer turnips and onions in a gratin dish, sprinkling nutmeg between layers. Pour cream over the top. Bake at 375° for 40 minutes, mashing turnips down occasionally.

This will make a turnip lover of anyone!

BROILED TOMATOES

yield: 6 servings

¼ cup mayonnaise
¼ cup Parmesan or Gruyère
  cheese, grated
¼ cup shallots or green onion,
  white part only, minced
2 Tablespoons parsley, minced
3 tomatoes, halved

Combine all ingredients except tomatoes and blend well. Gently spread mixture on tomato halves. Broil 4 inches from heat source 2-3 minutes, until lightly browned. Watch closely to prevent burning. Serve immediately.

STUFFED TOMATOES

yield: 6 servings
oven temperature: 400 °F

6 large tomatoes
½ teaspoon salt
1 (10-ounce) package chopped
  spinach, cooked
2 Tablespoons butter
1 large onion, chopped
3 stalks celery, chopped
1 cup green pepper, chopped
2 carrots, chopped
2 teaspoons parsley, chopped
¾ cup seasoned dry bread crumbs
⅓ cup milk
1 egg, beaten
1 Tablespoon Parmesan cheese,
  grated

Cut ¼-inch slice from the top of tomatoes; scoop out pulp and seeds. Reserve the pulp and discard the seeds. Sprinkle salt inside the tomato shell and invert to drain.
Press all the moisture out of the spinach.
Sauté onion, celery, green pepper, carrots and parsley in butter until tender. Combine vegetables, spinach, bread crumbs, milk and egg. Mix well.
Spoon vegetable mixture into tomatoes; place on lightly greased 8-inch square baking dish. Sprinkle cheese over filled tomatoes. Bake at 400° for 15 minutes.

SUMMER SQUASH FRITTATA

yield: 4-5 servings

6 slices bacon
Flour
Salt and pepper, to taste
¼ of a green pepper (optional)
1½ cups summer squash, sliced
½ cup onion, sliced
5 eggs, beaten
Monterey Jack cheese, grated

Fry bacon in skillet. Remove bacon and set aside. In a small bowl, season flour (enough to coat squash, onion and green pepper) with salt and pepper. Toss vegetables in flour mixture. Sauté vegetables in bacon drippings until lightly browned. Crumble bacon and mix with eggs. Pour the egg mixture over the vegetables in the skillet; cook over medium heat until partially set. Gently lift the egg mixture with a spatula so the uncooked liquid can run down and cook on the bottom of the skillet. When the eggs are nearly set, sprinkle with cheese; place under the broiler until the cheese melts. Cut in wedges and serve immediately.

SQUASH CASSEROLE

yield: 6 servings
oven temperature: 400°F

4-5 medium yellow squash, sliced
1 onion, sliced
½ green pepper, chopped
1 (16-ounce) can tomatoes,
   undrained, chopped
1 cup Cheddar cheese, shredded
1 teaspoon salt
Dash of pepper
4 slices bacon, cooked and
   crumbled

Boil squash, onion and green pepper together for 4 minutes; drain well. Add tomatoes, cheese, salt, pepper and bacon; mix well. Pour into buttered 2-quart casserole. Bake at 400° for 20-30 minutes.

SOUTH-OF-THE-BORDER SQUASH

yield: 6-10 servings
oven temperature: 325 °F

3 (10-ounce) packages frozen squash, or 2 pounds fresh squash
1 onion, chopped
1 (2-ounce) can green chilies, chopped
1 green pepper, chopped
2 eggs, beaten
½ cup mayonnaise
½ cup Cheddar or Monterey Jack cheese, grated
Salt and pepper, to taste
Parmesan cheese, grated

Steam squash, onion, chilies and green pepper together until tender, using a small amount of water. Drain. Mix with eggs, mayonnaise, cheese, salt and pepper. Pour into greased 1-quart casserole and sprinkle with Parmesan cheese. Bake at 325° for 45 minutes to 1 hour.

ZUCCHINI SLIPPERS

yield: 6 servings
oven temperature: 350 °F

6 medium zucchini
2 eggs, well beaten
1½ cups sharp Cheddar cheese, grated
½ cup cottage cheese
2 Tablespoons parsley, chopped
½ teaspoon salt (optional)
Dash pepper
½ cup fresh bread crumbs
¼ cup Parmesan cheese

Cook whole zucchini in salted boiling water until tender but still firm. Remove ends, cut in half lengthwise, and invert to drain. Mix eggs, Cheddar cheese, cottage cheese, parsley, salt and pepper. Fill each "slipper" with mixture and arrange in a greased 7 x 11-inch casserole. Top each "slipper" with a combined mixture of bread crumbs and Parmesan cheese. Bake at 350° for 15 minutes then 400° for 5 minutes.

SPICY HOT BLACK-EYED PEAS

yield: 6 servings

3 slices bacon
1 (17-ounce) can black-eyed peas
1 (16-ounce) can whole tomatoes,
  undrained and chopped
1 cup onion, chopped
1 large green pepper, chopped
1 clove garlic, minced
1 teaspoon cumin
1 teaspoon dry mustard
½ teaspoon curry powder
½ teaspoon chili powder
1 teaspoon salt
½ teaspoon pepper
Parsley, fresh, chopped

Cook bacon until crisp. Remove, crumble and reserve. Stir ingredients as listed into bacon drippings in skillet; bring to a boil. Reduce heat and simmer 20 minutes; stir occasionally. Pour into serving dish. Sprinkle with reserved bacon and parsley.

"HAPPY NEW YEAR!!!"

ARROZ ADIOS

yield: 6-8 servings
oven temperature: 325 °F

1 cup rice, raw
½ cup butter
Salt and pepper, to taste
1 (8-ounce) can green chilies
2 cups sour cream
½ pound Monterey Jack cheese,
  grated
½ cup Cheddar cheese, grated

Cook rice according to package directions. Add butter, salt and pepper. In casserole, arrange layers of rice, green chilies, sour cream and cheeses. Cover and bake at 325° for 1 hour.

RICE PILAF

yield: 8 servings
oven temperature: 350 °F

2 cups rice, raw
⅔ cup butter or margarine
4 cups chicken stock
¾ cup celery, chopped
¾ cup carrots, shredded
¾ cup parsley, chopped
½ cup green onion, tops included, chopped
1 cup pecans, chopped
Salt, to taste

Sauté rice in butter until lightly browned. Add stock and place in a 2-2½-quart casserole. Bake covered at 350 °F for 30 minutes. Add remaining ingredients; stir to blend. Return to oven for 30 minutes.

CHINESE FRIED RICE

yield: 6 servings

2 eggs
½ teaspoon dry sherry
3 Tablespoons oil, divided
2 Tablespoons scallions, chopped
3½ cups rice, cooked and cooled
1 cup ham, chicken, turkey or shrimp, cooked and diced
½ cup green peas, frozen
½ cup carrots, parboiled
4 teaspoons soy sauce
1 teaspoon salt

Beat eggs with sherry, and set aside. In a wok, heat 1 tablespoon oil to 375°; pour in eggs and scramble until very dry. Remove eggs from wok and set aside. Heat the remaining 2 tablespoons oil and sauté scallions. Add rice, meat, peas, carrots, soy sauce, salt and scrambled eggs. Stir-fry constantly for 8-10 minutes until ingredients are well mixed and heated.

You may want to substitute Chinese snow peas for the peas and carrots.

RICE ALMONDINE

yield: 8 servings
oven temperature: 350°F

6 Tablespoons butter
1 medium onion, chopped
1¼ cups rice, raw
1 (10½ ounce) can beef consommé
1 can water
1 (2-ounce) can sliced mushrooms, drained
Salt, to taste
¼ - ½ teaspoon pepper
½ cup almonds, slivered

In a skillet, over medium heat, melt the butter and sauté the onion until tender. Add the rice, consommé, water, mushrooms, salt, pepper and almonds. Stir gently until rice grains are separated and all ingredients are well mixed. Pour into lightly buttered 1½-quart baking dish. Cover and bake at 350° for 1 hour, stirring once during baking.

SAFFRON RICE WITH VEGETABLES

yield: 6 servings

1 (7-ounce) package saffron rice, cooked
1 cup margarine
1 small green pepper, chopped
1 large onion, chopped
1 (8½-ounce) can small party peas with liquid
1 (4-ounce) can mushrooms with liquid
1 (2-ounce) jar pimiento, chopped
Ripe olives, sliced
Parsley, chopped

While rice is cooking, melt ½ cup margarine in a large skillet and sauté green pepper and onion. Add rice, peas, mushrooms, pimiento, and ½ cup margarine. Cook over low heat for 20 minutes. Place in serving dish, garnish with olives and parsley.

BARLEY PILAF

yield: 6 servings
oven temperature: 350°F

½ pound mushrooms, sliced
6 Tablespoons butter
1½ cups onions, chopped
1 cup barley, fine or medium
1 (13¾-ounce) can condensed
  chicken broth
Water, 1 soup can
¼ teaspoon salt
¼ teaspoon pepper

In a large, heavy saucepan, sauté mushrooms 4-5 minutes in butter; remove mushrooms and cook onions for 10 minutes, stirring often, until golden brown. Mix in barley and continue cooking 5 more minutes; add mushrooms, broth, water, salt and pepper. Spoon mixture into 1½-quart casserole. Cover and bake at 350° for 1½-2 hours, or until barley is tender.

RED BEANS AND RICE

yield: 8 servings

¾ pound Italian sausage, sliced
  1-inch thick
¼ cup butter
1 large onion, chopped
½ cup celery, chopped
1 small green pepper, chopped
⅓ cup green onion tops, chopped
2 Tablespoons parsley, chopped
2 (15-ounce) cans New Orleans
  style kidney beans
2 Tablespoons ketchup
2 Tablespoons Worcestershire
  sauce
1 (8-ounce) can tomato sauce
⅛ teaspoon red pepper
Salt and pepper, to taste
1 cup rice, raw

Sauté sausage in butter for 5 minutes. Remove sausage and drain. Sauté vegetables in drippings for 5 minutes or until they begin to wilt. Add sausage, beans and remaining ingredients. Cover and bring to a boil. Simmer for 20-30 minutes. Cook rice according to package directions.

Serve red beans mixture over cooked rice.

FRUIT KABOBS

yield: 16 servings

32 fresh strawberries, whole
32 green grapes, seedless
32 fresh pineapple wedges
32 balls cantaloupe, honeydew, watermelon or combination
1 (6-ounce) can frozen limeade, thawed
16 wooden skewers or bamboo sticks

Pour undiluted limeade over fruit in a large bowl. Chill at least 2 hours. Put together by alternating fruit on skewers. Stick skewers into a melon half and serve.

BAKED PEARS

yield: 4 servings
oven temperature: 350°F

4 Bosc or Anjou pears, peeled
1 cup light brown sugar
3 Tablespoons butter
½ cup rum or orange juice

Halve and core pears. Place cut side down in a shallow baking dish. Sprinkle generously with brown sugar and dot with butter. Pour rum or orange juice in the side of the dish, taking care not to disturb the sugar. Cover and bake at 350° for 20 minutes. Remove cover and baste with liquid. Bake approximately 15 minutes longer or until pears are tender, basting frequently. Serve as a side dish, or with ice cream or whipped cream as a dessert.

HOT PINEAPPLE

yield: 6-8 servings

3 eggs
½ cup butter, no substitutes
1½ cups sugar
6 slices homestyle white bread,
    cubed
1 (15¼-ounce) can crushed
    pineapple with juice (not syrup)

Cut butter into small pieces. Beat eggs until fluffy. Add butter, sugar, bread and pineapple; mix well. Bake in a 2-quart casserole for 40-50 minutes.

Serve for brunch with ham or sausage. Good with barbecue.

HOT FRUIT SALAD

yield: 8 servings
oven temperature: 350°F

1 (16-ounce) can pineapple chunks,
    drained
1 (16-ounce) can pear halves,
    drained
1 (16-ounce) can sliced peaches,
    drained
32 ounces frozen unsweetened
    strawberries
½ cup butter
¾ cup brown sugar, firmly packed
1 Tablespoon cinnamon
1 (16-ounce) can applesauce

Combine pineapples, pears, peaches and strawberries and set aside.

Melt butter. Add brown sugar, cinnamon and applesauce; mix well. Pour over fruit mixture, dot with butter and bake at 350° for 1 hour.

Brunch dish!

BAKED APPLES

yield: 6-8 servings
oven temperature: 350°F

6 apples, peeled and thinly sliced
1 cup sugar
½ teaspoon nutmeg
¼ teaspoon cinnamon
3 cups soft bread crumbs
½ cup butter, melted

Mix apples, sugar, nutmeg and cinnamon. Blend bread crumbs with butter. Layer apples and crumbs alternately in buttered 1-quart baking dish. Cover and bake at 350° for 40 minutes.

Good with roast pork!

MICROWAVE BAKED APPLES

yield: 2-3 servings

2-3 baking apples
Vegetable cooking spray
Dark corn syrup
Light brown sugar, to taste
Cinnamon, to taste
Butter, thinly sliced

Peel apples leaving a strip around the middle and core all the way through the apple. Spray microwave-safe dish with cooking spray. Cover bottom of dish with dark corn syrup; add apples. Combine brown sugar, cinnamon and butter. Fill the apples with mixture; cover. Microwave for 5 minutes. Turn dish and cook 10 minutes.

TO SERVE: Fill each apple with syrup, cover with sweetened cream and dust with powdered sugar.

APPLE GRATIN

yield: 6-8 servings
oven temperature: 350°F

2 pounds Granny Smith apples, peeled, sliced
½ cup raisins
½ teaspoon cinnamon
¼ cup lemon juice
¾ cup brown sugar, firmly packed
½ cup flour
⅛ teaspoon salt
¼ cup butter, softened
1 cup sharp Cheddar cheese, grated

In a well buttered 1-quart casserole arrange apple slices. Sprinkle with raisins, cinnamon, and lemon juice (for sweeter apples use less lemon juice). Cut together with a fork: brown sugar, flour, salt, butter, and cheese and sprinkle over the apples. Bake at 350° for 30 minutes or until apples are tender.

JAMYE'S MUSTARD PICKLES

yield: 12 pints

4 quarts green tomatoes
1 cup salt
2 quarts white onion
6 bell peppers
½ large bunch celery
3½ pounds cabbage
8 cups vinegar
½ small box dry mustard
½ box celery seed
½ box ground cinnamon
½ box turmeric
1 cup flour
1 teaspoon cloves
2½ pounds sugar
½ cup pimiento, chopped
6 sour pickles, chopped

Chop tomatoes and add salt. Let stand overnight. Next morning squeeze out excess water. Chop the other vegetables; mix with tomatoes. Add 6 cups vinegar, dry mustard, celery seed and cinnamon and bring to a boil. Lower heat and cook for 1 hour. Mix turmeric, flour and 2 cups of vinegar to make a paste. Add to vegetables and cook for 20 minutes, stirring constantly to avoid scorching. Just before removing from the stove add pimiento and sour pickles. Fill jars while hot and seal.

DILLY BEANS

yield: 5-6 pints

3 pounds whole beans, strung
1 teaspoon red pepper
4 cloves garlic, chopped
2 cups water
4 large heads dill, chopped or 4
    Tablespoons dill seed
2 cups vinegar

Scald beans and pack into pint jars. Combine remaining ingredients and bring to a boil. Pour over beans and seal.

AUNT VONNIE'S PICKLED BEETS

yield: 3 quarts

1 gallon beets, including 1-inch of
    the tops
2 cups white vinegar
1 Tablespoon pickling spices
2 cups water
3 cups sugar

Boil jars and set aside, leaving in hot water. Bring lids to a near boil in a small saucepan and set aside, leaving in hot water. Cover beets with water and boil, covered until the beets are tender. Make a syrup by bringing vinegar, pickling spices, water and sugar to a boil and boiling about 3 minutes.
Peel hot, cooked beets and place in jars; cutting if too large. Pour syrup over beets to cover and within 1-inch of the jar top. Slip a non-metallic utensil down the side of the jar to bring up any bubbles. Seal. Turn upside down a few seconds and turn right side up. Cool and check seals.

DESSERTS

BUTTER CORNFLAKE BALLS

yield: 3 dozen
oven temperature: 325 °F

1 cup butter, softened
½ cup sugar
2 cups flour
1 teaspoon cinnamon
1 teaspoon vanilla
2 cups cornflakes, crushed
1 cup pecans, finely chopped
¼ cup powdered sugar

Combine all ingredients except powdered sugar and mix well. Roll into balls the size of a walnut and place on a cookie sheet. Bake at 325° for 30 minutes. After baking roll in powdered sugar.

LACE COOKIES

yield: 6 dozen
oven temperature: 325 °F

2 cups rolled oats
1 Tablespoon flour
2 cups sugar
½ teaspoon salt
1 cup butter, melted
2 eggs, beaten
1 teaspoon vanilla

Mix oats, flour, sugar and salt in a large bowl. Pour very hot butter over dry mixture and stir until the sugar is melted. Add eggs and vanilla. Stir well. Cover cookie sheets with aluminum foil. Drop ½ level teaspoon of cookie mixture on the foil, 2 inches apart. Bake at 325° for 10-12 minutes. Watch carefully! Let cookies cool on the foil, when they are fully cooled carefully pull off foil. Store in an airtight container.

TEA CAKES

yield: 3 dozen
oven temperature: 400 °F

½ cup butter
1 egg
1 cup sugar
1 teaspoon baking soda
6 Tablespoons buttermilk
1 teaspoon vanilla
4 cups flour

Cream butter, add egg and sugar. Mix baking soda with buttermilk and add to mixture. Add vanilla and enough flour to make dough and roll out. Cut like biscuits and sprinkle with sugar. Bake at 400 °F for 15 minutes or until brown.

CHOCOLATE PUFFS

yield: 5 dozen
oven temperature: 375 °F

½ cup butter
¾ cup cocoa
4 Tablespoons oil
2 cups sugar
4 eggs
2 teaspoons vanilla
1½ cups flour
2 teaspoons baking powder
Dash cinnamon
Powdered sugar

In a saucepan, melt the butter and add the cocoa and oil. Cool and stir in sugar, 1 cup at a time, beating well after each addition. Beat in eggs and add vanilla. Sift flour, baking powder and cinnamon together. Add to chocolate mixture and mix well. Cover and refrigerate for 12 hours.
Roll teaspoon of dough into ball and roll in powdered sugar.
Bake on a lightly greased cookie sheet at 375° for 10 minutes.

TUILES

yield: 24 cookies
oven temperature: 425 °F

1½ cups almonds, blanched and
thinly sliced
1 cup sugar
¾ cup flour, sifted
2 egg whites, lightly beaten
4 Tablespoons butter, melted and
cooled
Pinch of salt

Combine almonds, sugar and flour in medium mixing bowl. Stir in egg whites, butter and salt. Drop teaspoons of dough onto a greased baking sheet. Flatten cookies with a moistened fork. Bake at 425° for 8 minutes until golden brown. Transfer warm cookies one at a time to a rolling pin to curl and cool enough so that they hold their round shape. Return to oven to warm if cookies become too stiff to remove from pan.

SYRUP COOKIES

yield: 3-4 dozen
oven temperature: 375 °F

1 cup shortening
1 cup brown sugar
2 cups molasses
2 teaspoons ginger
1 teaspoon baking soda
2 teaspoons warm water
1 teaspoon salt
4½ cups flour

Cream together shortening and sugar. Mix molasses, ginger, baking soda dissolved in warm water and salt. Add flour 1 cup at a time, stirring well after each addition. Make a stiff dough. Roll dough out and cut with a cookie cutter. Bake at 375° for 3-5 minutes until golden brown.

ORIENTAL ALMOND COOKIES

yield: 4 dozen
oven temperature: 325 °F

2¾ cups flour, sifted
1 cup sugar
½ teaspoon baking soda
½ teaspoon salt
1 cup margarine
1 egg, slightly beaten
1 teaspoon almond extract
⅓ cup whole almonds

Sift flour, sugar, baking soda and salt together into bowl. Cut in margarine until mixture resembles corn meal. Add egg and almond extract; mix well. Shape dough into 1-inch balls and place 2 inches apart on ungreased cookie sheet. Place an almond on top each cookie and press down to flatten slightly. Bake at 325° for 15 to 18 minutes. Cool on rack.

LIME SUGAR COOKIES

yield: 5 dozen
oven temperature: 375 °F

½ cup butter, softened
½ cup sugar
⅛ teaspoon salt
4½ teaspoons fresh lime juice
1½ cups flour, sifted
2 Tablespoons sugar
2 teaspoons lime rind, grated

In a medium bowl with an electric beater, cream butter and sugar; beat in salt and lime juice. Add flour, stir with a wooden spoon until well blended. Chill, tightly covered, until firm enough to handle. Shape into two 4-inch long rolls. Wrap in plastic wrap and chill until firm enough to slice. Remove one roll from refrigerator. Cut into ⅛-inch slices. Place one inch apart on ungreased cookie sheet. Mix sugar and lime rind and sprinkle cookies with mixture. Bake at 375° for 6-8 minutes.

NO WAIT SUGAR COOKIES

yield: 2-2½ dozen
oven temperature: 350°F

⅔ cup shortening
1 cup sugar
1 egg
2 Tablespoons milk
1 teaspoon vanilla
2 cups flour
½ teaspoon baking powder
½ teaspoon baking soda
¼ teaspoon salt
½ teaspoon nutmeg

Cream shortening and sugar. Add egg, milk and vanilla. Stir in flour, baking powder, baking soda, salt and nutmeg. Divide dough in half and roll on a sugared and floured surface. Cut out cookies and bake on ungreased cookie sheet at 350° for 5-10 minutes. Cookies are not as dark as most sugar cookies. Do not overcook!

SHORTBREAD

yield: 4 dozen bars
oven temperature: 300°F

1 cup unsalted butter
½ cup sugar
Pinch of salt
¼ cup rice flour
2¼ cups flour
Sugar, optional

By hand (not with a spoon) cream sugar and butter together. Add the remaining ingredients; mixing until dough makes a ball. Press lightly into a 9 x 13-inch pan. Prick with fork tines and score into bars.

Bake at 300° for 45 minutes to 1 hour or until lightly browned. Cut through the scored edges immediately after removing from oven. Sprinkle with sugar.

APRICOT SQUARES

yield: 24 bars
oven temperature: 400°F

2 cups dried apricots, packed
1¼ cup sugar, divided
½ cup dark brown sugar
¼ cup water
2 cups flour
1 teaspoon salt
½ teaspoon baking soda
¾ cup butter, softened
1½ cups coconut
¾ cup pecans, chopped

TOPPING:
1 cup heavy cream
3 Tablespoons powdered sugar
¼ teaspoon almond flavoring

Cook apricots and drain well. Combine with ¼ cup sugar, brown sugar and water, cook 5 minutes more (stirring occasionally). Cool.

Sift together flour, salt and baking soda and set aside.
Cream butter with 1 cup sugar and beat well. Blend dry ingredients into sugar mixture; add coconut and pecans. Press 3 cups of this mixture into a 13 x 9-inch pan. Bake at 400° for 10 minutes. Remove pan from oven and reduce heat to 350°. Spread apricot mixture over the crust and sprinkle with the remaining crumb mixture. Bake at 350° for 15 minutes or until crust is golden brown. If it browns too fast cover with foil for the last few minutes.

TOPPING:
Whip cream and flavor with sugar and almond. Serve on top of each bar.

MERINGUE PECAN BARS

yield: 12-16 squares
oven temperature: 350°F

½ cup brown sugar
½ cup butter
2 eggs, separated
2 teaspoons vanilla, divided
1½ cups flour
1 teaspoon baking powder
1¼ cups brown sugar
½ cup pecans, chopped
½ cup coconut, shredded

Mix brown sugar, butter, egg yolks and 1 teaspoon vanilla. Blend well. Add flour and baking powder and press into an ungreased 9 x 9-inch pan. Beat egg whites until soft peaks form; add 1 teaspoon vanilla and brown sugar. Beat until glossy. Fold in nuts and coconut. Spread evenly over flour mixture. Bake at 350° for 25 minutes. Cut while warm.

NUT BARS

yield: 18-24 servings
oven temperature: 375°F

CRUST:
½ cup butter
1½ cups flour
½ teaspoon salt
¾ cup powdered sugar

TOPPING:
½ cup light corn syrup
2 Tablespoons butter
1 Tablespoon water
6 ounces butterscotch chips
12 ounces fancy mixed nuts

CRUST: Cut all ingredients together until it resembles a coarse meal. Pat into a 9 x 13-inch pan. Bake 375° for 12 minutes.

TOPPING: Combine corn syrup, butter, water and butterscotch chips in a double boiler. Pour over crust. Arrange nuts on top. Bake 5 minutes or until bubbly all over. Cut while still warm.

CHEESECAKE BARS

yield: 48 bars
oven temperature: 350°F

1 cup flour
¼ cup light brown sugar, firmly packed
1 cup pecans, finely chopped
½ cup butter, melted
2 (8-ounce) packages cream cheese
1⅓ cups sugar, divided
2 teaspoons vanilla, divided
3 eggs
2 cups sour cream

Cut together flour, brown sugar, pecans and butter. Press in bottom of a 9 x 13-inch pan. Bake 10-15 minutes, or until brown. Combine cream cheese, 1 cup sugar and 1 teaspoon vanilla. Add eggs and beat well. Pour onto crust and bake 20 minutes. Combine sour cream, ⅓ cup sugar and 1 teaspoon vanilla. Pour over baked filling and bake 3-5 minutes. Cool and refrigerate before cutting.

These are best eaten with a fork, not fingers!!

LEMON SQUARES

yield: 12 servings
oven temperature: 350°F

FIRST LAYER:
½ cup butter
¼ cup powdered sugar
1 cup flour
Pinch salt

FIRST LAYER: Cream ingredients. Pat mixture with your fingers into greased 8 x 8-inch pan. Bake at 350° for 15 minutes or until slightly browned.

SECOND LAYER:
2 eggs, slightly beaten
1 cup sugar
2 Tablespoons flour
Juice of 1 lemon
Pinch of salt

SECOND LAYER: Mix ingredients together. Pour over hot crust and return to oven for 20 minutes. Dust with powdered sugar when baked.

GRAHAM CRACKER BARS

yield: 20 servings

34 graham crackers
1 egg, well beaten
1 cup sugar
1 cup butter, melted
½ cup milk
1¼ cups coconut
1 cup pecans, chopped
1 cup graham cracker crumbs

FROSTING:
½ cup butter
4 Tablespoons cream
2 cups powdered sugar, sifted
1 teaspoon vanilla

Line a 9 x 12-inch pan with graham crackers.
Combine in saucepan the egg, sugar, melted butter and milk. Cook, stirring constantly until mixture boils. Remove from heat and add coconut, nuts and crumbs. Spread this mixture over crackers in pan. Immediately place remaining crackers on top. Frost, refrigerate, then cut.

FROSTING: Combine all ingredients and beat until creamy.

LEBKUCHEN

yield: 108 bars
oven temperature: 350°F

4 eggs
2 cups sugar
⅔ cup honey
1½ cups almonds, slivered
5 cups flour, sifted
1 teaspoon cinnamon
1 teaspoon ground cloves
1 teaspoon allspice
½ teaspoon baking soda
1 cup candied fruit, chopped

GLAZE:
8-12 ounces powdered sugar
Juice of 1 lemon
Water, to thin

Beat eggs until very light; gradually beat in sugar until light and fluffy. Add honey and almonds. In large bowl, sift dry ingredients together. Stir in candied fruit. Add dry ingredients to egg mixture, 1 cup at a time. Stir well after each addition. Spread mixture into 2 well greased 15 x 10-inch baking sheets. Bake at 350° for 15-18 minutes.

GLAZE: Mix glaze ingredients and glaze cookies while warm. Cool and cut cookies.

PEANUT BUTTER BROWNIES

yield: 16 servings
oven temperature: 350°F

½ cup crunchy peanut butter
⅓ cup butter, softened
¾ cup light brown sugar
¾ cup sugar
2 eggs
2 teaspoons vanilla
1 cup flour
1 teaspoon baking powder
¼ teaspoon salt
2 (6-ounce) packages semisweet
  chocolate morsels

In large bowl combine peanut butter, butter, brown sugar and sugar; beat until creamy. Beat in eggs, one at a time, then add vanilla. In a separate bowl, stir together flour, baking powder and salt. Gradually stir this into peanut butter mixture until well mixed. Stir in one package (6-ounces) chocolate morsels. Spread into 13 x 9-inch baking pan. Sprinkle second package (6-ounces) chocolate morsels over top of batter. Bake at 350° for 3 minutes and spread the chocolate topping. Bake for an additional 26 minutes.

NUTTY CHOCOLATE BARS

yield: 4 pounds candy

2 cups butter (no substitutions)
2 cups sugar
1¼ cups almonds, sliced or broken
1 (12-ounce) package milk
  chocolate morsels
1 (6-ounce) package milk chocolate
  morsels
1½ cups pecans, finely chopped

Melt butter slowly in large heavy saucepan. Add sugar and almonds. Cook over medium heat, stirring constantly until golden brown, (about ½ hour). If butter separates during cooking, skim oil off top. Pour the hot thick mixture into a well greased and floured jelly roll pan. Spread evenly. Pour chocolate morsels over hot mixture, spreading as they melt. Sprinkle pecans over all. Cool and break in pieces.

PRALINES

yield: 15 pralines

2 cups sugar
1 cup milk
9 large marshmallows
3 Tablespoons butter
¾ teaspoon vanilla
2 cups pecan halves

Combine sugar, milk and marsh-mallows in 4-quart saucepan. Cook stirring constantly over medium heat until soft ball stage or 234° on candy thermometer. Remove from heat, stir in butter and vanilla. Beat until creamy. Add pecans. Beat until mixture begins to thicken. Working rapidly, drop mixture by spoonfuls onto lightly buttered waxed paper. Cool. Store in airtight container.

"MY BROTHER JOHN'S ONLY RECIPE"

yield: 6-8 servings

2 teaspoons oil
1 pound white chocolate
3 cups pretzel sticks, very thin, broken into pieces
1 cup cocktail peanuts

Pour oil into a large pan and add white chocolate. Melt over low heat. Add pretzels and nuts to chocolate; stir to coat rapidly. Pour mixture on an aluminum foil covered cookie sheet. When cool, break into small pieces. Store in an airtight container.

PEANUT BUTTER ROLL CANDY

yield: 3¼ pounds

Flour
4 cups sugar
1 cup water, hot
1 cup light corn syrup
3 large egg whites
2 teaspoons vanilla
Dash salt
1 quart peanut butter

Prepare counter top by wiping off with a clean damp cloth. Sprinkle evenly with flour from a sifter. Have a tablespoon, table knife or spatula and rolling pin ready for preparing the candy and spreading the peanut butter. Combine sugar, water and corn syrup; cook until hard ball stage (260° on a candy thermometer). While syrup is cooking, beat egg whites stiff and dry. Leave the mixer running and slowly add some syrup (when it has reached hard ball stage) to the egg whites until they cook. Then still beating constantly you may pour faster until all syrup is used. Add vanilla and salt. Beat until mixture is the consistency of biscuit dough.

Roll out on counter to about ¼-inch thick. Spread with peanut butter and roll up as you would a jelly roll. Slice.

The entire quart of peanut butter may not be needed. The hard ball stage can be tested by dropping a drop of the syrup into cold water — it will sound like glass breaking when it touches the water.

CRACKER CANDY

yield: 2 dozen pieces
oven temperature: 400°F

40 saltine crackers (2 x 2-inch)
1 cup butter (no substitutions)
1 cup brown sugar
1 (12-ounce) package milk
  chocolate morsels

Place saltines, side by side, on a foil covered cookie sheet. Bring butter and brown sugar to a boil; boil 3 minutes. Spread mixture over crackers. Bake 5 minutes. Sprinkle morsels over baked crackers; let stand 5 minutes. Spread evenly. Refrigerate until hard. Remove foil; break into pieces.

SOUR CREAM MILK CHOCOLATE FUDGE

yield: 36 pieces

3½ cups sugar
2 Tablespoons light corn syrup
2 cups sour cream
6 Tablespoons butter
6 ounces milk chocolate, broken in
  pieces
1 teaspoon vanilla
1 cup nuts, chopped (optional)

Combine sugar, corn syrup, sour cream and butter in a heavy 3-quart saucepan. Cook over medium heat, stirring often with a wooden spoon. Cook to 254° on a candy thermometer. Remove from heat. Add milk chocolate, vanilla and nuts. Let stand 10 minutes. Stir until it begins to lose its sheen. Pour into a buttered 9 x 13-inch pan. Cut when cool. Sometimes all the chocolate will not melt. This gives the fudge a unique flavor.

Very rich but sooo good! Serve with plenty of cold milk!!

CHOCOLATE FUDGE

yield: 5 pounds

5 cups sugar
1 cup butter
1 (12-ounce) can evaporated milk
3 (6-ounce) jars marshmallow
  cream
1 scant Tablespoon vanilla
3 (6-ounce) packages semisweet
  chocolate chips

Heat sugar, butter and evaporated milk in a heavy saucepan over medium heat until mixture boils. Continue to boil for 8 minutes, stirring constantly. Remove from heat and add remaining ingredients. Stir until well blended. Pour into a buttered 8½ x 11-inch pan. Cool.

For a change ripple peanut butter through mixture after pouring into pan. Drained chopped maraschino cherries or nuts may be added after cooking. Keeps for a long time in the refrigerator.

MRS. WINFIELD DUNN'S CHOCOLATE PEPPERMINTS

yield: 18 muffins

1 cup butter
2 cups powdered sugar
4 eggs
4 (1-ounce) squares unsweetened
  chocolate, melted
2 teaspoons vanilla
½ teaspoon peppermint extract or
  oil of peppermint
Pecans, toasted and chopped

Cream butter and sugar. Add eggs one at a time, beating well after each addition. Add the chocolate, vanilla and peppermint extract. Taste and add more peppermint if desired. Sprinkle bottoms of paper muffin cups with toasted pecans. Fill cups with chocolate mixture. Freeze.

MOUND'S CANDY

yield: 12 dozen

2 (16-ounce) boxes powdered sugar
½ cup margarine
1 teaspoon vanilla
1 (14-ounce) package coconut
1 (14-ounce) can sweetened
  condensed milk
¾ cake paraffin
1 (12-ounce) package semisweet
  chocolate chips

Mix sugar, margarine, vanilla, coconut and condensed milk together in a large bowl. Shape into 1-inch balls. Chill. Melt paraffin and chocolate chips together. Dip coconut balls into chocolate and cool on waxed paper. Refrigerate in an airtight container.

CARAMEL CORN

yield: 8 quarts
oven temperature: 200 °F

2 cups brown sugar
½ cup dark corn syrup
1 cup butter or margarine
1 teaspoon vanilla
Pinch cream of tartar
Salt, to taste
½ teaspoon baking soda
8 quarts popped corn, unpopped
  kernels removed

In a saucepan, mix sugar, syrup and margarine. Bring to boil and cook 5 minutes. Remove from heat and add vanilla, cream of tartar, salt and baking soda. Stir until it turns lighter in color and increases in volume. Put the popcorn in a very large container, pour the mixture over the popcorn and toss to mix. Place in a roasting pan. Bake at 200° for 1 hour stirring 2 or 3 times during baking. Pour on waxed paper and separate to cool. Store in an airtight container.

ALMOND CRUNCH

yield: 24 pieces

1 cup butter or margarine
1¼ cups sugar
2 Tablespoons light corn syrup
2 Tablespoons water
2 cups almonds, chopped, divided
1 (12-ounce) package chocolate
   chips

In a heavy skillet melt butter, sugar, corn syrup and water. Boil to hard crack stage (300° on a candy thermometer). Quickly add 1 cup nuts and pour into a heavily greased 9 x 13-inch pan. Cool completely.

Turn out on waxed paper. Melt chocolate chips and quickly spread half the chocolate on top of brittle. Sprinkle with ½ cup nuts. Cool. Then turn whole thing over. Spread with rest of chocolate and nuts. Cool and break into pieces.

MAPLE PECANS

yield: 2½ cups

1½ cups sugar
½ cup milk
¼ teaspoon salt
1 teaspoon light corn syrup
1 teaspoon maple flavoring
2½ cups pecans

Mix sugar, milk, salt and corn syrup. Cook to a soft ball stage or 234° on a candy thermometer. Add maple flavoring and nuts. Stir until mixture starts to set up. Pour all at once onto waxed paper. Separate pieces with a fork. Cool and store in covered container.

English walnuts may be substituted for pecans.

SPICED PECANS

yield: 4 cups
oven temperature: 300°F

1 egg white
1½ Tablespoons water
4 cups pecans
¾ cup sugar
1 teaspoon salt
½ teaspoon ground cloves
1½ teaspoons cinnamon
½ teaspoon nutmeg

Beat egg white and water and stir in pecans. Mix sugar, salt and spices together and sprinkle over pecans. Coat pecans well. Spread in a shallow pan (well-buttered) and bake at 300° for 30-40 minutes, stirring occasionally.

DIVINITY

yield: 64 1-inch squares

2 cups sugar
Pinch of salt
½ cup water
½ cup light corn syrup
2 egg whites, beaten stiff not dry
1 cup pecans, chopped
½ teaspoon vanilla
¼ teaspoon almond extract

In a saucepan, mix sugar, salt, water and corn syrup. Cover and cook slowly over low heat until mixture boils. DO NOT STIR. Uncover and cook without stirring until syrup threads and flies when small amount is lifted with a tablespoon into air above the pan. Beat egg whites. Slowly add very small amounts of the hot mixture into bowl with the egg whites. Beat until thick. Add nuts. Pour into a buttered 8 x 8-inch pan. When cool cut into squares. Divinity may also be dropped by the teaspoonful onto waxed paper. Divinity should not be made on a humid day; but you may add up to ¼ cup powdered sugar to the mixture while it is very hot, to thicken.

FUNNEL CAKES

yield: 6 servings

Oil
1⅓ cups milk
2½ cups self-rising flour
2 eggs
¼ cup sugar
Powdered sugar

Heat 2 inches of oil to 375° in a 3-quart pan. Beat remaining ingredients, except powdered sugar until smooth. Holding your forefinger over the end of a ½-inch diameter funnel pour about ½ cup batter into the funnel. Drip batter into oil, making circles from the center out. Control the flow of batter with your finger. Fry until light brown, then turn and fry the other side. Drain. Sprinkle with powdered sugar. Serve immediately.

DO NOT keep these tightly covered as cakes become soggy.

POUND CAKE

yield: 10-12 servings
oven temperature: 350°F

1½ cups butter or margarine, softened
1 (16-ounce) box powdered sugar
6 eggs, room temperature
½ cup cold water
1 teaspoon vanilla extract
½ teaspoon lemon extract
4 cups flour, sifted

Cream butter and sugar together. Add eggs, one at a time; beat until it looks like whipped cream. Combine water and extracts in measuring cup. Add flour and liquid alternately to butter, sugar and egg mixture; beating well after each addition. Grease and flour 2 loaf pans, lining bottoms with wax paper. Pour in batter, and bake at 350° for 1 hour.

FIVE FLAVOR POUND CAKE

yield: 10-12 servings
oven temperature: 325 °F

5 eggs, beaten
1 cup butter
½ cup shortening
3 cups sugar
3 cups flour
½ teaspoon baking powder
½ cup milk
½ teaspoon coconut flavoring
1 teaspoon of each flavoring:
  Rum
  Vanilla
  Butter
  Lemon

GLAZE:
1 cup sugar
½ cup water
Cream of tartar
1 teaspoon of each flavoring:
  Coconut
  Rum
  Butter
  Vanilla
  Lemon
  Almond

Beat eggs, add butter and shortening; add sugar. Add flour and baking powder alternating with milk. Add flavorings. Bake for one hour 15 minutes in a greased and floured tube pan.

GLAZE: Combine sugar, water and cream of tartar in saucepan. Bring to boil. Boil about three minutes. Add flavorings. Pour over hot cake.

This unusual flavor combination tastes marvelously like butterscotch!!

SHERRY NUT CAKE

yield: 3 loaves
oven temperature: 275°F

4 cups flour
1 teaspoon baking powder
3 cups raisins
4 cups pecans, broken
1½ cups butter, no substitutes
2 cups sugar
6 eggs
½ cup sherry
1 cup sherry for topping

Mix the flour, baking powder, raisins and pecans well. Cream butter and sugar and add eggs, then alternately add flour mixture and the sherry.

Butter 3 bread loaf pans and put in equal amounts of the batter. Bake at 275° for 80 minutes or bundt pan for 2½ hours. As soon as they are removed from oven, pour ⅓ cup sherry over each loaf or 1 cup over bundt; let stand 6 hours in pan. Wrap each loaf in aluminum foil and seal tightly in a plastic bag. Refrigerated this cake will keep for 6 months.

This recipe can also be put in a tube pan as one cake, but bake for 2½ hours and as soon as it is removed from oven, pour 1 cup sherry over top of cake and let cool 6 hours.

When serving, slice thin.

This recipe is over 100 years old!!

PINEAPPLE CARROT CAKE

yield: 10-12 servings
oven temperature: 350°F

1¾ cups sugar
1¼ cups oil
4 eggs
2 cups flour
2 teaspoons baking powder
2 scant teaspoons baking soda
1 teaspoon salt
2 teaspoons cinnamon
3 cups carrots, grated
½ cup nuts, chopped

ICING:
1 (16-ounce) package or box
   powdered sugar
1 (8-ounce) package cream cheese
¼ cup butter or margarine
2 teaspoons vanilla
1 small can pineapple, crushed,
   drained and dried well

Cream sugar and oil together. Add eggs. Blend in dry ingredients. Mix well. Add carrots and nuts. Bake in three 9-inch round cake pans (greased and floured) at 350° for 25-30 minutes.

ICING: Mix icing ingredients together and frost cool cake between layers, top and sides.

GRANDMA'S SAUCE

yield: 4 cups

1 egg
1 cup sugar
¼ cup butter, melted
1 teaspoon vanilla
1¼ cups heavy cream, whipped

Beat egg in large bowl with electric mixer until thick and lemon colored. Gradually add sugar, beating until thickened, about 2 or 3 minutes. Stir in melted butter and vanilla using rubber spatula. Gently fold in whipping cream. Chill at least one hour.

CHOCOLATE CAKE

yield: 3-layer cake
oven temperature: 350°F

2 eggs, beaten
2 cups buttermilk
2 teaspoons vanilla
½ cup butter
4 (1-ounce) squares unsweetened
 chocolate
2½ cups flour
½ teaspoon salt
2 cups sugar
2 teaspoons baking soda

ICING:
½ cup evaporated milk
2 teaspoons vanilla
1 (16-ounce) box powdered sugar
4 (1-ounce) squares unsweetened
 chocolate
½ cup butter

Beat eggs with buttermilk and add vanilla. Melt the butter and chocolate in a double boiler. Sift together dry ingredients and add to egg mixture. Add chocolate mixture. Beat thoroughly. Pour into 3 greased 8-inch cake pans and bake at 350°F for 30 minutes.

ICING: Add milk and vanilla to sifted sugar. Melt chocolate and butter together and add to first mixture. If icing is not thick enough to spread nicely, add more sifted powdered sugar.

CAMP-OUT CAKE

yield: 12 servings

1 (15¼-ounce) can crushed
 pineapple, undrained
1 (16-ounce) can cherries,
 undrained
1 box yellow cake mix
¼ cup butter or margarine

In the bottom of a Dutch oven, dump pineapples and cherries and juices. Dump in cake mix and stir to moisten leaving fruit essentially in place on bottom of oven. Dot top with butter. Place Dutch oven over 5-8 charcoal briquets arranged in checker-board pattern. Cover and place 7-10 briquets on lid. Cook 45-60 minutes.

OATMEAL CAKE

yield: 12 servings
oven temperature: 350°F

1½ cups hot water
1 cup oats
½ cup shortening
1 cup sugar
1 cup brown sugar
2 eggs
1 teaspoon cinnamon
½ teaspoon nutmeg
½ teaspoon salt
1 teaspoon vanilla
1⅓ cups flour
1 teaspoon baking soda

ICING:
6 Tablespoons butter, melted
⅔ cup brown sugar
¼ cup heavy cream
1 cup coconut
1 cup nuts, chopped
1 teaspoon vanilla

Pour hot water over oats and let stand. Cream shortening and sugars. Add eggs, and then cinnamon, nutmeg, salt and vanilla. Gradually add flour and baking soda to the oat mixture. Combine the oat and shortening mixtures, pour into greased and floured 9 x 13-inch pan and bake at 350° for 30 minutes.

ICING:
Mix all ingredients together and spread on top of cooled cake. Broil 2 minutes under the broiler watching closely to prevent scorching.

EASY MOCHA CAKE

yield: 8-10 servings

1 package chocolate cake mix and
the ingredients listed on the box
½ cup brown sugar
½ cup sugar
4 Tablespoons cocoa
1 cup strong coffee, cold

Prepare chocolate cake mix according to directions, and pour into greased 9 x 13-inch pan. Mix together remaining ingredients and pour over the top of the cake. Bake according to box directions. Serve warm with ice cream or whipped topping.

PERFECT FLUFFY WHITE FROSTING

yield: frosts one cake

1 egg white
⅔ cup sugar
¼ cup light corn syrup
3 Tablespoons water
¼ teaspoon salt
⅛ teaspoon cream of tartar
1 teaspoon vanilla

Combine all ingredients except vanilla in top of double boiler, over rapidly boiling water. Beat with electric mixer about 5 minutes or until mixture stands in peaks. Remove from heat and add vanilla. Continue beating until it reaches spreading consistency.

Very good on Angel Food or Devils Food cakes!!

CHOCOLATE ANGEL CAKE

yield: 10-12 servings
oven temperature: 375 °F

¼ cup cocoa
¾ cup cake flour
1½ cups plus 2 Tablespoons sugar, divided
1½ cups egg whites (about 12)
1½ teaspoons cream of tartar
¼ teaspoon salt
1½ teaspoons vanilla

Blend together cocoa, flour and ¾ cup plus 2 tablespoons sugar. In a large bowl, beat egg whites, cream of tartar and salt until foamy. Gradually add remaining ¾ cup sugar, 2 tablespoons at a time. Beat until stiff peaks form. Fold in vanilla, sprinkle cocoa mixture over the egg white mixture. Fold in gently just until dry ingredients disappear. Spoon batter into tube pan. Bake at 375° for 30-35 minutes. Invert cake pan over funnel and let hang until completely cooled.

It is important to have the ungreased tube pan ready while you prepare the cake batter. This may be frosted, if desired. It is also important that this recipe not be overcooked.

CARAMEL ICING

yield: frosts a 2-layer cake

1 cup brown sugar
½ cup butter (no substitutes)
¼ cup milk
2 cups powdered sugar
1 teaspoon vanilla

Combine brown sugar and butter in medium saucepan stirring constantly; bring to a boil for 2 minutes. Add milk and let mixture return to a boil. Remove pan from heat and let stand until cool. Add powdered sugar and vanilla; beat until spreading consistency.
This icing never gets hard.

CHEESE CAKE

yield: 20 servings
oven temperature: 325 °F

1 pound cream cheese, softened
1 pound ricotta cheese
1½ cups sugar
4 eggs, slightly beaten
1 teaspoon vanilla
3 Tablespoons flour
2 Tablespoons cornstarch
3 Tablespoons lemon juice
½ cup butter, melted
2 cups sour cream

Blend cream cheese and ricotta cheese in a large mixing bowl. Gradually cream in sugar, add eggs and beat well until smooth. Stir in vanilla, flour, cornstarch and lemon juice. Add butter and mix until smooth; blend in sour cream.
Bake in a greased springform pan for 1 hour in a 325° oven. After baking 1 hour, turn oven off and leave in oven for 2 hours. Cool; then refrigerate.
May be served plain or topped with blueberry or cherry pie filling.

IRISH CREAM WHISKEY CHEESE CAKE

yield: 8 servings
oven temperature: 375 °F

CRUST:
Chocolate chip cookies with nuts
Butter, melted
FILLING:
½ cup sugar
½ teaspoon vanilla
2 (8-ounce) packages cream cheese, softened
3 eggs
1 (8-ounce) bar German chocolate, melted
½-¾ cup Irish cream whiskey
Whipping cream, whipped

CRUST: Crush the cookies and combine with enough butter to make a coarse meal. Spread into a 10-inch pie pan.
FILLING: Beat together the sugar, vanilla and cream cheese. Add eggs one at a time. Then add the chocolate and the liqueur. Pour into pie crust. Bake at 375° for 20 minutes.
Serve with whipped cream around the edges.

CHOCOLATE CHEESECAKE

yield: 12 servings
oven temperature: 375 °F

CRUST:
1¼ cups graham cracker crumbs
¼ cup sugar
¼ cup cocoa, scant
⅓ cup butter, melted

CAKE:
2 (8-ounce) packages cream cheese, softened
¾ cup sugar
⅓ cup cocoa
2 eggs
⅓ cup strong coffee
⅓ cup coffee liqueur
1½ teaspoons vanilla extract

TOPPING:
1 cup sour cream
2 Tablespoons sugar
2 teaspoons coffee liqueur
Chocolate, shaved, optional

CRUST: Combine graham cracker crumbs, sugar, cocoa and melted butter. Press into bottom of 9-inch springform pan. Bake at 300° for 5 minutes. Cool.

CAKE: Beat cream cheese until light and fluffy; gradually add sugar and cocoa. Beat in eggs, one at a time. Stir in coffee liqueur and vanilla; pour onto crust. Bake at 375° for 25 minutes. (The filling will be soft.)

TOPPING: Mix sour cream, sugar and liqueur; spread over hot cheesecake. Bake at 425° for 5 minutes. Let cool to room temperature. Chill 8 hours before serving. The sides of the springform pan may be removed when cake reaches room temperature.
Before serving, garnish with shaved chocolate.

MINIATURE CHEESECAKES

yield: 48 cheesecakes
oven temperature: 350°F

Butter
1 (13½-ounce) package graham
  cracker crumbs
2 (8-ounce) packages cream cheese,
  softened
¾ cup sugar
3 eggs, separated
¾ cup sour cream
2½ Tablespoons sugar
1 teaspoon vanilla

Butter 4 miniature muffin tins on the sides and bottoms. Sprinkle tins with graham cracker crumbs and shake so the cups are completely covered.

Mix together cream cheese, sugar and 3 egg yolks. Beat 3 egg whites stiff and fold into cream cheese mixture. Spoon into muffin cups, filling each almost to the top. Bake at 350° for 15 minutes. Cool. They will fall as they cool.

Mix sour cream, sugar and vanilla together and drop on the inner circle of each cooled cheesecake. Bake at 400° for 5 minutes.

PLANTATION PRUNE CAKE

yield: 12-16 servings
oven temperature: 350 °F

2 cups cooked prunes with juice
2½ cups flour
1 teaspoon baking powder
1 teaspoon salt
1 teaspoon ground allspice
1 teaspoon ground cinnamon
1 teaspoon ground nutmeg
1 cup pecans, finely chopped
3 eggs
1 cup sugar
½ cup brown sugar
1 cup oil
½ cup buttermilk
2 cups apples, chopped

VANILLA GLAZE:
1 cup sugar
½ teaspoon baking soda
½ cup buttermilk
1 Tablespoon light corn syrup
½ cup margarine
1 teaspoon vanilla
½ cup pecans, crushed

Grease and flour a tube pan. Drain liquid from prunes into a 2 cup measuring cup. Pit prunes, then cut each into 3-4 pieces. Place in the measuring cup with the prune juice to make 2 cups (pour off any extra liquid over 2 cups).

Sift flour, baking powder, salt, allspice, cinnamon and nutmeg into a medium size bowl, stir in pecans. In a large bowl of electric mixer beat eggs well at high speed. Slowly beat in sugar until mixture is fluffy. Beat in oil, then buttermilk. Stir in prunes and apples. Beat in flour mixture a third at a time until well blended. Pour into prepared pan. Bake in moderate oven at 350° for 1 hour, or until top springs back when lightly pressed with fingertip. After cooling cake 10 minutes in the pan on a wire rack; loosen cake around edges. Cool.

VANILLA GLAZE: Combine sugar, baking soda, buttermilk, corn syrup and margarine in a saucepan. Heating slowly and stirring constantly, bring to a boil and cook 2 minutes. Remove from heat, stir in vanilla and pecans. Pour over cake.

PRUNE CAKE

yield: 12 servings
oven temperature: 350°F

1 cup prunes, pitted
1½ cups sugar
2 cups flour
1 teaspoon baking soda
¼ teaspoon salt
1 teaspoon cinnamon
1 teaspoon nutmeg
1 teaspoon allspice
3 eggs, beaten
1 cup oil
1 cup buttermilk
½ cup nuts, chopped
1 teaspoon vanilla

SAUCE:
1 cup sugar
½ cup buttermilk
½ teaspoon baking soda
1 Tablespoon light corn syrup
½ teaspoon vanilla
¼ cup butter

Stew prunes; drain, cool and mash. Sift together sugar, flour, baking soda, salt and spices. Add eggs, oil, buttermilk, prunes, nuts and vanilla to sifted ingredients. Mix until well blended. Pour into greased and floured 9 x 13-inch pan. Bake at 350° for 35-40 minutes. Cool cake and prick with fork.

SAUCE: Bring sauce mixture to a slow boil and whip to blend. Pour sauce over cake.

DRIED APPLE CAKE

yield: 1 bundt cake
oven temperature: 300 °F

3 cups dried apples, chopped
3 cups sugar, divided
1 cup butter
2 eggs
3 cups flour
2 teaspoons baking soda
½ teaspoon salt
1 teaspoon each:
  allspice
  cloves
  nutmeg
  cinnamon
1 cup sour milk, or buttermilk
1 teaspoon lemon extract
1 teaspoon vanilla extract
1 cup chopped nuts
1 cup raisins, plumped

Cover apples with water and soak 5-6 hours or overnight. Wring out excess moisture and run through a food mill. Measure 2-3 cups apples and mix in a saucepan with 2 cups sugar; cook until thick. Cool.

In a very large bowl cream butter and 1 cup sugar; beat in the eggs. Combine flour, baking soda, salt and spices. Alternately add dry ingredients and sour milk to the creamed mixture. After the batter is well mixed add lemon and vanilla extract. Add the chopped nuts and apple mixture to the batter.

Pour into 2 high-sided loaf pans or a tube pan.

Bake at 300° for 1½ hours or until toothpick comes out clean.

This cake keeps very well if it is tightly wrapped and actually becomes moister after a day or two. If the cake dries out pierce the top with a fork and drizzle apple juice or apple brandy over the top and seal in plastic wrap and foil for a day or two.

To make sour milk add 1 Tablespoon lemon juice or 1 Tablespoon vinegar to 1 cup of milk.

To plump raisins, heat with ½ teaspoon soda and let cool.

APPLE DELIGHT CAKE

yield: 10-12 servings
oven temperature: 325 °F

3 cups sifted all purpose flour
1 teaspoon baking soda
1 teaspoon ground cinnamon
2 cups sugar
3 eggs
1¼ cups oil
1 teaspoon vanilla
¼ cup orange juice
2 cups apple, grated — do not peel
1 cup walnuts, chopped (or
  pecans)
1 cup coconut, flaked

BUTTERMILK SAUCE:
1 cup sugar
½ cup butter
½ teaspoon baking soda
½ cup buttermilk

Sift flour, baking soda and cinnamon together, set aside. Combine sugar, eggs, oil, vanilla and orange juice with electric mixer until well mixed. Gradually add flour mixture until well blended. Fold in apples, nuts and coconut. Pour into a greased and floured tube pan. Bake at 325° for 1½ hours or until top springs back. Cool cake in the pan on a wire rack for 15 minutes and then remove from the pan to a plate. Puncture top of cake with a wooden pick or skewer.

SAUCE: Combine all ingredients for sauce in a saucepan, cook over medium heat until it boils. Pour slowly over the top of the cake until all the sauce is absorbed. Let stand one hour before serving.

COCONUT CAKE

yield: 12-15 servings
oven temperature: 350 °F

CAKE:
1 (18½-ounce) package yellow cake
  mix
1 (3-ounce) package vanilla instant
  pudding mix
1⅓ cups water
4 eggs
⅓ cup oil
2 cups flaked coconut
1 cup walnuts or pecans, chopped

FROSTING:
4 Tablespoons butter, divided
2 cups flaked coconut
1 (8-ounce) package cream cheese
2 teaspoons milk
3½ cups powdered sugar, sifted
½ teaspoon vanilla

CAKE: Blend cake mix, pudding mix, water, eggs and oil in large mixing bowl. Beat at medium speed for 4 minutes. Stir in coconut and nuts. Pour into 3 greased and floured 9-inch layer pans. Bake at 350° for 35 minutes, remove from oven and cool on racks.

FROSTING: Melt 2 tablespoons butter in skillet. Add coconut; stir constantly over low heat until golden brown. Spread coconut on absorbent paper toweling to cool. Cream 2 tablespoons butter with cream cheese; add milk and sugar alternately, beating well after each addition. Add vanilla. Stir in 1¾ cups of toasted coconut. Spread on tops and sides of cake layers. Sprinkle top with remaining ¼ cup coconut.

Refresh shredded coconut by soaking it in ½ cup milk before using in your favorite recipe.

Set hot cake pans on a damp cloth after removing from the oven; after 10 minutes the cakes slip out easily.

SLICE OF THE SOUTH BLACKBERRY PIE

yield: 8 servings
oven temperature: 350°F

CRUST:
2¼ cups flour
¾ cup unsalted butter, sliced (no substitutions)
½ teaspoon salt
6-7 Tablespoons ice water
Powdered sugar

FILLING:
¼ cup butter, melted
5 cups blackberries, not packed
½ cup brown sugar
¼ cup sugar
3 Tablespoons cornstarch
2 Tablespoons blackberry flavored brandy
Sugar

Using the steel blade, in a food processor, combine flour, butter and salt until it is the texture of coarse meal. With the blade running, slowly add ice water. Process 10-15 seconds.
Divide dough into 2 balls with one slightly larger. Roll dough on a board sprinkled with powdered sugar. Roll larger ball for bottom crust and place in a deep dish pie plate. Roll out smaller ball and cut into 10 or 12 strips for lattice work.

PIE: Combine butter and blackberries in a saucepan. In a separate bowl, combine sugars and cornstarch. Add to the berries and heat until the sugars and juice are well mixed. Stir in brandy and pour into pie crust. Weave the strips of dough on the top for the lattice work; sprinkle with sugar. Bake at 350° for 50-60 minutes.

RHUBARB PIE

yield: 6-8 servings
oven temperature: 350 °F

2 eggs, beaten
1 cup sugar
2½ cups rhubarb, sliced
1 (9-inch) unbaked pie shell

Mix together all ingredients and pour into pie shell. Bake at 350 °F for one hour.

APPLE WALNUT COBBLER

yield: 8 servings
oven temperature: 350 °F

1½ pounds tart cooking apples (4 cups thinly sliced)
1 cup sugar
¾ cup walnuts, chopped
½ teaspoon ground cinnamon
1 cup flour, sifted
½ cup evaporated milk
1 egg, well beaten
½ cup butter, melted
Whipped cream flavored with cinnamon and sugar, to taste, or ice cream

Peel and thinly slice apples. Place apples in an 8-inch round baking dish. Mix sugar, ½ cup walnuts and cinnamon. Sprinkle over apples. Sift together flour, sugar, baking powder and salt. Combine evaporated milk, egg and melted margarine. Add to the dry ingredients all at once and mix until smooth. Pour over the apples. Sprinkle with ¼ cup walnuts. Bake 55 minutes at 350°. Serve warm with cinnamon flavored whipped cream or ice cream.

CRUMB CRUST APPLE PIE

yield: 12 servings (2 pies)
oven temperature: 325 °F

Pie crust for 2 pies (double crust
  pie dough)
7 pounds cooking apples, peeled
1 cup flour
1 cup sugar
1 cup brown sugar
6 Tablespoons butter or margarine
2 teaspoons cinnamon
2 teaspoons lemon juice
1 teaspoon nutmeg
Salt

TOPPING:
1 cup oatmeal
1 cup flour
1 cup brown sugar
⅔ cup butter
¾ cup coconut
¾ cup pecans

This pie is the best baked in a large cast iron skillet. Place pie crust dough in the skillet or 2 pie plates. Arrange apples in crust and cut together the flour, sugar, brown sugar, butter, cinnamon, lemon juice, nutmeg and salt. Sprinkle over the apples.

TOPPING: Mix together the oatmeal, flour and brown sugar and cut in the butter. Toss in coconut and pecans. Spread over apple mixture. Bake at 325 °F for 1¼ hours.
This can be baked in a 13 x 9-inch pan.

FRESH PINEAPPLE PIE

yield: 8 servings
oven temperature: 425 °F

¾ cup sugar
¼ cup cornstarch
¼ teaspoon salt
¼ teaspoon nutmeg
4 cups fresh pineapple, drained
  and diced
1 Tablespoon margarine
Pastry for double 9-inch pie

Mix dry ingredients together. Toss with fruit. Turn into pastry lined pie plate. Dot with margarine and cover pie with pastry. Seal and flute edge. Make several slits in top crust. Bake at 425° for 15 minutes; reduce to 350° and bake 40 minutes longer.

PUMPKIN PIE

yield: 8 servings
oven temperature: 350°F

1 cup sugar
¼ cup butter or margarine,
    softened
1 egg
1 Tablespoon flour
¼ teaspoon nutmeg
1 teaspoon cinnamon
Pinch of ginger
1 cup pumpkin
1 cup milk
1 (9-inch) pie shell, baked

Mix all ingredients together. Pour into pie shell. Bake at 350°F for 1 hour.

SCOTTISH HIGHLAND PIE

yield: 12-14 servings
oven temperature: 375°F

1 cup evaporated milk
3 Tablespoons butter
1 (6-ounce) package chocolate
    chips
½ cup butterscotch chips
3 eggs, slightly beaten
1½ cups sugar
3 Tablespoons flour
½ teaspoon salt
2 teaspoons vanilla
2 cups nut meats, scant
2 pie shells, unbaked

Mix milk, butter, chocolate chips and butterscotch chips in a saucepan and stir over low heat until melted. In a separate bowl beat eggs; add sugar, flour and salt. Combine 2 mixtures together then add vanilla and nut meats. Pour into pie shells and bake at 375° for 35 minutes.

Nut meats are chopped nuts!

SOUTHERN CITRUS PIE

yield: 8 servings

CRUST:
4 Tablespoons butter
½ cup brown sugar, firmly packed
1½ cups wheat flakes cereal,
   slightly crushed
½ cup nuts, chopped

FILLING:
3 eggs, separated
½ cup sugar
½ teaspoon lemon peel, grated
½ teaspoon orange peel, grated
¼ teaspoon lime peel, grated
3 Tablespoons lemon juice
2 Tablespoons orange juice
1 teaspoon lime juice
1 cup heavy cream

CRUST: Melt butter and brown sugar together. Simmer one minute then add cereal and nuts. Spread on cookie sheet and set aside to cool.

FILLING: In large bowl beat egg whites with mixer on high until soft peaks form. Add sugar gradually until stiff peaks form. Set aside. Beat egg yolks until thick and lemon colored. Fold into egg whites. In a medium bowl, combine peels, juices and cream and beat on high until soft peaks form. Fold into egg mixture.
Crumble cooled crust mixture and place half of it in bottom of a buttered pie plate. Spoon in filling and top with remaining crumbled crust. Freeze until firm — at least 8 hours or overnight. Allow to thaw slightly before serving.

BUTTERMILK PIE

yield: 6-8 servings
oven temperature: 350°F

2 cups sugar
¼ cup butter or margarine
3 Tablespoons flour, heaping
3 eggs
1 cup buttermilk
1 teaspoon vanilla
Dash nutmeg (optional)
1 9-inch pie crust, unbaked

Cream sugar and butter; add flour and mix well. Add the eggs one at a time until well blended. Mix in buttermilk, vanilla and nutmeg. Pour into pie crust and bake at 350° for 45-60 minutes or until browned.

OATMEAL PIE

yield: 6-8 servings

¾ cup sugar
¾ cup dark corn syrup
¾ cup quick cooking oatmeal
½ cup butter or margarine, melted
½ cup coconut, shredded
2 eggs, well-beaten
1 9-inch pie crust, unbaked
Whipped cream or non-dairy
    whipped topping (optional)

Mix all the ingredients together and pour into the pie crust. Bake at 350°F for 50-60 minutes. Serve topped with whipped cream.

Great for people who can't eat pecans!

SUPERB FUDGE PIE

yield: 8 servings
oven temperature: 350°F

½ cup butter
3 (1-ounce) squares unsweetened
  chocolate
4 eggs
3 Tablespoons light corn syrup
1½ cups sugar
¼ teaspoon salt
1 teaspoon vanilla
9-inch pie shell, unbaked

Melt together butter and chocolate and cool slightly. Beat eggs until light. Beat in corn syrup, sugar, salt and vanilla; add chocolate mixture. Mix thoroughly and pour into an unbaked pie shell. Bake at 350° for 25-30 minutes. Top should be crusty but filling not completely set. DO NOT OVERBAKE.

Delicious served warm and topped with vanilla ice cream!

CHOCOLATE YOGURT PIE

yield: 8 servings

2 (1-ounce) squares unsweetened
  chocolate
1 (14-ounce) can sweetened
  condensed milk
1 teaspoon vanilla extract
1 (8-ounce) carton vanilla yogurt
1 (12-ounce) carton frozen non-
  dairy whipped topping, thawed
1 (9-inch) graham cracker crust

Melt chocolate in a glass quart measure in the microwave at 100% power for 1-2 minutes. Stir in the sweetened condensed milk and the vanilla. Microwave at 100% power for 3 minutes, stirring occasionally. Cool completely. When completely cooled, fold in yogurt and non-dairy whipped topping. Pour into pie shell. Refrigerate until serving time.

THE BEST PECAN PIE

yield: 6-8 servings
oven temperature: 425°F

½ cup butter
1 cup light corn syrup
1 cup sugar
3 eggs, beaten
½ teaspoon lemon juice
1 teaspoon vanilla
Dash of salt
1 cup pecans, chopped
1 (8-9-inch) unbaked pie shell

Brown butter in saucepan until golden brown, DO NOT BURN! Cool. In separate bowl combine corn syrup, sugar, eggs, lemon juice, vanilla, salt and pecans; stir. Blend in browned butter. Pour mixture into unbaked pie shell. Bake at 425° for 10 minutes, then lower temperature to 325° for 40 minutes.

STANDARD PASTRY

yield: 1 pie crust

8-9-inch crust:
1 cup flour
½ teaspoon salt
⅓ cup plus 1 Tablespoon
    shortening
3 Tablespoons cold milk

10-inch crust:
1⅓ cups flour
½ teaspoon salt
½ cup shortening
5 Tablespoons cold milk

Measure flour and salt into bowl. Cut in shortening (use pastry blender or 2 knives) until mixture resembles coarse corn meal. Stir milk in (use fork now) until all flour is moistened and dough pulls away from bowl. Gather into ball and roll out on floured board, handling as little as possible (the longer you work with dough the tougher it gets).

⧗ EASY-AS-PIE PASTRY

yield: 1 double crust

3 cups flour
1 teaspoon salt
1 cup shortening
1 egg, beaten
⅓ cup cold water
1 teaspoon vinegar

Blend flour, salt and shortening. Mix egg with water and vinegar. Pour over flour mixture; blend and shape into a ball. Chill. When ready to use, roll out. Bake at 450°.

Keeps for days in airtight container in refrigerator.

NEVER FAIL MERINGUE

8 Tablespoons sugar, divided
1 Tablespoon cornstarch
½ cup water
⅛ teaspoon salt
½ teaspoon vanilla
3 egg whites

Combine 2 tablespoons sugar and cornstarch in small saucepan and add water. Cook over medium heat, stirring constantly until soft mounds form. Add 6 tablespoons sugar gradually to egg whites and salt, beating well after each addition. Add vanilla and cooled cornstarch mixture and continue beating until meringue stands in soft peaks. Cover pie with meringue and brown in oven, if desired.

UPPER CRUST BLACKBERRY SORBET

yield: 1 quart

1 cup sugar
1 cup water
2 pints blackberries, washed,
  frozen may be substituted
3 large tart apples, peeled and
  cored
2 Tablespoons apple jack, or
  blackberry liqueur
¼ cup orange juice

In a saucepan over medium heat, combine sugar and water. Cook until sugar dissolves and the mixture almost comes to a boil. Chill in refrigerator.
Purée the blackberries and apples; sieve to remove the seeds. Combine all ingredients in a chilled ice cream freezer container and freeze.
More sugar syrup may be used according to the tartness of the berries.

PEACHES N' CREAM ICE CREAM

yield: 1 gallon

3 cups peaches, fresh or frozen,
  mashed
1 Tablespoon lemon juice
3 cups milk
4 cups heavy cream
1½ cups sugar
1 teaspoon vanilla extract
¼ teaspoon almond extract
¼ teaspoon salt

Sweeten peaches to taste and add lemon juice. In a large bowl combine milk, cream, sugar, vanilla, almond extract and salt. Add peaches to mixture and chill. Freeze in ice cream freezer.

CHOCOLATE ICE CREAM

yield: 12 servings

2 cups milk
1 cup sugar
2 eggs
10 Tablespoons cocoa, scant
5 Tablespoons flour
4 cups heavy cream
1 teaspoon vanilla

Cook milk, sugar, eggs, cocoa and flour in double boiler until thick like boiled custard. Add heavy cream and vanilla. Freeze in ice cream freezer.

MERINGUE ICE CREAM PIE

yield: 1 10-inch pie
oven temperature: 350°F

3 egg whites, beaten stiff
1 teaspoon baking powder
¼ teaspoon salt
1 cup sugar
1 cup graham cracker crumbs
½ cup pecans, chopped
1½ quarts coffee ice cream
Chocolate or hot fudge sauce

Add the baking soda and salt to the egg whites. Slowly add sugar; beating constantly. Fold in cracker crumbs and nuts. Spoon into a well greased and floured 10-inch pie pan. Bake at 350° for 30 minutes; turn oven off and let pie cool in the oven 4-5 hours.

Fill crust with ice cream. Serve with chocolate or hot fudge sauce.

ICE CREAM PIE

yield: 1 10 inch pie

1 cup evaporated milk
1 (6-ounce) package chocolate
   chips
1½ cups miniature marshmallows
Vanilla wafers
1½-2 quarts vanilla ice cream,
   softened

Stir milk and chocolate over low heat until chocolate melts and thickens. Add marshmallows and stir until melted. Cool. Line a 10-inch pie pan with wafers and spoon on a layer of ice cream. Spoon chocolate over the top. Repeat layers. Freeze 5 hours before serving.

STRAWBERRY CRUNCH

yield: 12 servings
oven temperature: 300°F

2½ cups crisp rice cereal
1 (3½-ounce) can flaked coconut
1 cup pecans, coarsely chopped
½ cup butter, melted
¾ cup brown sugar
½ gallon strawberry ice cream

Spread cereal, coconut, pecans and melted butter in jelly roll pan and bake at 300° for 30 minutes. Stir occasionally for even browning. Remove from oven and blend brown sugar into hot mixture. Pat ½ of cereal mixture in bottom of 9 x 12-inch rectangular dish. Cut ice cream into one inch slices and cover crunchy mixture. Press remaining cereal mixture on top. Cover with foil and freeze 6 hours.

BLUEBERRY DESSERT

yield: 10-12 servings
oven temperature: 350°F

CRUST:
¾ cup margarine, melted
1½ cups flour
½ cup brown sugar
1 cup pecans, chopped

TOPPING:
1 (8-ounce) package cream cheese,
   softened
½ cup milk
¾ cup sugar
1 container frozen non-dairy
   whipped topping
1 (16-ounce) can blueberry pie
   filling

CRUST:
Mix margarine, flour, brown
sugar and pecans. Press into a
buttered 9 x 13-inch metal pan.
Bake in 350° oven until lightly
brown, about 15 minutes. Cool
completely.

TOPPING:
Blend cream cheese, milk and
sugar. Fold in whipped topping.
Spread mixture over cooled crust.
Top with blueberry pie filling.
Refrigerate.

POTS de CREME

yield: 4-6 servings

1 (6-ounce) package chocolate
   chips
2 eggs
3 teaspoons very strong coffee
1 teaspoon dark rum
1 Tablespoon orange liqueur
¼ cup non-fat milk, hot, scalded

In a blender or food processor,
whirl chocolate chips, eggs, coffee, rum and orange liqueur until
chocolate is finely chopped,
about 30 seconds. Add milk and
blend again until chocolate is
dissolved. Pour into 4-6 custard
cups, pots or small coffee cups.
Chill until set, about 2 hours.

APRICOT DESSERT

yield: 24-30 servings

FILLING 1:
3 cups dried apricots
¾ cup sugar

CRUST:
3 cups graham cracker crumbs
¾ cup walnuts, chopped
9 Tablespoons butter, melted

FILLING 2:
4½ cups powdered sugar, sifted
9 Tablespoons butter
¾ teaspoon vanilla
3 eggs

TOPPING:
1½ cups heavy cream, whipped
6 Tablespoons graham cracker
   crumbs

FILLING 1:
Cover the apricots with water and cook until very tender. Drain and mash sugar and apricots together until they are pureed. Cool.

CRUST:
Combine crumbs, walnuts and butter; pat into 2 (two) 13 x 9-inch pans. Freeze for 30 minutes.

FILLING 2:
In a medium bowl, cut the powdered sugar and butter into a fine meal. Add eggs and vanilla and beat until fluffy. Spoon over crust. Cover with apricot mixture.
Just before serving, top with whipped cream and sprinkle with cracker crumbs.

COEUR de la CREME

yield: 6 servings

2 cups heavy cream
1 (8-ounce) package cream cheese, softened
1 cup powdered sugar, sifted
1 teaspoon vanilla

SAUCE:
1 (10-ounce) package frozen strawberries or raspberries
2 Tablespoons kirsch

Mix the cream and part of the sugar.
Mix together the cream cheese, vanilla and the remaining sugar. Combine the cream mixture and the cream cheese mixture. Cover a 4 cup mold with cheesecloth and fill with the mixture. Refrigerate 12 hours. When ready to unmold lift out gently with the cheesecloth; gently peel off the cheesecloth to retain shape of mold.
SAUCE:
Combine sauce ingredients in a blender. Pour over entire coeur de la creme or spoon over individual serving.

SPUMONI SAUCE

yield: 2 cups

½ cup mixed candied fruit, chopped
¼ cup pecans, chopped
½ cup light corn syrup
¼ cup sugar
¼ cup orange juice
½ teaspoon rum flavoring

Combine fruit, pecans, corn syrup, sugar and orange juice. Bring to a boil and simmer 1 minute. Remove from heat and stir in rum flavoring; chill.

Great served over pudding or ice cream.

CREAM PUFFS

yield: 8 servings
oven temperature: 400°F

PUFFS:
1 cup water
½ cup butter
1 cup flour, sifted
4 eggs

FILLING:
⅔ cup sugar
5 Tablespoons flour
⅛ teaspoon salt
3 egg yolks
¼ cup cold milk
1½ cups milk, scalded
1 teaspoon vanilla
3 egg whites, beaten

ICING:
2 (1-ounce) squares unsweetened
   chocolate
1½ Tablespoons butter
⅔ cup powdered sugar, sifted
2 Tablespoons milk

PUFFS:
Heat water and butter to boiling point in saucepan. Stir in flour and stir constantly until mixture leaves the sides of the pan and forms a ball (about 1 minute). Remove from heat and cool. Beat in eggs one at a time, beating mixture until smooth and velvety. Drop from spoon onto greased baking sheet. Bake at 400°F for 45-50 minutes. Makes 8 large puffs. When cool cut tops off with a knife. Scoop out any filaments of soft dough.

FILLING:
Mix sugar, flour, salt, egg yolks and milk together. Stir into scalded milk. Cool until thick. Add vanilla and beaten egg whites. Fill cream puffs and replace tops.

ICING:
Melt chocolate and butter in top of a double boiler. Remove from heat, stir in powdered sugar and milk blending until mixture is smooth and spreading consistency. Spread on the tops of the filled cream puffs. Serve cold.

WHITE CHOCOLATE MOUSSE

yield: 12 servings

9 ounces imported white chocolate, broken into pieces
3 egg yolks
⅜ cup powdered sugar, divided
2 cups heavy cream
3 egg whites
¼ teaspoon cream of tartar

SAUCE:
1 (10-ounce) package frozen raspberries, thawed
1 Tablespoon kirsch
2 Tablespoon sugar

Heat chocolate in a double boiler until it melts. Remove immediately as it scorches easily! Mix the egg yolks and ⅛ cup (2 tablespoons) sugar and add to the chocolate. Set aside. Whip the cream with ⅛ cup sugar. Whip egg whites, cream of tartar and ⅛ cup sugar to stiff peaks. Add enough cream to the chocolate mixture to achieve a thick stirring consistency. Fold chocolate into whipped cream, blending just enough to achieve uniform color. Gently fold egg whites into chocolate mixture just to uniform color. Chill in cups or shallow parfait glasses.

SAUCE:
Blend raspberries in a blender and strain to remove pulp and seeds. Add kirsch and sugar. Spoon over mousse before serving.

Imported chocolate is a must because it is made with cocoa butter. This recipe is not very difficult and is very pretty!!

PUMPKIN ROLL

yield: 12-15 servings
oven temperature: 375 °F

3 eggs
1 cup sugar
¾ cup canned pumpkin
1 teaspoon lemon juice
¾ cup flour
1 teaspoon baking powder
2½ teaspoons cinnamon
1 teaspoon ginger
½ teaspoon nutmeg
½ teaspoon salt
1 cup nuts, finely chopped
Powdered sugar

FILLING:
2 (3-ounce) packages cream cheese,
    softened
4 teaspoons butter
½ teaspoon vanilla
Lemon peel, grated (optional)

Beat eggs on high speed for five minutes. Gradually beat in sugar. Stir in pumpkin and lemon juice. Sift together flour, baking powder, cinnamon, ginger, nutmeg and salt and fold into pumpkin mixture. Pour into a greased and floured 10 x 15-inch pan. Top with nuts. Bake for 15 minutes.

FILLING: Mix filling ingredients and set aside. Immediately turn cake out on a towel sprinkled with powdered sugar. Start at narrow end and roll cake and towel together and cool. Unroll and spread filling onto cake. Reroll. Cover loosely and refrigerate.

PRALINE SAUCE

yield: 3½ cups

1½ cups brown sugar
⅔ cup light corn syrup
4 Tablespoons butter
1 (5⅓-ounce) can evaporated milk
½ teaspoon vanilla extract

Combine brown sugar, corn syrup and butter; bring to boil. Remove from heat and cool. Add milk and vanilla; blend well. Serve over ice cream.

RASPBERRIES ON A CLOUD

yield: 8-10 servings
oven temperature 250 °F

NEST:
4 egg whites, room temperature
½ teaspoon cream of tartar
1 cup sugar
1 teaspoon vanilla
1 cup pecans, chopped, optional

SAUCE:
2 Tablespoons cornstarch
⅔ cup sugar
2 pints fresh raspberries or
   2 (10-ounce) packages frozen
   raspberries
2 Tablespoons lemon juice, freshly
   squeezed

Beat egg whites with electric mixer until frothy. Add cream of tartar and vanilla, continue beating until double in volume. Mix in sugar a tablespoon at a time until meringue is stiff and glossy. Fold in pecans. Form individual meringues by dropping 2 tablespoons onto a cookie sheet, lined with brown paper, hollow out center with the back of a spoon to form a nest. A pastry bag can also be used to flute the meringues. Bake in a 250° oven for 50 minutes. Turn off oven and leave in oven another 10 minutes to dry out. Remove and cool. Store in an airtight container. Freezes well.

SAUCE: Mix cornstarch with sugar in the top of a double boiler over simmering water. Add raspberries and gradually stir until thick and shiny. Add lemon juice. Refrigerate if not serving immediately.
Serve meringue nest with a scoop of vanilla ice cream topped with raspberry sauce.

BLUEBERRY BUCKLE

yield: 6-8 servings
oven temperature: 375°F

1 cup sugar
½ cup margarine
1 egg
½ cup milk
2 cups flour
2 teaspoons baking powder
¼ teaspoon salt
2 cups blueberries, fresh or frozen

TOPPING:
½ cup sugar
⅓ cup flour
¼ cup margarine
2 teaspoons cinnamon

Mix sugar, margarine and eggs. Stir in milk. Sift together flour, baking powder and salt and add milk mixture. Gently blend in fruit. Spread the batter in a greased 9 x 9-inch pan.

TOPPING: Prepare topping by cutting together the sugar, flour, margarine and cinnamon. Sprinkle over the batter
Bake at 375° for 45-50 minutes.

ALMOND TART

yield: 8 servings
oven temperature: 400°F

PASTRY:
1 cup flour
½ cup butter
3 Tablespoons almond liqueur

FILLING:
⅔ cup almond liqueur
⅓ cup sugar
½ cup heavy cream
1 cup sliced almonds

PASTRY:
Mix flour and butter with pastry blender or knife. Stir in liqueur; press on bottom and sides of 9-inch pie plate. Bake at 400° for 15 minutes.

FILLING:
Combine all filling ingredients, pour into baked pie shell. Bake at 350° for 45 minutes or until brown.

COLD LEMON SOUFFLE

yield: 4-6 servings

1 Tablespoon gelatin
¼ cup cold water
3 egg yolks
1 cup sugar
½ cup lemon juice
Zest of 1 lemon
1 teaspoon vanilla
2 cups heavy cream, whipped
3 egg whites
Pinch cream of tartar

In a saucepan soften gelatin in water and heat gently until gelatin dissolves. Beat the egg yolks until light and lemon colored. Continue beating and gradually add sugar until it forms a ribbon. Beat in lemon juice, lemon zest, vanilla and hot gelatin; when gelatin begins to congeal and has the consistency of lightly whipped cream, add a little cream and then fold in the remaining cream. Whip the egg whites with the cream of tartar and fold into cream mixture. Turn gently into 1½-quart souffle dish and chill several hours before serving.

WINE JELLY

yield: 8 servings

2 cups sugar
4⅔ cups cold water, divided
2 lemon rinds, cut into pieces
3 envelopes gelatin
2 cups sherry
1 cup rum
Juice of 3 lemons
Heavy cream, whipped

Bring sugar, 2 cups of cold water and lemon rind to a boil and boil 15 minutes. Soak gelatin in ⅔ cup water. Pour hot mixture over gelatin and stir until dissolved. Add remaining 2 cups water, sherry, rum and lemon juice. Chill thoroughly. Spoon into serving dishes and top with whipped cream.

TOFFEE SHORTBREAD

yield: 6-8 servings
oven temperature: 325 °F

CRUST:
1 cup flour
½ cup butter
2 Tablespoons sugar

FILLING:
½ cup butter
½ cup condensed milk
1 Tablespoon corn syrup
1 Tablespoon sugar
¼ teaspoon vanilla

TOPPING:
2 (1-ounce) squares unsweetened
  chocolate, melted

CRUST:
Mix ingredients and press evenly in a shallow cake pan. Bake at 325° until golden and cool.

FILLING:
Mix butter, milk, corn syrup and sugar in a saucepan and bring to a boil. Cool and add vanilla. Spoon onto crust; chill for 2 hours.

TOPPING:
Pour melted chocolate over shortbread and chill 1 hour. Slice into thin wedges — very rich!

CHRISTMAS BOILED CUSTARD

yield: 10-12 servings

2 quarts milk
6 eggs
1 cup sugar
½ cup brown sugar
1 heaping Tablespoon flour
15 large marshmallows
1 Tablespoon vanilla

Heat milk in a double boiler. Mix eggs, sugar, brown sugar and flour until smooth and pour into milk a little at a time. Stir constantly over low heat until thick, about 10-20 minutes. DO NOT BOIL. After mixture thickens, add marshmallows and stir until dissolved. Cool and add vanilla. Refrigerate and serve cold.

BLACK BOTTOM CUPCAKES

yield: 20 servings
oven temperature: 350°F

1 (8-ounce) package cream cheese,
  softened
1 egg
⅓ cup sugar
⅛ teaspoon salt
1 (6-ounce) package chocolate
  chips
1½ cups flour
1 cup sugar
½ cup cocoa
1 teaspoon baking soda
½ teaspoon salt
1 cup water
⅓ cup oil
1 Tablespoon white vinegar
1 teaspoon vanilla

Combine cream cheese, egg, sugar and salt and beat well with mixer. Stir in chocolate chips. Set aside.
Mix flour, sugar, cocoa, baking soda and salt for batter. Add water, oil, vinegar and vanilla and beat well with mixer.
Line muffin tins with paper liners. Fill ½ full with batter and top each with a heaping teaspoon of cream cheese mixture. Sprinkle each with a little sugar. Bake at 350° for 30-35 minutes.
No frosting needed!

"MOTHER'S CHOCOLATE SAUCE"

yield: 6 servings

5 Tablespoons cocoa
1 cup water
2 cups sugar
2 Tablespoons butter
1 teaspoon vanilla
¼ teaspoon salt

Bring cocoa and water to a boil and boil for 4 minutes. Add sugar and heat until sugar dissolves. Then add butter, vanilla and salt; remove from heat and stir until butter is absorbed. May be served hot or cold.

LIGHT
& LEAN DISHES

SKEWERED PASTA AND VEGGIES

yield: 24 servings

72 cheese filled tortellini, uncooked (can use part or all spinach tortellini, if desired)
⅔ cup water
1 teaspoon cornstarch
1 teaspoon dry basil
1 teaspoon dry oregano
½ teaspoon sugar
½ teaspoon dry mustard
¼ teaspoon garlic powder
¼ teaspoon onion powder
¼ teaspoon salt
½ cup cider vinegar
2 green peppers, sliced
1 package whole mushrooms
12 small cherry tomatoes, cut in half
24 wooden skewers

Cook tortellini according to package directions, omit salt and fat. Drain and set aside. Combine cornstarch, sugar, herbs, and spices in a saucepan. Gradually stir in water and vinegar. Bring to a boil and cook 30 seconds. Stir with a wire whisk. Let cool. Alternate tortellini, mushrooms, tomatoes, and green peppers on 24 wooden skewers. Put in a pan and marinate at least 4 hours. Drain marinade before serving, if desired.

21 calories per serving
.7 grams fat
0 mg cholesterol

79 mg sodium
4 grams carbohydrate
1 gram protein

LAYERED MEXICAN DIP

yield: 16 servings
oven temperature: 400°F

Non-stick vegetable spray
½ pound ground turkey,
   browned and drained
1 large onion, diced
2 pounds vegetarian refried
   beans
3 cups non-fat mozzarella
   cheese, grated
1 cup non-fat Cheddar cheese,
   grated
1 can (16 ounce) diced tomatoes
   and green chilies
1 can (4 ounce) chopped green
   chilies
1 cup fat-free sour cream

Spray pan with non-stick spray and brown onion. Add cooked ground turkey. Stir refried beans into turkey mixture. Spray 9 x 13 inch pan with non-stick cooking spray. Spread turkey mixture on bottom of pan, pour green chilies over turkey and bean mixture. Sprinkle half of the cheese over chilies. Pour tomatoes over cheese and then sprinkle remaining cheese on top. Bake 20 to 25 minutes. Cool slightly, then add sour cream to top. Serve with low-fat tortilla chips.

160 calories per serving
6 grams fat
22 mg cholesterol

432 mg sodium
14 grams carbohydrate
12 grams protein

WHITE CHILI

yield: 8 - 10 servings

1 can (16 ounce) northern beans
6 cups canned chicken broth
2 cloves minced garlic
2 medium onions (one to sauté, one for beans)
2 cans (4 ounces each) chopped green chilies
2 teaspoons ground cumin
1½ teaspoons dried oregano
¼ teaspoon ground cloves
¼ teaspoon cayenne pepper
4 cups chicken breasts, cooked and diced
2 cups Monterey Jack cheese, grated
Non-stick vegetable spray

Combine beans, chicken broth, and one onion in crockpot on high. Cook 4 hours. Sauté the other onion in non-stick spray. Combine chilies and seasonings and add to bean mixture. Add chicken to bean mixture. Cook 2 more hours. To serve, top with grated cheese.

266 calories per serving
9 grams fat
67 mg cholesterol

631 mg sodium
14 grams carbohydrate
32 grams protein

RASPBERRY CONGEALED SALAD

yield: 8 servings

1 cup unsweetened applesauce
1 large box (.6 ounces) sugar-free raspberry jello
12 ounces diet sugar-free gingerale
8 ounces crushed pineapple in its own juice

Heat applesauce to the boiling point. Stir in jello. Add gingerale and mix. Pour into an 8" x 8" pan. Chill until lightly set. Fold in pineapple. Chill until set. Cut into 8 servings.

Serve on shredded lettuce with a dollop of fat-free mayonnaise.

48 calories per serving
.1 grams fat
0 mg cholesterol

32 mg sodium
12 grams carbohydrate
.6 grams protein

⌛ CRANBERRY ORANGE SALAD

yield: 6 - 8 servings

2 heads Boston lettuce
2 heads Bibb lettuce
1 cup cranberries (use fresh or dried)
1 large can mandarin oranges, drained
1 small red onion, sliced and separated into rings

SALAD DRESSING:
1 container (8 ounce) low-fat raspberry yogurt
2 Tablespoons vinegar
1 Tablespoon lite maple syrup

Wash lettuce; pat dry; tear into bite size pieces. Add cranberries, mandarin oranges, and red onion slices. Top with raspberry vinaigrette dressing.

SALAD DRESSING: Mix well.

84 calories per serving
8 grams fat
1 mg cholesterol

32 mg sodium
17 grams carbohydrate
4 grams protein

CHICKEN SALAD ORIENTAL

yield: 4 servings

2 Tablespoons water
2 Tablespoons safflower oil
4 teaspoons low-sodium soy
  sauce
2 Tablespoons cider vinegar
¾ teaspoon ground ginger
¼ teaspoon garlic powder
⅛ teaspoon pepper
⅛ teaspoon sugar
2 cups chicken breasts, cubed
  and cooked
1 package (6 ounce) frozen snow
  pea pods, thawed and dried
¼ cup green onions, chopped
1 cup bean sprouts
¼ cup celery, chopped
½ cup water chestnuts, sliced

Combine vinegar, oil, water, soy sauce, ginger, pepper, garlic powder, and sugar in a jar with a lid; shake well. Toss chicken, pea pods, onions, and bean sprouts with dressing. Chill overnight. Before serving, add celery and water chestnuts.

220 calories per serving
7 grams fat
73 mg cholesterol

269 mg sodium
10 grams carbohydrate
29 grams protein

MARINATED CHICKEN

yield: 4 servings

4 boneless, skinless chicken
  breasts
½ teaspoon pepper
1 teaspoon salt
1 teaspoon dried sage
½ teaspoon dried thyme
¼ to ½ teaspoon cayenne pepper
1 clove minced garlic
2 Tablespoons white wine

Mix all dry ingredients. Sprinkle wine on chicken, then shake on dry marinade. Let stand about one hour. Spray grill rack with vegetable spray. Grill over hot coals until cooked (about 12 to 15 minutes).

79 calories per serving
2 grams fat
36 mg cholesterol

570 mg sodium
.8 grams carbohydrate
13 grams protein

FESTIVE CHICKEN

yield: 4 servings

1 pound chicken parts, boned
  and skinned
¼ cup frozen orange juice
  concentrate (unsweetened),
  thawed
1 Tablespoon vegetable oil
1 Tablespoon red wine vinegar
¼ teaspoon ground ginger
1 Tablespoon minced onion
  flakes

Place chicken in a large zip-lock bag. Combine remaining ingredients in a small bowl and pour over chicken. Marinate 4 or 5 hours in bag, making sure chicken is evenly coated. Broil or grill until done (about 15 minutes). Turn chicken frequently and baste with marinade while grilling.

200 calories per serving
7 grams fat
79 mg cholesterol

89 mg sodium
8 grams carbohydrate
25 grams protein

Be sure to watch chicken carefully, over cooking can make it tough and dry.

GREEN PEPPER STEAK

yield: 4 servings

4 Tablespoons low-sodium soy
  sauce
2 Tablespoons cooking sherry
1 clove garlic, minced
½ teaspoon sugar
½ teaspoon salt
Divide above into 2 servings
½ pound lean round steak, cut
  into thin strips
½ teaspoon salt-free season-free
  accent
1 green pepper, sliced
1 onion, diced
3 teaspoons black bean sauce
¾ cup water
1 tomato, diced
2 Tablespoons cornstarch
¼ cup water
Non-stick vegetable spray

Sprinkle meat with accent. Combine first five ingredients and pour ½ of sauce mixture over meat and marinate. Sauté onion and green pepper in non-stick vegetable spray. Cook meat in sauce mixture. Add onion and green pepper, then the second serving of sauce mixture, and ¾ cup of water. Bring to a boil. Combine diced tomato and cornstarch with ¼ cup water and stir until thick. Pour over meat and serve with rice.

178 calories per serving
5 grams fat
48 mg cholesterol

525 mg sodium
12 grams carbohydrate
20 grams protein

BEEF DIJON

yield: 4 servings
oven temperature: broil

1 pound lean, boneless sirloin
  steak, trimmed
2 Tablespoons Dijon mustard
2 Tablespoons Burgundy wine
1 teaspoon ground pepper
2 cloves garlic, minced
1 cup fresh mushrooms, sliced
1½ Tablespoons all-purpose
  flour
1 cup low-sodium, fat-free beef
  broth
½ cup Burgundy wine
¼ teaspoon pepper
¼ teaspoon salt
Non-stick vegetable spray

Combine mustard, wine, ground pepper, and garlic. Coat steak on both sides with mustard mixture, and place in a shallow dish. Cover and refrigerate 8 hours. Place steak on rack coated with vegetable cooking spray. Place rack in broiler pan. Broil 4 inches from heat (with oven door partially opened) for 4 to 5 minutes on each side. Let stand 5 minutes. Thinly slice steak across grain; keep warm. Sauté mushrooms in non-stick skillet with cooking spray, stirring constantly, over medium heat until tender. Add flour, cook one minute, stirring constantly. Gradually add beef broth and ½ cup wine. Cook until thickened, stirring constantly. Add salt and pepper. Serve over meat.

213 calories per serving
7 grams fat
80 mg cholesterol

435 mg sodium
7 grams carbohydrate
28 grams protein

BAKED ORANGE PORK CHOPS

yield: 4 servings
oven temperature: 350°F

4 pork tenderloin chops
  (5 ounces each)
½ cup orange juice
  (unsweetened)
1 Tablespoon soy sauce (may use
  low-sodium)
1 Tablespoon honey
2 teaspoons minced onion flakes
¼ teaspoon dry mustard
½ teaspoon orange peel, grated
⅛ teaspoon dried thyme

Broil chops on a rack in a pre-heated broiler, turning once, until lightly browned. Place browned chops in a shallow baking pan. Combine remaining ingredients and pour over chops. Cover and bake one hour.

Serve chops over cooked brown rice, garnished with orange slices.

232 calories per serving
9 grams fat
83 mg cholesterol

324 mg sodium
9 grams carbohydrate
28 grams protein

ALFREDO SAUCE

yield: 2¾ cups

2 cups non-fat cottage cheese
2 Tablespoons butter buds
3 Tablespoons Parmesan cheese, grated
½ cup evaporated skim milk
½ teaspoon chicken bouillon cubes
½ teaspoon basil
¼ teaspoon white pepper

Combine all ingredients with electric blender. Blend until smooth. Pour into small saucepan. Cook over low heat until heated, stirring constantly.

86 calories per serving
.8 grams fat
6 mg cholesterol

495 mg sodium
7 grams carbohydrate
13 grams protein

PRIMAVERA FETTUCCINE

yield: 6 servings

1 package (12 ounce) fettuccine, cooked without salt or fat
1 package (10 ounce) frozen snow pea pods, thawed
1 green pepper, sliced
1 cup fresh broccoli, cut into bite size pieces
½ cup mushrooms, sliced
1 small onion, chopped
Non-stick vegetable spray

Sauté onion with vegetable spray until tender. Add snow peas, green pepper, broccoli, and mushrooms. Cook until tender, stirring constantly. Add Alfredo Sauce and toss gently.

339 calories per serving
2 grams fat
6 mg cholesterol

509 mg sodium
57 grams carbohydrate
23 grams protein

MISSISSIPPI RICE

yield: 6 servings
oven temperature: 400°F

1 cup onions, chopped
1 cup celery, chopped
1 cup raw rice
2 beef bouillon cubes
2 cups boiling water
½ cup low-fat margarine

Mix onions, celery, and rice. Add bouillon mixture and top with margarine. Bake for 45 minutes to one hour.

192 calories per serving
8 grams fat
.1 mg cholesterol

492 mg sodium
28 grams carbohydrate
3 grams protein

BLACK BEANS AND RICE

yield: 4 to 6 servings

1½ cups uncooked brown rice
1 can (10 ounce) diced tomatoes
   and green chilies w/juice
1 can (16 ounce) black beans,
   drained

Cook rice according to package directions. After 5 minutes, add black beans, tomatoes, and chilies. Cook on low for 15 minutes or until rice is cooked.

103 calories per serving
1 gram fat
0 mg cholesterol

487 mg sodium
21 grams carbohydrate
3 grams protein

GRILLED MIXED VEGETABLES

yield: 4 servings

1 yellow squash
1 zucchini
1 green pepper
1 small onion
6 large mushrooms
Non-fat Italian dressing

Cut vegetables into one inch chunks. Place on large piece of aluminum foil. Sprinkle with low-fat or non-fat Italian dressing. Close up foil and place on grill for about 15 minutes. May substitute or add any other vegetables.

26 calories per serving
.3 grams fat
0 mg cholesterol

3 mg sodium
6 grams carbohydrate
1 gram protein

FLAVORED GREEN BEANS

yield: 6 servings

1 quart fresh green beans
2 chicken bouillon cubes

Add bouillon cubes to green beans while simmering.

39 calories per serving
6 grams fat
3 mg cholesterol

197 mg sodium
7 grams carbohydrate
3 grams protein

CHOCOLATE ECLAIR CAKE

yield: 15 - 2¼" x 2½" servings

2 boxes (9 ounces) sugar-free instant vanilla pudding
3½ cups skim milk
1 (12 ounce) container lite whipped topping
45 (2¼" x 2½") rectangles graham crackers (2 packages plus one rectangle from third package of a one pound box)
1 (6 ounce) sugar-free, fat-free hot fudge packet (or 4 - 1½ ounce pouches from local yogurt shop)

Pour pudding and milk into a bowl. With an electric mixer at lowest speed, beat about 2 minutes until blended. Fold whipped topping into cold pudding. Line the bottom of a 9" x 13" pan with 15 - 2¼" x 2½" graham crackers. Spread ½ of the pudding mixture over the graham crackers. Layer 15 more crackers over pudding mixture. Spread the remaining pudding mixture over these crackers. Place 15 more crackers over pudding mix. Drizzle fudge pouches over top graham crackers and spread. (Do not heat fudge before putting on cake.) Refrigerate cake at least 24 hours before serving. Cut into 15 - 2¼" x 2½" cracker servings.

Good recipe to make a day or two ahead of serving time.

172 calories per serving
5 grams fat
0 mg cholesterol

127 mg sodium
29 grams carbohydrate
4 grams protein

EASY CHOCOLATE CAKE

yield: 8 servings
oven temperature: 350°F

¾ cup all-purpose flour
2 Tablespoons cocoa
  (unsweetened)
½ teaspoon baking soda
½ teaspoon butter buds
¼ cup plus 1 Tablespoon sugar
2 Tablespoons safflower oil
1 teaspoon chocolate extract
1 teaspoon vanilla extract
1 Tablespoon low-fat yogurt,
  plain
¼ cup plus 2 Tablespoons cold
  water
Non-stick vegetable spray

Combine dry ingredients; mix until blended. With a spoon, make a well in the center. In a small bowl, combine remaining ingredients and mix. Pour into well in dry mixture. Stir until all ingredients are moistened. Place batter in a 4 x 8 inch non-stick loaf pan or one sprayed with cooking spray. Bake 15 minutes. Cool in pan on wire rack. Top with confectioners sugar.

122 calories per serving
5 grams fat
0 mg cholesterol

53 mg sodium
18 grams carbohydrate
2 grams protein

BANANA SPLIT CAKE

yield: 8 servings

24 graham crackers, crushed
1 large package sugar-free
   instant vanilla pudding
3 cups skim milk
4 bananas, sliced
1 container (8 ounce) cool whip
   lite
2 cups strawberries, sliced
2 small cans crushed pineapple
   (in own juice), drained

Spread graham crackers in 9 x 13 inch dish. Prepare pudding according to package directions. Cover crackers with pudding mixture. Layer bananas, then cool whip followed by strawberries and pineapple. Refrigerate.

212 calories per serving
4 grams fat
0 mg cholesterol

101 mg sodium
44 grams carbohydrate
4 grams protein

ORANGE CINNAMON ROLLS

yield: 10 servings
oven temperature: 350°F

1 Tablespoon liquid margarine
3 Tablespoons sugar
1 Tablespoon frozen orange
   juice concentrate
   (unsweetened), thawed
½ teaspoon cinnamon
1 package (10 ounce) canned
   biscuits (10)

Combine margarine, sugar, orange juice concentrate, and cinnamon. Spread evenly over bottom of 9" pie pan. Arrange biscuits evenly on top of mixture in pan. Bake 20 to 25 minutes, until golden brown. Cool in pan one minute, then invert onto a serving plate. Serve warm for best flavor.

110 calories per serving
5 grams fat
0 mg cholesterol

260 mg sodium
18 grams carbohydrate
2 grams protein

Wine List and Food Pairings

WHITE WINES

- Chardonnay: Usually a medium to full-bodied, dry wine. Apples and applesauce, citrus, tropical fruits such as pineapple and banana; vanilla, butter, butterscotch, occasionally ginger, tea and tropical floral scents.

Poultry and game birds, veal and pork, rabbit, fish and pasta preparations which feature cream and/or butter; mushrooms; herbs such as tarragon, chervil, marjoram.

- Sauvignon Blanc (Fumé Blanc): Medium to light-bodied and dry. Fresh-cut grass, dried hay or straw, summer herbs, vegetables such as bell peppers and green beans, sometimes melons and figs.

First courses, seafood, ethnic dishes-pastas, curries, salsas, spicy sausages, asparagus with flavored mayonnaise, vegetable dishes, luncheon salads, olive-oil based dishes, fresh tomato sauces, goat cheese, dill.

- Chenin Blanc: Light to medium-bodied, normally off-dry to semi-sweet. Melons, pears, peaches, sweet apples.

Braised chicken, sushi and other Oriental dishes with sauces based on mixtures of soy, garlic, ginger, scallions, honey, rice vinegar; poultry; pork cooked with fruits; Indonesian curries; vegetable and fruit salads; poppy seed dressing; mild cheeses such as Teleme and Jarlsburg.

- Gewurztraminer: Light to medium body; usually semi-sweet, occasionally off-dry, can also be made into an intriguing dessert wine. Uniquely spicy and floral/fruity.

Spicy cuisines such as Chinese, Mexican and Indian; stuffed cabbage, mild sausages, fruit salads.

- Riesling (Johannesburg Riesling, White Riesling): Light to medium bodied; semi-sweet to off dry; the classic grape for the luscious, late-harvest dessert wines. Delicately aromatic, a mix of floral and fruity scents.

Crabmeat, appetizers and finger foods, prosciutto and melon, pork, foods marinated in sweet/sour marinades, salads dressed with citrusy dressings.

RED WINES

- Cabernet Sauvignon: Medium to full-bodied, tannic and dry. Blackberry, cassis, green olive, bell pepper, dried herbs, tobacco, cedar, leather, oak.

  All kinds of beef-steaks, roasts, hamburgers; lamb; pork; duck; game meats; cheeses such as fresh goat cheese, Parmesan, aged Asiago, Stilton, creamy Gorgonzola; herbs such as thyme, savory, rosemary.

- Merlot: Medium to full-bodied, less tannic than Cabernet, dry. Black cherry, red and ripe summer fruits, occasionally a wisp of bitter orange, Cabernet-like, but softer, fruitier.

  Same as Cabernet; stews, braised beef, pizzas, hearty pastas.

- Zinfandel: Medium to full-bodied but is made by some producers in a lighter, quaffable style; dry. Raspberries, licorice, black pepper and spice.

  Hamburgers, beef, lamb, venison and game; hearty pastas such as ones with meat or sausage sauces; Cioppino; roast turkey; all sorts of stews; pizza; aged Gouda; sweet paprika.

- Pinot Noir: Medium to light-bodied, dry; because the grape has little naturally-occurring tannin, the wine has a silky texture and leaves a lingering freshness in the mouth. Cherries, wild cherries, pansies and violets, smoke, earth, occasionally barnyard.

  Lamb, duck, turkey game birds, Beef Bourguignon, Coq au Vin, dishes prepared with a light smattering of chiles or green salsa, wild mushrooms, barbecued pork ribs, Moroccan dishes, rabbit, semi-soft and soft ripening cheeses.

PINK WINES

- Rosé, White Zinfandel, Cabernet Blanc, Blush, Blanc de Noirs: These wines vary in color from white to light red, in aroma from strawberry or melon and apricot to herbal; in taste from dry to sweet. At their best (choose the most current vintage), these wines should be clean and fresh.

  Many pink wines are appropriate, and delicious, with almost any food. Try pink wines with smoked foods; quiche; ham and pork; barbecued sausages; picnic foods of all kinds; Mexican and Thai cuisines.

INDEX

High South Publications
JOHNSON CITY JUNIOR LEAGUE
P. O. Box 1082
Johnson City, TN 37605

Please send _____ copies of **TREASURES OF THE SMOKIES, Tempting Recipes
from East Tennessee** at $16.95 each _____
Please send _____ copies of **SMOKY MOUNTAIN MAGIC** at $10.25 each _____
Postage and Handling .... $ 2.00 each _____
Tennessee residents add 8¼% sales tax each .... each _____
TOTAL $ _____

Name _____

Street _____

City _____ State _____ Zip _____

Proceeds from the sales of these books are used to support community projects.

- -

High South Publications
JOHNSON CITY JUNIOR LEAGUE
P. O. Box 1082
Johnson City, TN 37605

Please send _____ copies of **TREASURES OF THE SMOKIES, Tempting Recipes
from East Tennessee** at $16.95 each _____
Please send _____ copies of **SMOKY MOUNTAIN MAGIC** at $10.25 each _____
Postage and Handling .... $ 2.00 each _____
Tennessee residents add 8¼% sales tax each .... each _____
TOTAL $ _____

Name _____

Street _____

City _____ State _____ Zip _____

Proceeds from the sales of these books are used to support community projects.

- -

High South Publications
JOHNSON CITY JUNIOR LEAGUE
P. O. Box 1082
Johnson City, TN 37605

Please send _____ copies of **TREASURES OF THE SMOKIES, Tempting Recipes
from East Tennessee** at $16.95 each _____
Please send _____ copies of **SMOKY MOUNTAIN MAGIC** at $10.25 each _____
Postage and Handling .... $ 2.00 each _____
Tennessee residents add 8¼% sales tax each .... each _____
TOTAL $ _____

Name _____

Street _____

City _____ State _____ Zip _____

Proceeds from the sales of these books are used to support community projects.